3 Catalan Dramatists

Engendra Theaterbooks
George E. Wellwarth
General editor

T. M.

3
Catalan
Dramatists

Edited by
George E. Wellwarth

Engendra Press
Montreal   1976

Contents

Introduction

The problem of minor-language literatures has always been an
extremely vexing one. The root of that problem lies in the dearth
of translators. Speakers of Icelandic, Estonian, Bulgarian, Czech, or
Catalan have the literatures of the principal languages of the world
available to them. Translators from French, German, English, and
Spanish abound in every language community; but translators of
literary sensitivity and linguistic proficiency who can transpose
the minor languages to the major ones are extremely rare. Readers
of French, German, Spanish, English or one of the other major
languages — "major" being defined in this context according to the
number of speakers — consequently always have the uneasy
suspicion, frequently a fully justified one, that they are missing out
on some important parts of the world's literary heritage. All too
often, to be sure, the literature they are missing, while stylistically
admirable in its own language and of absorbing interest to those
who are members of the culture it represents, is too provincial, too
tightly linked to the specific concerns of the cultural group for
which it is written, to be of interest to outsiders.

In this connection, the Swiss playwright Friedrich Dürrenmatt
made an astute critical distinction in a lecture delivered in New
York in 1960 entitled "Amerikanisches und Europäisches Drama."
Dürrenmatt divided dramatic literature into *Grossmacht* or Great-
Power literature and *Kleinstaat* or Small-State literature. His point
was that the political status of a country must determine the
nature of that country's drama if its drama is to have any
significance beyond its own borders. In the present-day world
there are only two Great-Power nations: the United States and the
Soviet Union. The latter has given up all pretence to the
production of literary work as a result of the application in even
more intensified form of the same principles of censorship
practiced in Spain. Consequently, only American writers can
practice "Great-Power" literature, which is the realistic depiction
of current society in that country. The political prominence of a
nation forces the rest of the world to take an interest in its
everyday affairs. A "Small-State" writer, as Dürrenmatt shrewdly
points out (justifying the method that has made him world
famous), must take his own society as a model for the world as a
whole. He must create stage worlds that, while remaining
recognizably national to his own compatriots, will become

1

meaningful to the rest of the world as well. He must, in other words, write symbolically, not realistically.

The plays included in this book clearly follow Dürrenmatt's prescription for universalizing "Small-State" literature. This is true despite the fact that the Catalan writer faces a problem not usually faced by writers from smaller countries. That problem is that he does not come from a country at all; or, more precisely, he comes from a specific area which he considers to be a country but which is not officially recognized as such and in which his own language — the lifeline of his distinctive cultural heritage — is not even the officially recognized language. He comes from the eastern littoral of the Iberian Peninsula, from the Balearic Isles, and from the extreme southern part of France. The languages that he *must* learn are Spanish and French, depending on which part of Catalonia he lives in. Indeed, from the end of the Spanish Civil War up to very recently, it was forbidden to teach Catalan in Spanish schools; and to this day no Catalan newspaper is permitted to be published even in Barcelona, the capital of Catalonia. This suppressive attitude on the part of the Spanish government has had the paradoxical but predictable result of stimulating an extraordinarily rich and profuse outpouring of Catalan poetry, novels, essays, and plays.

With the sole exception of Salvador Espriu, who has confined his writing principally to poetry and who is universally recognized as the Dean of Catalan Letters at the present time, the most important and best-known Catalan writer today is Manuel de Pedrolo. Had he been born and brought up a few miles to the west, Pedrolo would be studied in every modern Spanish literature course now given and would be recognized as one of the world's leading writers. Pedrolo has written several closely reasoned polemical essays on the subject of the responsibility of the Catalan writer to his native language. In these essays Pedrolo displays a profound contempt for the Catalan writer who chooses to abandon his own language for gain and notoriety. He backs up his argument by asserting that the native Catalan speaker can never write with the same ease and stylistic confidence in Spanish as in Catalan. The common impression that the visitor to Catalonia carries away of all educated Catalans being completely bilingual because of their facility at switching back and forth between Catalan and Spanish in mid-sentence is erroneous. Pedrolo maintains that this apparent bilingualism is artificial and has been forced on Catalans as a result of political circumstances. To the Catalan, Spanish is a foreign language that he has been obliged to learn. Pedrolo expands

2

on this theme in another essay, in which he points out that a language is known in direct proportion to the political power wielded by the state in which it is spoken and that it is translated to a degree in direct proportion to the state's international political visibility. These facts have hitherto condemned the Catalan writer to obscurity, just as the dominance of the central Spanish government has condemned his "country" to obscurity.

The provincialism that is an inevitable characteristic of literature written in a language struggling for its autonomy and that is, consequently, prevalent in much of contemporary Catalan literature is not at all evident in the work of the three authors included in this book. Indeed, were it not specified that these plays constitute a part of contemporary Catalan literature, there would be no way of inducing the fact from the texts. The plays deal with universal concerns and are as meaningful in the context of other cultures as they are in Catalan culture. The three works by Pedrolo are obviously allied to, if not influenced by, the theater of the absurd. Pedrolo's vision is of a world in which men fight desperately, stubbornly, instinctively to push back the knowledge of the indefinable menace that they feel surrounding them. His favorite image is that of an enclosed space, usually a room. This room is the world to its inhabitants, who feel trapped in it and hate it, but who generally have an even greater fear of what lies outside. Pedrolo's plays are metaphysical dramas that show humanity stripped down to its essentials. The action of these plays never consists of what we might call social movement: the recognizable everyday actions, that is, of human beings. In many dramatic works, of course, these "social" actions are merely the outward indication of an inner essence that they represent or symbolize. In Pedrolo's plays we see the skeletal inner essence: reality laid bare, without the "clothing" of social movement, unobscured by the web of conventional gesture that covers reality and ameliorates our apprehension of it in everyday life and in ordinary drama. His plays are not set in a specified time or place but in an extraterrestrial ultimate reality where the Platonic essences of being exist. They show us the reality for which the reality we know is the name. Samuel Beckett is the only other playwright to have accomplished this transposition effectively. There are, moreover, certain other obvious analogies that are worth pointing out. José Monleón has suggested that Pedrolo's predilection for the image of the room derives ultimately, as does Pinter's, from Sartre's *No Exit*. This is undoubtedly true, but it should be noted that both Sartre and Pinter use the room or enclosed space image quite differently from Pedrolo. In Sartre's play the action, although taking place in a putative Hell, is completely bound to ordinary reality. *No Exit* is a psychological drama whose claim is that Hell is within ourselves and in our relations to other people, those relations comprising the outward and superficial manifestations of our inner impulses. Both Pedrolo and Beckett would have shown the inner emptiness and stasis which the actions of the characters are an attempt to disguise. Sartre, in other words, demonstrates that in order to cover up the hell of the knowledge of our essential nullity we create a web of conflicting actions and character traits that constitute a new hell of misunderstandings, hatreds, and self-loathing. Pinter, on the other hand, uses the room image as a haven from the world. Pinter's characters gather in rooms that are womb-like structures where they cower in embryonic regression, jealously guarding themselves against invasion from the darkness outside. When they are torn loose from their cocoons and forced out of their warm, well-lighted caverns it is at once a birth and a death. In Pedrolo's plays the rooms are either all that there is — they seem to be floating in a vacuum — or they are as cold and forbidding as the outside. Like Beckett, Pedrolo is uncompromising. He holds out no comforting hand.

Cruma (1957) is a play that shows the quintessence of life, existence pared down to its most skeletal. The scene is a bare room with blank, white walls. The man who lives there, the "Resident," has only a chair and an ashtray. He is visited, every day, by a friend, the "Visitor." Each day these two do something different to distract themselves and keep out the memory of the past, the threat of the present, and the dread of the future. This time when the Visitor enters he finds the Resident measuring the walls. This is the "game for today" — the thing that they must do to keep out thought. This obsession of theirs is rather reminiscent of the "old jokes" and the attempted hanging in *Endgame* and *Waiting for Godot*, just as the Visitor's warning that the appearance of the ashtray (it was not there the day before) presages an inundation of inanimate objects — and thus a violation of the skeletal purity in which they live and which they try to preserve with the jealous and self-absorbed care of men tiptoeing on eggshells — recalls Ionesco's *The New Tenant*. The game the two men play turns out to be a flop, for they find that the numbers have disappeared from their tape measures, which are now completely blank. They cannot measure the room anymore — they cannot, that is, make any sense of their world. The world did, perhaps, make sense once when it was simpler and the products of technology and thought had not yet encroached on human life so utterly. "Cruma" is the name of an Etruscan unit of measurement which, like everything else Etruscan, is lost to us. The world the Etruscans knew could, perhaps, have been measured or understood by them, but the world as it is cannot be measured or understood by us.

Another facet of the play is the Resident's inability to relate to other people. His world is enclosed by the walls of his room. He is, as it were, a monad floating through existence unaware of the other particles he meets. People pass through his room to an inner room, where, he tells his friend, all are dead, but he cannot distinguish these people and insists that they are "nobody." When the Visitor goes to the bathroom, a completely different man, the "Stranger," comes out, but nothing will convince the Resident that this is another person. If he did admit the difference he would then have to relate to another person — which would mean breaking his carefully constructed cocoon and letting chaos in. Pedrolo's depiction of the Resident's life and character shows us his vision of what each person's life really is at the core: a struggle to maintain the pitifully minimal amount of personal autonomy he has by living in as self-centered a fashion as possible.

In *The Room* (*Tècnica de cambra*, 1959), again, there is no escape: the room *is* the world, *is* life. The scene is a dormitory room in a hostel. Miscellaneous objects are scattered about. One by one, seven young people are introduced into the room by an invisible landlady whose voice can be heard fulsomely praising the room's comforts. The seven people are different types of humanity — domineering, submissive, selfish, and so on. They are not caricatures in any sense, however. As they come in, each carries an empty suitcase, preempts a space in the room and some objects from the shelves, and settles down. But this room is the world, and there are neither enough beds nor enough objects to go round. What Pedrolo shows us here with consummate dramatic skill is a microcosm of life and its conflicts played out in the compass of this ordinary room. At the end the characters are called out of the room by the voice of the landlady, one by one, just as they were introduced. They leave — for they have no choice — some reluctantly, some resignedly, discarding their earthly dross as they go. At the end the room is again empty, but the eternal cycle of life begins afresh as we hear the voice of the landlady lauding the room to a new tenant. *The Room* is a bold experiment, for the representation of life as a whole in everyday terms runs the danger of becoming trite; but Pedrolo succeeds in making the dramatic

5

image into which he has compressed his view of life a valid and workable one.

Full Circle (*Situació bis*, 1958) is a more socially oriented play than the other two. The leaders of the rebellion against an apparently senseless imposed social order themselves become the representatives of that order and suppress those whom they incited to rebel with the same mindless ferocity exercised by the previous rulers. The play is essentially a powerful political parable, in which Pedrolo speaks of the corruptive effect of power and of the faithlessness of political victors to the ideals for which they fought. Political revolutionaries are like Cronus, swallowing their children lest they in turn be deposed. Their rebellion founders on the reef of their own insecurity and insincerity, both malleable raw materials in the process of conversion from pristine idealism to the moral putrefaction that the possession of power brings. As the disappointed rebel leader in Genet's *The Balcony* remarks after it is all over, "No truth was possible."

Josep Benet i Jornet is a much younger man than Pedrolo — who was born in 1918 — and most of his plays to date have been concerned with specific problems of Catalan society. In *The Ship* (*La nau*, 1969), however, he uses the conventions of science-fiction as his framework and thus, while still maintaining the concern with Catalan affairs subtextually, he universalizes his theme and makes a knowledge of Catalan society entirely unnecessary to an appreciation of the play. The "Ship" of the title is an enormous spaceship containing a million people on its way from Drudania (the Earth) to colonize the farthest stars. Benet's parable is based on the Fall of Man, which has given a group of unscrupulous business entrepreneurs (the business being religion) the opportunity to control all men by playing on their desire to believe and on their feelings of guilt and fear. The spaceship *is* the world, and the Fall consisted of its blast-off. The Earth was the Garden of Eden and in seeking to leave it and discover the secret of the universe by trying to reach the stars, men fell from grace — or so they are told by the entrepreneurs to whom they have fallen victims. Allegorically speaking, the Ship is the world closed off and bounded by the arbitrary rules of religion and government. When Dan opens the window at the end, he opens up the possibilities of the mind of man unfettered by the restrictions of tradition. The window looks out upon the cold, bare spaces where only existential freedom is possible, and where neither religion nor repressive government has any place — where there is no room for the manipulations of the technicians who make the human psyche their field of operation.

With Jordi Teixidor we enter another world altogether. Using a technique directly derived from Brecht's epic theater, he presents the legend of the Pied Piper of Hamelin as an anti-capitalistic fable. Stylistically, the Brecht play to which Teixidor has the closest affinity is *Galileo;* thematically, however, he differs from Brecht in having less confidence in the solutions he espouses. Teixidor is a realist and presents problems; Brecht was always troubled by the Utopian itch and could never stop himself from implying the existence of solutions. With Brecht the wish was frequently father to the man, and reason tended to be muffled by propaganda. Though Teixidor is writing only some twenty-five years after Brecht, he is no longer able to delude himself into optimistic thinking. It is interesting to note that his play is dramatically weaker than any Brecht work (except such childishly didactic potboilers as *The Yea Sayer* and *The Nay Sayer*) precisely because he will not permit himself to indulge in hope. The rulers of Pimberg are clearly shown as callous and self-seeking, but the Shoemaker can do no more than assert that there is something wrong with their actions although he cannot put his finger on the flaw in their rationalizations. Teixidor implies that there *is* a solution, but that it has not yet been discovered. Above all, no practicable alternative has been found. The Shoemaker's idealistic desire to end suffering remains visionary. It is noteworthy that while this play had a long and successful run in Catalonia, it was banned by the censors after its first performance in the Spanish version.

Catalan theater abounds in talented writers who, one hopes, will follow the lead of Pedrolo, Benet, and Teixidor, and begin writing in a mode that is meaningful beyond the boundaries of Catalonia.

January, 1976   G.E.W.

Cruma

(Cruma)

Manuel de Pedrolo

English version by George E. Wellwarth

CHARACTERS

Visitor
Resident
Nagaio
Stranger
Girl

Entrance hall and corridor of an apartment. The front door is at the far end of the hall. There is a large window at the back. The corridor has two doors. Everything is plain and white. The only piece of furniture is a chair in the hallway, the only other object being an ashtray on the floor next to the chair. The window and all three doors are closed. The corridor runs the whole length of the stage, ending in an archway which leads to an interior room.

At the rise of the curtain a man of uncertain age is seated on the chair, smoking. He leans over to tap the ash from his cigarette into the ashtray at his feet. After a few moments he gets up, takes a tape measure out of his pocket, and starts to measure the walls more or less at random. The bell rings. The man remains still, uncertain what to do. The bell rings again, and this time he makes up his mind to go and open the door. Enter another man of uncertain age.

Visitor: Hi!

Resident: Hi! (*They leave the door. The* **Visitor** *walks into the hall.*)

Visitor: Everything the same. (*He looks around.*) Everything's always the same.

Resident (*shutting the door*): Nothing ever changes.

Visitor: No, never. The walls, white . . .

Resident: Yes.

Visitor: The pure air . . . (*Notices the tape measure in the* **Resident**'s *hand.*) What's that?

Resident (*looks at it*): A tape measure.

Visitor: What for?

Resident: For measuring.

Visitor: Measuring what?

Resident: Things. All sorts of things.

Visitor: Is that the game for today?

Resident: Yes, I just got through inventing it.

Visitor: Good. (*He takes a tape measure from his pocket.*) I'll help you.

Resident: Thanks.

Visitor: Where shall we start?

Resident: Wherever you like. (*He bends down and stubs out the butt of his cigarette in the ashtray.*)

Visitor (*apparently noticing the ashtray for the first time*): An ashtray? You didn't have that yesterday . . .

Resident: No.

Visitor: Where'd it come from?

Resident: I don't know. Someone brought it and now it's here.

Visitor (*shaking his head*): That's bad.

Resident: Bad? Why?

Visitor: If you're not careful you'll get swarmed under by objects.

Resident (*apologetically*): It's such a little thing . . .

Visitor (*severely*): But it's a thing! That's how it starts.

Resident: If you like, I'll get rid of it.

Visitor: No, it's here now. Besides, I feel like smoking. (*He takes a cigarette from his pocket and lights it; then he pulls the chair over to one side, picks up the ashtray and puts it on the chair.*) Fine, now we can start.

Resident: I've started already.

Visitor: What have you measured?

Resident: I don't know . . . (*Gesturing vaguely.*) Over there.

Visitor: Let's get on with it, then. (*He goes over to some part of the wall to continue the measurements. A young girl comes out from the farther end of the corridor, goes to the front door, opens it, and leaves. The two men look at each other.*)

Resident: Did you see that?

Visitor: Somebody passed through . . .

Resident: No, not somebody. A girl.

Visitor: Went right by us as if she didn't exist.

Resident: For us nobody exists. But a girl . . .

Visitor: A girl exists less than anybody.

Resident: But I remember . . .

Visitor: What?

Resident (*shaking his head*): No . . . I don't know. Everything's always been the same, hasn't it?

Visitor: Always. Me alone. You alone. Others alone.

Resident: Always playing.

Visitor: Always playing. At being together. At doing something. Right now, at measuring . . .

Resident: At measuring?

Visitor: Yes, have you forgotten? You invented it.

Resident: You may be right. But what's the point of it?

Visitor: I don't know. But right now it's the only thing to do — so let's measure.

Resident (*after a pause*): Let's measure. (*They start measuring the doors and walls, slowly and lackadaisically, one of them in the hallway, the other in the corridor.*)

Voice (*from outside*): Nagaio!

Visitor (*turning to the* **Resident**): What did you say?

Resident: Me? Nothing.

Visitor: You said "Nagaio" in a very peculiar tone of voice! . . .

12

Resident: That wasn't my voice. It came from outside.

Visitor: Outside?

Resident: Yes, obviously.

Voice (*loudly*): Nagaio!

Visitor: There is an outside, then?

Resident: Sure, that's where you came from.

Visitor (*somewhat surprised*): Ah, yes — outside!

Voice: Nagaio!

Visitor: Well then, who is it?

Resident: I don't know. We could open the window.

Visitor: Really? Are you sure we can open it?

Resident: Yes.

Visitor: You're not absolutely sure, are you? Have you ever tried it?

Resident: No, not really. But I've always known I could open it. (*He goes to the window at the back of the hallway.*) Shall I open it?

Visitor: I don't know . . .

Resident: You scared?

Visitor: Scared? What nonsense! Why should I be scared? You yourself said that I'm from outside.

Resident: I didn't mean to offend you.

Visitor: You haven't offended me. You were right. We're all from outside.

Resident: Shall I open it, then?

Visitor: Yes.

The **Resident** *opens the window wide. On the other side of the stairwell there is an identical window which is shut.*

Resident (*sticking his head out*): Nobody to be seen.

Visitor (*coming over to him*): Or heard either.

Resident: No.

Visitor (*hesitantly*): Maybe if you called . . .

Resident: You want to?

Visitor: You could try, couldn't you?

Resident: I don't know . . . You want to know something? I don't dare.

Visitor (*looking out*): Nobody there . . . You want me to shout?

Resident: What if something happens?

Visitor: What could happen?

Resident: I don't know. That's why I'm scared to do it myself.

The front door opens. Both men turn their heads to it. The same girl

13

who went out comes in rapidly. She goes through the corridor and out the other end. The **Visitor** *follows her, as if fascinated, but remains onstage, not daring to go further.*

Visitor (*looking at the* **Resident**): That was . . .
Resident: Yes, a girl. Nobody.
Visitor: The same one?
Resident: I don't know. They're all the same.
Visitor (*peering in the direction where the girl has gone*): And if . . . and if you were to go there too?
Resident: Where? What do you mean?
Visitor (*nodding in the direction of the archway*): There . . . What's over there?
Resident: The dining room or the living room.
Visitor: The living room? It couldn't be!
Resident: I know that already.
Visitor: There's no place that could be a living room back there, and we're not nowhere. Let's go . . .
Resident: That's why you can't follow her.
Visitor: And you?
Resident: Me neither. I tried it once.
Visitor (*impatiently*): And what happened?
Resident (*shrugging his shoulders*): Nothing. They were all dead.
Visitor (*moving away rapidly*): Ah!
Resident (*with a touch of panic in his enjoyment*): Really dead.
Visitor: Is that why we can't leave this corridor?
Resident: You can. You come and go through it.
Visitor: Have I come before?
Resident: Every day. Don't you remember?
Visitor: Maybe. I'm not sure. Where do I come from?
Resident: I don't know. From outside. You've never wanted to talk about it.
Visitor (*goes to the chair, puts the ashtray on the floor, and sits down*): That's funny. I seem to have forgotten all about it.
Resident: I can't believe that. You're keeping something from me. Like everybody else.
Visitor: No. If you like you can come with me some day.
Resident: Where?
Visitor: I don't know. To other corridors.
Resident: Are there only corridors out there?
Visitor: I don't know. But people go back and forth. Other people — they're always other people . . .
Resident: Like these girls?

Visitor: What girls?

Resident: The ones that pass through.

Visitor: Do many pass through?

Resident: I don't know. Girls come and go. One. Many. How would I know?

Voice (*from outside but much louder since the window is still open*): Nagaio!

Both men jump and look at each other.

Visitor: Did you hear that?

Resident: Yes.

Visitor (*gets up, goes to the window and looks outside*): I don't see anyone.

Resident: There's never anybody to be seen.

Voice: Nagaio!

Resident: It might be better to close it.

Visitor: No. We could play at this today.

Resident: At what?

Visitor: At looking at them . . . at people.

Resident: But what about the measurements?

Visitor: That's right, we were just about to finish up the measurements. (*Leaving the window.*) Between the two of us we'll finish that right away.

Resident: But we'll have to start all over again. I've forgotten everything.

Visitor: We ought to have some paper and a pencil.

The **Resident** *rummages around in his pockets and comes up with a whole pile of things: a stone, a piece of wood, a piece of string, a nail, a handkerchief, a rubber heel. He puts all of them on the chair and goes on rummaging. Finally he finds a pencil stub.*

Resident: I've got it! (*Triumphantly.*) A pencil!

Visitor: And now a piece of paper . . .

Resident (*rummages some more but does not find anything*): I don't have any. Maybe you . . .

Visitor (*rummages in his turn and comes up with exactly the same things as the* **Resident***; finally he finds a pencil stub*): No, I don't have any paper . . .

Resident (*looking at the things the other has put on the chair next to his*): Hey, wait a minute . . . how come you also . . .

Visitor: What?

Resident: Have the same things I do!

Visitor (*looking*): Hey, yes! You're right!

Resident: That's strange.

Visitor: Strange? Why!

Resident: Well, because . . . why are they the same?

Visitor: Shouldn't they be?

Resident: No. Everyone carries around the things he wants to.

Visitor: Well, I want to carry these things around!

Resident: Me too. It's the most peculiar thing.

Visitor: Everything's peculiar enough. All you have to do is think about it.

Resident: What's that you say?

Visitor: That all you have to do is think about it.

Voice: Nagaio!

Visitor (*sticking his head out of the window*): And at times it's better not to think about it. Because we have nothing to do with that out there.

Resident: With that out there, no. But with these things . . .

Visitor (*interrupting him with a gesture*): Stop! I have it!

Resident: What?

Visitor: I know why we're both carrying the same things around: because that's what we decided to do the last time we saw each other.

Resident (*skeptically*): You sure?

Visitor: Certainly! I'm absolutely sure. Didn't we decide to do some measuring today?

Resident: You're right.

Visitor: Well then, that's why they're the same.

Resident: Maybe. But you certainly have a peculiar way of solving problems . . .

Visitor: What problems? You think there are some problems here?

Resident: Aren't there?

Visitor: I don't know. It's a point of view.

Voice: Nagaio!

Resident (*sticking his head out of the window*): I'd like to know what point of view this other . . .

Visitor: Maybe they're calling us.

Resident (*startled*): Us?

Visitor: Could be.

Resident (*shaking his head*): No. Neither one of us is named Nagaio.

Visitor: How do we know that? We might be.

Resident (*a bit irritably*): You're joking, aren't you?

16

Visitor: No. Anyone could be Nagaio. Nobody knows the name they give him.

Resident: That who gives him?

Visitor: Others.

Resident (*pensively*): Would you say so?

Visitor: Would I say what?

Resident: I'd say that if others . . . that's to say, if the names . . . No, that's not it . . .

Visitor: Now I don't understand you.

Resident: I don't either. It's something to think about.

Visitor: Meanwhile we ought to go on measuring.

Resident: Yes, that's right. But what about the paper? We don't have any paper.

Visitor (*looking around*): No, we don't have any . . .

Resident: Then we'll have to forget all about it.

Visitor (*still looking around*): Wait a minute. Yes . . . yes, that's it!

Resident: What?

Visitor: We don't need any paper.

Resident: We don't?

Visitor: No. We've got the walls. They're white.

Resident: No, not the walls! Precisely for that reason.

Visitor: Precisely for what reason?

Resident: Because they're white.

Visitor: We could erase afterwards . . .

Resident: No. They won't be the same anymore.

Visitor: What do you mean?

Resident: They're the only pure thing we have, don't you see?

Visitor (*pensively*): Yes, that's true enough. We don't have any other alternatives left, though.

Resident: No, we don't. And you can imagine the time it'll take.

Visitor: Well, what shall we do, then? We've got to have some place to mark down the measurements . . .

Resident: Maybe we could just let the whole thing go.

Visitor: Let what go?

Resident: The measuring, man.

Visitor (*energetically*): No, absolutely not that!

Resident: After all, it isn't really all that necessary . . .

Visitor: Never mind. We've undertaken to measure — so we have to measure.

Resident: All right, maybe so . . . But if we can't write on the walls . . .

Visitor: Hold it — I think I have it!

Resident (*slightly alarmed*): You do?

Visitor: Yes. The handkerchief!

Resident: The handkerchief?

Visitor (*producing a crumpled and dirty handkerchief*): We'll write on this.

Resident (*doubtfully*): It's pretty dirty.

Visitor: So it is. Let's see yours.

Resident (*producing a colored handkerchief*): It's not all that dirty.

Visitor: But it isn't white.

Resident: No, that's true. So what'll we do?

Visitor: We could wash mine.

Resident: No, that wouldn't be any use.

Visitor: No. Maybe we could do something else ...

Resident: What?

Visitor: Borrow a piece of paper.

Resident: From whom?

Visitor: I don't know. From someone — anyone.

Resident: There isn't anyone.

Visitor: In there ... (*He indicates the interior room with his head.*)

Resident: No. They don't have anything at all.

Visitor: We could wait for one of those girls to pass through ...

Voice: Nagaio!

Visitor (*listening*): They've started calling again.

Resident (*upset*): Yes.

Visitor: Let's wait for one of those girls to pass through.

Resident: Not me. I'm not waiting for anything.

Visitor: Why not?

Resident: I've never seen any girl.

Visitor: Sure you have, man! Don't make so much ...

Resident: I still like your handkerchief more.

Visitor (*looking at it uncertainly*): Every time I look at it it gets dirtier. If you hadn't said anything ...

Resident: I know. It slipped out. But it's just that it really was dirty.

Visitor: Not all that dirty.

Resident: In any case it doesn't cost anything to try it.

Visitor (*puts the handkerchief on the floor after smoothing it out and draws lines on it with the pencil*): It looks as if it'll do after all. We'll leave the pencil there ...

Resident (*looking over his shoulder*): It'd be better if I did the measuring and you took notes.

Visitor: But if we both measured, we'd be through sooner.

18

Resident: I don't want to finish sooner.

Visitor: You don't?

Resident: No. What would we do afterwards?

Visitor: You're right. We'd have to invent something else.

Resident: I'll sing out the figures to you.

Visitor: Right. I'll sit down here.

He sits down on the floor, smooths out the handkerchief, and holds one end of it fast by putting the chair legs on it.

Resident (*after waiting for the preparations to end*): Ready?

Visitor: Ready.

Resident: First the door. (*He goes to the door but hesitates once he gets there.*)

Visitor (*noticing the hesitation*): What's the matter?

Resident: It's just that I don't know what's the best way to measure it. Should I measure if from top to bottom or from one side to the other?

Visitor (*getting up and going to the door*): Well now ... (*He examines the door with great care.*) I don't know for sure, mind you, but it seems to me that all in all it would be much better to start with the length.

Resident: I don't see any objection to that.

*The **Visitor** goes back to his place. The **Resident** starts measuring but finds that he cannot reach all the way to the top of the door.*

Resident: I'm going to need the chair.

Visitor: The chair?

Resident: Certainly — I can't reach the top.

Visitor: But I need the chair too. For the handkerchief.

Resident: I didn't think of that. (*Pause.*) In that case I don't see how we're going to do it ...

Visitor: There is a way.

Resident: I don't see it. What is it?

Visitor: You could climb up on my shoulders.

Resident: I don't think much of that; I might fall.

Visitor: Well, in that case nothing else occurs to me.

Resident: The chair would be just the right solution.

Visitor: But I can't let you have the chair. I've already told you that.

Resident: I know ... Oh, it's all just too complicated!

Visitor: Maybe you could start at the bottom . . .

Resident: Sure, but what about afterwards?

Visitor: Afterwards something or other will occur to us . . .

Resident: You think so?

Visitor: I'm not absolutely certain.

Resident: All right. (*He goes to the angle of the corridor, under the window, and places the tape measure on the floor.*) Ready?

Visitor (*sitting down beside the handkerchief*): Whenever you like.

The **Resident** *slowly measures the wall at the far end of the hallway. The tape does not reach all the way to the end. Seeing this, he hesitates, then leaves it lying and goes to the chair.*

Visitor: How's it going?

Resident: I need something to mark the place where the tape ends.

Visitor: Oh!

The **Resident** *takes the stone and puts it down on the floor to mark the end of the tape. He then picks up the tape and proceeds to measure the short remaining length. When he has done this, he turns around.*

Resident: That's that.

Visitor: Very good. (*Ready to take notes.*) How much is it?

Resident (*peers at the tape and scratches the back of his neck*): I don't know.

Visitor: What do you mean, you don't know? Look at the numbers, man!

Resident: The thing is there aren't any numbers!

Visitor (*gets up and goes over to look at the tape*): You're right. It doesn't have any numbers!

Resident: What do we do now?

Visitor: Let's use mine. (*Takes it out of his pocket and offers it.*) Here.

Resident (*takes it and looks at it*): But this doesn't have any numbers either!

Visitor: It doesn't? (*Both of them examine it.*) I could have sworn it had some . . .

Resident: Me too.

Visitor (*astonished*): You too? But you've never seen it before!

Resident: I meant mine. It used to have numbers too.

20

Visitor: I don't understand it . . .

Resident: The fact is we don't understand anything.

Visitor: We can't accomplish anything. Everything betrays us . . .

Resident (*confidentially*): I know how we can do it!

Visitor: How?

Resident (*stretching out his hand*): With this.

Visitor: With what?

Resident: With the hand. We can measure by the width of the palm.

Voice: Nagaio!

Visitor (*sticking his head out the window*): Do they always call like that?

Resident: Yes, always. I don't know! (*Reproachfully.*) We were talking about the hand!

Visitor: Ah, yes, the hand. We can measure by its width.

Resident (*bending down to begin work*): Now watch how . . .

The **Visitor** goes back to his place and watches how the other measures palm by palm. Before he gets to the end, the window across the way opens, and a mature but still good-looking woman dressed in a bathrobe looks out. The two men raise their heads at the sound of the window being opened but do not get up until the woman begins speaking.

Nagaio: (*leaning out and looking down*): Who called me?

Visitor: Is that Nagaio?

Resident: I don't know; it must be.

Nagaio (*looking at the two men since no one has replied from below*): Did you two call me, maybe?

Visitor (*to* **Resident**): What's she saying?

Resident: I don't know.

Visitor: But she did say something to us?

Resident: I don't know.

Nagaio: Who called me?

Visitor: Answer her.

Resident: What shall I say?

Visitor: Something — anything.

Resident (*to the woman, pitifully*): We're two . . .

Nagaio: Did you call me?

Visitor (*jumping into the conversation*): We're measuring . . .

Nagaio: What do you want?

Resident (*becoming animated*): We're measuring with our hands since the tape measure turned out to be blank.

Nagaio: Do you live here?

Resident: It sounded to us as if they were calling from below.

Nagaio: I don't remember ever having seen you before.

Visitor: It must be someone who wanted to see you.

Nagaio: Do you want me for anything? I was just taking a bath . . .

Resident: Maybe it was the janitor — I don't know . . .

Nagaio: You can see I came out just as I was.

Resident: It was just a short while ago that they called you.

Nagaio: I had a little time since today is Saturday, so I thought I'd take advantage of it.

Visitor: We were only measuring . . .

Nagaio: Isn't Caterina there yet?

Resident: Since we don't have any paper, we're taking notes on a handkerchief.

Nagaio: She told me she was going, but she didn't even come to say good-bye to me.

Visitor: If you don't have anything to do and want to help us . . .

Nagaio: Well, since you're new lodgers here . . . My name's Nagaio.

Visitor: All in all, three might be more amusing . . .

Resident: And we'd probably do a better job.

Nagaio: I'll be with you shortly. I still have to comb my hair.

Visitor: Do you live alone?

Nagaio: I'm expecting visitors later.

Resident: You haven't said yes or no to us.

Nagaio (*closing the window*): See you soon. So long.

Visitor: Well?

Resident: What do you mean, well?

Visitor: Just that. What did she say?

Resident: Didn't you understand what she said?

Visitor: Not a word. How about you?

Resident (*discouraged*): Me neither.

Visitor: Are you trying to say that that's all?

Resident: I don't know. But either she or we . . .

Visitor (*grabbing his arm*): We? What are you trying to say?

Resident (*pensively*): Take it easy, I don't know. It's as if we were alone.

Visitor: Who?

Resident: Us. You and me.

Visitor: I don't understand it. She was there. (*He points.*) But it's just as if she hadn't been.

Resident: That's just what I'm trying to say.

Visitor (*impatiently*): Trying to say, trying to say! But who can figure it out? And that voice that was calling her . . . What was it calling her for?

Resident: Maybe it wasn't calling her at all. Maybe she isn't Nagaio.

Visitor: Maybe not — that's right.

Resident: How could we find out?

Visitor: You that interested?

Resident: No, but if I only worried about things that interested me . . .

Visitor: Ah, I see. (*He goes to the chair and starts to collect what he had taken from his pocket.*) There's no sense pretending you're going to go on being good company.

Resident: And you?

Visitor: Me neither. That's why I'm going.

Resident: You're going? Do you mean you don't want to measure any more? . . .

Visitor: Any more? But we've hardly started!

Resident: That's precisely why, man.

Visitor: No, I've had enough. (*Takes the handkerchief, folds it up and sticks it in his pocket. He looks at this hands.*) I've got myself all dirty; I'll have to wash.

Resident (*pointing to the second door in the corridor*): There.

Visitor: I know.

He goes to the door. The **Resident** *turns round and starts to pick up the things still left on the chair. Meanwhile the* **Visitor** *opens the door of the bathroom and enters, bumping into the* **Stranger,** *who is just coming out. The two look at each other for a moment; then the* **Stranger** *steps aside to let the* **Visitor** *by. The latter inclines his head and enters while the* **Stranger** *comes out, shutting the door behind him. The* **Resident,** *who has just finished putting everything in his pocket, turns round.*

Resident (*to the* **Stranger**): All through?

Stranger: All through with what?

Resident: Your hands . . .

Stranger: What about my hands?

Resident: Didn't you want to wash your hands?

Stranger: Sure; what about it?

Resident: Well then, you're all through. You were pretty quick about it too.

Stranger: You think so?

Resident: Yes, but you didn't have to hurry so much . . . Hey, listen, I've thought of something else.

23

Stranger: What?

Resident: We could put numbers on the tapes.

Stranger: What tapes?

Resident: What do you mean, what tapes? Ours!

Stranger: I don't have any tape.

Resident: You always have to kid around . . .

Stranger: What about you? You're making things up.

Resident: Not now. We were measuring and . . .

Stranger: What were we measuring? What?

Resident (*with an expansive gesture*): Well, everything. The doors. The walls.

Stranger: Not me.

Resident: Sure you were.

Voice: Nagaio!

Stranger: And I say no.

Resident (*going to the window*): They're starting to call her again.

Stranger: Call who?

Resident: Nagaio.

Stranger (*joining him at the window*): And who is Nagaio? Why do you keep talking about things I don't know anything about?

Resident: You know as much as I do.

Nagaio (*opening the window opposite and looking out*): Did you call me again?

Stranger: Are you Nagaio, then?

Nagaio: Did you call me?

Stranger: Someone called you, sure enough.

Nagaio: It wasn't you?

Stranger: All right . . . maybe it could be that it might have been us. We could have been it if we had known that a girl like you . . .

Nagaio (*complacently*): Don't sweet-talk me!

Stranger: It's the truth, pure and simple. And anyway you didn't let me finish.

Resident (*to the* **Stranger**): What are you talking about? Is that Nagaio?

Stranger: Search me. I suppose so. (*To the woman.*) Your name is Nagaio, isn't it?

Nagaio: Yes. Why?

Stranger: Because my friend here asked me.

Nagaio: But I told you that before!

Stranger: Before? But I just got here! I've never seen you before.

Nagaio: Just a few moments ago.

Stranger: I assure you I haven't. I wouldn't have forgotten a girl

24

like you . . .

Nagaio: Don't flatter me!

Stranger: I'm not, so far — and you won't let me finish this time either.

Resident (*to the* **Stranger**): What are you talking about?

Stranger: What's the matter with you? Can't you hear?

Resident: Yes, but . . .

Stranger: Well then, shut up and listen.

Resident: It's just that I don't understand.

Stranger (*to* **Nagaio**): He says that he doesn't understand.

Nagaio: What?

Stranger: Everything that we're saying.

Nagaio: Is he deaf?

Stranger: No. That's to say, I don't think he is. (*To the* **Resident.**) That's right, isn't it?

Resident: What's that?

Stranger: I'm asking you if you're deaf!

Resident: Deaf? (*Annoyed.*) And why should I be deaf?

Stranger: It just looked that way to me. (*To* **Nagaio.**) No, he isn't deaf.

Nagaio: Well, he's kind of peculiar, isn't he?

Stranger: Yes, that's true — just a little. He only says things that don't make any sense.

Resident: Are you talking about me?

Stranger: Oh, you understood that, did you?

Resident: Of course! But don't say things that don't make any sense! You're the one who's not making sense!

Stranger: Me? Allow me to remind you that you're the one who was talking about measurements . . .

Resident: So? Didn't you agree to it? Didn't you, when all's said and done, pull out a dirty handkerchief to mark them down?

Stranger: A handkerchief? (*He pulls a clean folded handkerchief out of his pocket.*) This one?

Resident (*looking at it*): No, not that one. It was dirty.

Stranger (*offended*): But I don't carry a dirty handkerchief around!

Resident: Don't tell me any stories!

Stranger (*to* **Nagaio**): I don't know what he's talking about. Never mind him, though . . . (*He leans further out of the window.*) Are you alone?

Nagaio: Yes. Why?

Stranger: I don't know. It just occurred to me that you might be afraid.

25

Nagaio: Afraid? Well, from time to time . . .

Stranger: And what about now?

Nagaio: Now? Well now, I don't know. I'm expecting a visit.

Stranger: That's what I thought. I'll be right over.

Nagaio: Is it you I'm expecting?

Stranger: Why not?

Resident: Do you mind explaining what this is all about?

Stranger: One moment. (*To* **Nagaio.**) Just let me straighten him out and then I'll be with you.

Nagaio: I'll be waiting — don't be long. (*She leaves the window.*)

Stranger: And now what do you want?

Resident: I want to know what's going on. Who is that woman, for a start?

Stranger: Nagaio. Don't you know that? She's waiting for me . . .

Resident: You mean she's waiting for us.

Stranger: No, no, just for me.

Resident: Impossible.

Stranger: Oh, really?

Resident: Yes. Both of us or . . . it's all the same now anyway. We can't go over there.

Stranger: I don't know about you. I can, all right.

Resident: No, neither one of us can. Don't you know that there's no one there?

Stranger: What do you mean, there's no one there? There's a woman there, and not all that bad-looking either.

Resident (*laughing contemptuously*): Don't be so credulous . . .

Stranger: Credulous? She told me herself that she was waiting for me.

Resident: Bah! You made all that up yourself.

Stranger: All right then, I'll tell you all about it afterwards. She . . . (*He stops because the girl who passed through previously has returned. She comes out of the room at the end of the corridor and goes to the front door.*) Hey, wait a minute! Who's that?

Resident: The same as the other one: nobody.

Stranger: You're crazy. (*To the girl, at the precise moment she passes in front of him.*) Hello there . . .

Girl: Hello.

Stranger: Don't we know each other?

Girl (*stopping*): Not that I know of, no.

Stranger: I just thought we did . . . My name's Claudi.

Girl: Mine is Filo.

Stranger: Filo . . . that's a very pretty name.

Girl: Claudi isn't so bad either.

26

Stranger: No, but Filo . . .

Resident (*interrupting him*): What are you talking about?

Stranger: What am I talking about? I'm talking with Filo.

Resident: With Filo? And who is Filo?

Stranger: She is. Don't you think she's pretty — real pretty?

Resident: Here we go again!

Stranger (*to the* **Girl**): Can you tell me what's the matter with him?

Girl: With whom?

Stranger: With him.

Girl: Him? What do you mean?

Stranger: Well, then . . . (*He thinks better of it.*) No. Let's skip it. Are you going out?

Girl: Yes, in a minute.

Stranger: That's funny. I was just going out too. Can I keep you company?

Girl: Well . . . I don't know if . . .

Stranger (*slyly*): After all, we've discovered that we both have nice-sounding names . . .

Girl (*smiling*): Well, in that case . . . (*She goes to the front door, the* **Stranger** *following.*)

Resident (*stopping him*): But do you really want to go away already?

Stranger: I'm accompanying her.

Resident: But . . .

Stranger (*seeing that the* **Girl** *has opened the door and is about to disappear*): I'll talk to you another time, okay?

Resident: But . . .

Stranger: See you soon. (*He hurries after the* **Girl.**)

Resident: But . . . (*He opens the window and sees* **Nagaio** *looking out. She catches sight of the* **Stranger** *on the landing of the staircase.*)

Nagaio: Aren't you coming?

Voice of the Stranger (*embarrassed*): I . . . I'm just going out for a moment to buy something . . .

Nagaio: No, you're going with her . . .

Voice of the Stranger: I assure you . . .

Nagaio: Never mind assuring. And you, Caterina . . .

Voice of the Stranger: Her name isn't Caterina, it's Filo.

Nagaio: I didn't think you'd have gone away without saying good-bye to me. We're friends, after all . . .

Voice of the Girl: But I'm not going away, I tell you!

Nagaio: And what about these men, then?

Voice of the Girl: What men? Do you mean Claudi?

Nagaio: And who's Claudi?

Voice of the Stranger: That's me.

Voice of the Girl: That's him.

Nagaio (*pointing to the other window*): I mean those others . . .

Voice of the Girl: What others?

Nagaio: I don't know. Maybe there isn't even one at the window right now.

Voice of the Girl: There shouldn't be anyone there.

Voice of the Stranger: Oh yes, just some poor fellow.

Voice of the Girl: I don't know who you're talking about. But you two . . . do you two know each other?

Voice of the Stranger: Well, we . . . oh, vaguely.

Voice of the Girl: Are you supposed to be together?

Nagaio: We were supposed to see each other, yes.

Voice of the Girl (*irritated*): Well then, as far as I'm concerned . . . (*She can be heard running downstairs.*)

Voice of the Stranger: No, Filo. Wait! . . . (*Runs after her.*)

Nagaio: Claudi! (**Claudi** *does not answer, and* **Nagaio** *continues to lean out of the window until she can no longer see him.*)

Resident (*to* **Nagaio**): Do you mind telling me what's going on? (**Nagaio** *takes no notice of him.*) Nagaio — that's to say, that really is your name, isn't it? (*The woman slowly closes the window.*) There you are! Alone again. Always the same! (*Irritated, he slams the window shut, breaking one of the panes. And if one of the panes doesn't break it's all the same.*) It's enough to make you sick!

He goes to the chair, sits down, rolls a cigarette, and lights up. He throws the match into the ashtray, which is on the floor. Then he hears a weak knock on the door. He gets up and plods heavily to the door. There is more knocking and he realizes that it is coming from the other direction. He stops, surprised, and goes back toward the bathroom, the door of which he opens.

Visitor (*coming out*): Somebody locked the door on me.

The **Resident** stares at him, mouth open, without saying a word.

Visitor (*noticing this behavior*): What's the matter with you? Is that so peculiar?

Resident: But, but . . . Were you in there?

Visitor: Don't you see I was?

Resident: No . . . And then, who . . .

Visitor: Exactly! That's just what I wanted to ask you. Because there was somebody else here.

Resident: Somebody else here . . .

Visitor: Somebody who came out of here when I went in. He locked me in . . .

Resident (*shaking his head*): Impossible. You're joking. That was you. I saw perfectly well that it was you.

Visitor: Who?

Resident: The other one . . . I mean the one you call the other.

Visitor: But I was right in here . . .

Resident: No. You went out with that girl . . .

Visitor: With what girl?

Resident: I don't know. With no one. With someone. The girls that pass by, everyone that passes by, those who come and go, those . . . one of them.

Visitor (*seizing his arm*): Stop it! I don't know what you're talking about . . .

Resident: You went out together.

Visitor: You can see yourself that I'm still here.

Resident: And you were talking to her . . .

Visitor: To whom?

Resident: To her. You were talking to her. And she was talking to you. And Nagaio, or whoever she is, also. I mean the other one.

Visitor: What other one?

Resident: The one at the window. You were going to go with her, she was waiting for you, but you went out with the other one, maybe because she was prettier and younger . . . But how? (*Desperately.*) How could you do it?

Visitor: But I didn't do anything!

Resident (*accusingly*): Yes, you did, too! I saw you. With my own eyes. (*He touches them.*)

Visitor: But I couldn't have gone out there and still be here . . .

Resident: I don't know if you could or not. You do some peculiar things!

Visitor: There has to be some sort of mix-up here.

Resident: No such thing. I know what I'm talking about.

Visitor: So do I. The fact is that you've always imagined things, and, what's worse, you've always tried to impose them on others. Just as an example, if it hadn't been for you it would never have occurred to me to measure this particular house.

Resident: And what's that got to do with it? Where's the imagination in that?

29

Visitor: I don't know, but . . . Yes, that's it: the tape measure without numbers . . .

Resident: Well, what about it? Is it my fault if there aren't any?

Visitor: But perhaps there are some . . . (*He takes his tape measure out of his pocket and looks at it. Then, without saying anything, he turns round and hides it.*)

Resident: Well? Are there any?

Visitor (*slightly irritated*): No, I guess there aren't. But there are other things as well.

Resident: What other things?

Visitor: We haven't been able to make any contact with Nagaio or whoever she is.

Resident: You have, all right.

Visitor: No, I talked to her a lot, but she and I weren't talking about the same thing. In short, I ask myself . . .

Resident: What?

Visitor: Whether you and I are talking about the same thing.

Resident: We understand each other well enough!

Visitor: Maybe it just seems that way to us. We certainly don't understand each other when you accuse me of having gone out with a girl.

Resident: It's not that we don't understand each other. It's that you deny it.

Visitor: But maybe I deny it because I don't know what you mean.

Resident: I could hardly make myself clearer!

Visitor: No. But the fact is that I haven't budged from this place. So how could I have gone out? There's some word here, something, I don't know what, that doesn't have the same meaning for both of us. Or maybe you're not talking to the man you think you're talking to. Or else I . . .

Resident: Or you what?

Visitor: Or maybe I'm not talking with whom I think I'm talking, or where I think . . .

Resident: Of course you are! We were measuring . . . or planning to measure . . . don't you remember?

Visitor: Sure I do, but it doesn't help.

Resident: Why?

Visitor: I've always been planning to measure with everyone.

Resident: What do you mean, with everyone? Who is everyone?

Visitor: Somebody else — other people. Anyone. Everyone measures or plans to. How should I know that it's you?

Resident: You?

Visitor: Yes. Everyone's like you, properly looked at.

Resident: In other words you've lied to me!

Visitor: I have?

Resident (*excitedly*): This time I've caught you at it, friend! You said that there wasn't anyone there . . .

Visitor: That's what *you* said.

Resident: We both said it.

Visitor: Not me. I just listened.

Resident: Listened to what?

Visitor: To you saying it.

Resident: And you agreed.

Visitor: I don't know about that. I've got no way of telling whether you're right or not. And there's no way you could have known if that man went out with the girl . . .

Resident: That doesn't mean a thing.

Visitor: It means that he went out . . . And if it was me that went out, you wouldn't have anyone here.

Resident: All you're saying is that you've misled me.

Visitor: No. What I'm saying is that you're dealing with phantoms.

Resident (*tapping him*): You're a phantom?

Visitor: If I'm not, the other one is. One of the two.

Resident (*after a moment, pensively*): No, this whole thing is a practical joke that you've cooked up . . .

Visitor: With the measuring business as well?

Resident: With . . . (*He stops because at this point the **Stranger** and the **Girl** enter by the front door.*) Well, what do you say now?

Visitor: What do I say to what?

Resident (*pointing to the two*): To that. You didn't go out with her . . .

Visitor: No. That's him, the other one. The one in the bathroom.

Resident: There's never been anyone in the bathroom.

Visitor (*stepping into the **Stranger**'s way*): One moment, if you please.

Stranger (*stopping*): What's the matter?

Girl (*not stopping*): Aren't you coming?

Stranger: Of course I am. (*He goes on.*)

Visitor: Just a moment, I tell you.

Stranger (*to the **Girl***): He says it'll only be a moment . . .

Girl: Who does?

Stranger: I don't know. Him.

Girl: But I can't wait.

Stranger: Go ahead. I'll follow you.

Girl: You won't be able to alone. You have to come now.

Stranger (*to the* **Visitor**): You hear her. It's got to be now. (*He starts to follow her.*)

Visitor (*intercepting him*): But this is more important!

Stranger: What is?

Visitor: This — clearing up this mistake.

Girl (*impatiently*): Are you coming or aren't you?

Stranger: Yes.

Visitor: No.

He holds him firmly to prevent him from leaving. The **Girl** *goes to the door leading to the interior room. The* **Stranger** *struggles with the* **Visitor,** *but the* **Girl** *disappears before he can free himself.*

Resident (*vaguely ironic*): Despite everything you're not going to make me believe it.

Visitor (*turning round*): What?

Resident: That there's someone else.

The **Stranger,** *profiting by the* **Visitor**'s *distraction, runs off towards the inner room but cannot enter. When the* **Visitor** *grabs him again, the* **Stranger** *pounds desperately on the door that bars his way.*

Visitor (*catching him*): Come here!

Stranger: Open up! Open the door!

Resident (*coming over*): A door?

Stranger (*knocking on it*): Yes, the door!

Resident: It's never been there before. (*All three stand looking at the door.*)

Stranger (*after a pause*): Well, it's here now.

Resident: I don't understand it. You've mixed everything up here.

Visitor: Well, it's going to get cleared up right now. In the first place, there's two of us, two completely different persons. Him and me.

Resident (*laughs*): No, no!

Visitor (*grabbing him by the lapels*): What's the matter, don't you have any eyes in your head?

Resident: It's all a joke.

Visitor (*turning desperately to the* **Stranger**): You tell it to him.

Stranger: What do you want me to tell him?

Visitor: That you're somebody else!

Stranger: Somebody else? No, I'm me!

Resident (*triumphantly*): You see?

Visitor: No. I mean he's him. He's the one who was in the bathroom.

Stranger: Yes, that's true, all right. I went in there to wash my hands.

Visitor: Yes, but when?

Stranger: I don't know.

Resident (*to the* **Visitor**): You went in there to wash your hands . . .

Visitor: Yes, but after him. When he came out.

Stranger: Wouldn't it make more sense for you to open the door? I want to get together with Filo again.

Resident: What Filo?

Stranger: Her.

Resident: There's nobody there.

Stranger: What do you know about it?

Resident: Naturally I know all about it. I live here!

Stranger: You?

Resident: Yes, me.

Stranger: And you don't know who lives in the house?

Resident: Nothing. Nobody.

Visitor: He's always lived alone.

Stranger: But Filo . . . You all saw her, right?

Resident: There's no Filo here.

Stranger: But there has to be something or other there. On the other side of this door . . .

Resident: The dead.

Visitor: That's right, the dead.

Stranger: It can't be!

Resident: Get together with yourself.

Visitor: What's that?

Stranger: What's that?

Resident: I said, get together with yourself. You can't say yes and no at the same time.

Visitor: I said yes, he said no.

Resident (*holding his head*): That's enough — I'm fed up!

Visitor: There's no getting any sense into you. We have an objective situation here . . .

Resident: Objective? What about the way you're getting it tangled up?

Visitor: There's nothing to be done. He's him and I'm me.

Resident: Maybe. And maybe you're Filo as well. And you say you want to get together with her again?

Visitor: Not me.

Stranger: Me — I do.

Resident: It's the same thing. (*He goes to the door and opens it with a slight touch.*)

Stranger: Oh! You know how to do it . . .

Resident: Sure. Come on then, go ahead.

Stranger: Thanks, eh? Many thanks. (*He goes in.*)

Resident: There you are.

Visitor: Yes, there you are. But what? What does it mean?

Resident: Not a thing. I know that. But now we're back where we were at the beginning.

Visitor: We've always been the same as at the beginning.

Resident: But now you won't be able to argue with me about whether you're you.

Visitor: I've never argued about it. But now I'm here and he's . . . on the other side.

Resident: No. Nowhere. He doesn't exist. He's never existed. Nor has Filo, nor . . .

Voice: Nagaio!

Resident: Nor has Nagaio.

Visitor: Nor have you, nor have I . . .

Resident: Nor you, nor I. Now we can finally get back to our business.

Visitor: Yes. (*Knock at the door.*) That's to say, who knows? (*Pause.*) Aren't you going to open?

*The **Resident** hesitates but finally shrugs his shoulders and goes to the door.*

CURTAIN

The Room

(Tècnica de cambra)

Manuel de Pedrolo

English version by Jill R. Webster

CHARACTERS

Cluc
Samir
Belet
Valva
Cacansa
Cleda
Alona
Voice of the Landlady

ACT 1

A rectangular room. Two doors at right angles, at the back on the right. On the left, placed towards the back, two divan beds. Towards the front some large shelves, possibly containing the following objects: a hammer, a key-ring crammed with keys, three different sorts of books, a couple of pencils, a saw, two sheets of paper, a bar of soap, a comb, lipstick, handcuffs, three or four packets of cigarettes, matches, four full bottles of whisky, glasses, an ashtray, a pack of cards, an envelope full of small keys, a dozen clothes pegs, eight plates, a jersey, an alarm clock, three empty boxes, a tie, a neat bundle of sticks, a fan, an iron, a pocket knife, a bicycle wheel, a mask with humble features and a box of thread and needles, all of them heaped together in an untidy way. In the foreground on the right a full-length mirror fixed to the wall and an additional table make up the contents of the room.

As the curtain is raised, the stage is empty. After a suitable time, the **Landlady's Voice** *is heard:* You've been fortunate, young man! The room, as you'll see, is pleasant and has all the comforts you could wish. We've taken care of your well-being without sparing any efforts, and it's with pride I can assure you that up to now none of the guests who've passed through this house have had any reason to complain. That's the reason we don't even have a complaints book! *(She is silent, while the rattling of chains and bolts and the opening of a lock can be heard, an operation which should give the impression of being a bit complicated. Immediately, while the door in the background opens to let through* **Cluc,** *a young man wearing a very loose jacket and carrying a large suitcase in his hand, the voice, whose owner is still unseen, takes up again.)* Look and judge for yourself. A room like a whole land, large and welcoming, in which besides all the indispensable things you'll find all those other superfluous objects which make life more pleasant. I'm sure that you'll be happy here, as all those who have preceded you have been happy, and that you'll wish to stay for a long while. Make yourself at home! *(The voice is silent and the door closes with the same laborious accompaniment.)*
Cluc *(leaving the suitcase on the floor)*: Perfect . . .

He goes into the room, hesitant, looking around him; he goes up to the beds, with his hand he tries the resilience of the springs, then turns to the shelves, touches some objects, full of curiosity, but afterwards crosses the room to the spot where he has left the case, picks it up, puts it on the small table and opens it. It is empty. Without hurrying, he begins a series of trips to transfer one by one the saw, a bottle, two plates, an empty box. Then he picks up the bicycle wheel and contemplates it doubtfully. He puts it down again at the same time as the **Landlady's Voice** *is heard once more, and from this moment, while the woman speaks, he closes the suitcase quickly, puts it down on the ground, where it was before, and then sits down by the foot of the bed in the background, close to the shelves. He picks up a packet of cigarettes, opens it and lights up one.*

Landlady's Voice: It's not worth mentioning nor's there probably any point to it, but the house has always had a reputation for its formality and the great comfort it affords to its guests. Everything possible in the way of comfort has been provided with the aim of making your stay pleasant. Now you'll see your room where you can lead a reasonable life without any worries. (*Noise of chains and bolts, etc., and the door opens on* **Valva** *dressed in a simple skirt with pockets and a very tight blue jersey. She is also carrying a suitcase in her hand.*) Here it is, a room like few others, full of nice little details, and solid furniture which it only remains for you to keep in good condition. I leave you in good company since it is the rule of the house only to take in people who are serious and in all ways respectable. I hope you will be happy. (*The door shuts with the usual noises, which are repeated each time.*
Valva *leaves her suitcase on the floor and looks at* **Cluc.**)
Cluc (*who the whole time has not ceased to observe her*): Hullo!
Valva: Hullo!
Cluc: It seems we're destined to be companions.
Valva: Yes. (*She goes over to the first bed, and lets herself fall on to it.*)
Cluc: My name's Cluc.
Valva: And I'm Valva.
Cluc (*touching the bed with his hand*): Perhaps you'll be more comfortable here.
Valva: I don't know. (*Then she seems to notice the mirror and gets up to look at herself in it.*) My hair's very untidy.
Cluc: (*pointing with a gesture to the shelves*): You'll find a comb there.

The girl goes over to the shelves and routs around until she finds it.

Valva: There's also a lipstick. (*She picks it up.*)
Cluc: Yes, I've already seen it.

Valva *moves again in the direction of the mirror, and proceeds to do her hair in front of it, leaving the lipstick on the table.* **Cluc** *has followed her and watches her in silence.*

Valva: What are you looking at so hard?
Cluc: You're so different . . .
Valva: Everyone's different, right?
Cluc: Perhaps so, but I meant in another way.
Valva: Of course, I'm a woman.

However, both of them look towards the door, because once again the voice of the **Landlady** *is heard.* **Cluc** *goes back to the divan bed and the girl hurriedly picks up the lipstick and puts it in her suitcase with the comb. She shuts the suitcase and goes to sit where she was in the beginning.*

Landlady's Voice: Welcome to this communal home where I'm sure days of happiness await you. I expect you already have some details of the house, situated in an ideal position, with healthy and bracing air, which you'll have the good fortune to enjoy. I'm always discreet in my praise but you should be aware of the numerous advantages which it has to offer to a new arrival. As far as the room you've been given is concerned, the only thing I should tell you is that it's on the best floor in the house. Allow me to do you the honors. (*Noise of chains, etc., and the door opens on* **Samir** *dressed in a long shirt, and carrying the inevitable suitcase.*) Look well around you and tell me if it's possible to find a more pleasant room. Here you can live a full and enviable life just like all the other guests we've had since the rooming house has been here. I'm confident you'll stay a long time. Good luck.

The door closes and **Samir** *turns towards the other two, leaving the suitcase on one side.*

Samir: A little annoying, eh?
Cluc: Yes; she repeats herself.
Samir: Have you two been living here long?
Cluc: Relatively. Time to wrap up something and . . . (*He stops suddenly.*)

Samir: Did you say wrap up?

Cluc: Just a way of speaking.

Samir (*he goes towards the bed and points to* **Valva**): And her?

Cluc: That's Valva.

Samir: Hullo, Valva.

Valva: How are you?

Cluc: My name's Cluc.

Samir: Samir. (*They shake hands.*) I hope we'll get on. (*He sits down beside* **Valva.**) And with you too. Yes, especially with you.

Valva: Why especially with me?

Samir: You seem very nice . . .

Valva *stares at him for a while and then gets up. She walks over to the suitcase, puts the lipstick into it and goes over to the mirror and continues to do her hair in front of it.*

Samir (*after watching all these actions he turns to* **Cluc**): I find an indefinable something about her . . .

Cluc: Yes, she's different.

Samir: That's it; different.

Cluc: She's a woman.

Samir: Yes. (*He smiles.*) I like her.

Cluc: Leave her alone. (*He pauses.*) There must be some others coming . . .

Samir: However, you're not sure, eh?

Cluc: No, not at all sure.

Samir: And if no one else comes, what then?

Cluc: It's too soon to worry about that.

Samir: I would say the same in your position. (*He gets up.*) It's not fair.

Cluc: Perhaps not. I could make up for it with other things . . .

Samir: What kind of things?

Cluc: Things I have. Come with me. (*He gets up and leads him to the case, opens it, and displays its contents.*) What appeals to you most?

Samir (*when he has looked at everything*): Nothing. She appeals to me most.

Cluc (*trying to tempt him*): Look — this box. (*He opens it.*) It's an empty box and you could put what you want into it . . .

Samir: But, supposing I don't have anything!

Cluc: That's immaterial. You could have something later on.

Samir (*examining the box*): Do you really like it? Do you really think it's something worthwhile?

40

Cluc: It sure is. There's nothing like a good box. (*But then he puts it away hastily, and shuts the suitcase because outside the* **Landlady's Voice** *can be heard again.* **Valva** *also hastily puts down the lipstick and comb, and they all go back to the beds and sit down as before,* **Cluc** *on the one against the shelves,* **Valva** *and* **Samir** *on the other.*)

Landlady's Voice: I've only good words for people like you who make such excellent choices. You couldn't have found a rooming house which is more convenient or more comfortable, or where for a modest price you can enjoy all the advantages which time places at your disposition. I'm sure that you'll be happy to prove that you've made a good choice, which promises you, as is only right, a pleasant and beautiful existence. I've reserved a room for you, which even the most demanding person couldn't complain about. (*Noise of chains, etc., and* **Cacansa** *appears at the threshold of the door. She is dressed in outdoor clothes and is carrying a suitcase in her hand.*) What do you say to it? It's at your service, carefully designed to fulfill your every need; so I'll leave you now with the select company that goes with the room. Make yourself at home!

The door shuts but the girl's eyes never leave it. Then she turns to the others.

Cacansa: What's all that about?

Samir: What're you talking about?

Cacansa: My reception.

Cluc: It seems it's the custom — we've all had to go through it. (*He gets up and approaches her.*) Why not put your suitcase down. (*He picks it up and places it beside his own.*) Come and sit down, you must be tired.

Cacansa: No, not really — more curious. (*She looks around her.*) A mirror! (*She rushes towards it.*) I've always wanted to look at myself in a mirror . . .

Cluc (*who has followed her*): That's understandable. You're very pretty!

Cacansa: Really? (*She turns to* **Samir.**) Do you think I'm pretty too?

Samir: It's enough if one of us does, isn't it? (*He turns to* **Valva** *and takes her hand.*)

Cacansa (*laughing*): Aha, I see! (*To* **Valva.**) But you're not saying anything!

Valva: Perhaps you want me to say that I think you're pretty too?

Cacansa (*shakes her head*): No, it's all the same to you. (*She looks at herself.*) How pale my lips are! If only I had something to paint them with . . .

Valva: I could lend you my lipstick.

Cacansa: Have you got one?

Valva (*going to her case*): Yes.

Cacansa (*follows her*): What else have you got? (*Both of them bend over as* **Valva** *opens the suitcase.*)

Samir (*to* **Cluc**): I suppose you're no longer interested in giving that box up?

Cluc: No, but in any case, if you want one there are some others over there. (*He points to the shelves.*)

Samir: Whose are they?

Cluc: First come, first served. There are lots of things. (*He goes over there and begins to rout around whilst the two girls stand up,* **Cacansa** *with the lipstick in her hand.*)

Cacansa: Aren't you going to put on any lipstick?

Valva: I haven't had time to yet.

Cacansa (*looking at her attentively*): Of course, your lips are naturally red. You don't need the lipstick as much as I do . . .

Valva: Perhaps you'd like to keep it?

Cacansa: If you don't mind . . .

Valva: Supposing I need it one day, will you lend it to me?

Cacansa: Of course. My word, you're kind! (*She hugs her warmly and goes over to the mirror, where she begins to put on some lipstick.* **Valva** *returns to her bed, just as* **Cluc** *crosses the room with the iron in his hand.*)

Samir (*who has been watching him*): Where are you going with that?

Cluc (*casually*): It could get lost here. It's better to keep an eye on it. (*But at that moment the* **Landlady's Voice** *is heard once more, and he goes back again to the shelves where he leaves the iron before returning to his bed.* **Cacansa** *continues to put on her make-up.*)

Landlady's Voice: Come in, have no fear, for we'll welcome you with open arms, as is the rule in this rooming house, which you've so wisely chosen. You must've already noticed its ideal position, on which I have to congratulate both you and myself, but wait until you see your room, where everything has been arranged to please the eyes and lighten the heart. I've no doubt that you'll feel quite at home, and will get along marvellously with all the companions awaiting you there. (*Usual noise of chains and bolts until the door opens to let in* **Cleda,** *dressed in slacks and a* *blouse and also weighed down by a suitcase.*) Well, how d'you like it? You really can't find words to express your surprise and satisfaction, right? It's a large, light room, clean and welcoming, where life goes on peacefully. I hope you'll stay a long time and be happy here. (*The door closes, and the girl, with a brusque gesture, throws the case to one side and immediately faces the others who are looking at her.*)

Cleda: Well?

Cluc: Nothing.

Samir: Make yourself at home.

Cleda (*as **Cacansa** leaves the lipstick on the little table, and traces the outline of her mouth with her fingers*): You can save that talk for the landlady. (*She takes a step forward and shakes her head, as if to push back her hair.*) My name's Cleda.

Cluc: And I'm Cluc. If you'd like to sit beside me . . .

Cleda (*she shrugs her shoulders*): What for? (*To **Samir**.*) And you two?

Samir (*pointing to his companion*): We're Samir and Valva.

Cacansa (*still in front of the mirror*): And I'm Cacansa.

Cleda (*going towards the beds and looking vaguely around the room*): What a dump! (*She apes the landlady.*) A light room, clean and welcoming; bah!

Valva: Everything depends on us.

Cleda: We'll see. (*She turns to the little table, as **Cluc** gets up from the bed and goes to fetch the iron. She notices **Cacansa**'s pencil.*) A lipstick (*she examines it*) . . .

Cacansa: It's mine.

Cleda: Why?

Samir: Do you always ask why?

Cleda: Of course I do.

Valva: I've given it to her.

As **Cacansa** looks at her reprovingly, **Cleda** moves over to her own suitcase and opens it, with the intention of hiding the lipstick. **Cluc** puts the iron down almost next to her.

Cleda: What've you got there?

Cluc (*shutting the suitcase hastily*): Things.

Samir (*going up to **Cleda***): You can't do that!

Cleda (*half turning round*): What? Ask him what he's got in the case?

Samir: No, keep the lipstick. She told you it was hers.

Cleda: Things change hands. (*She shuts the suitcase and stands up while* **Cluc** *glides across to the other side of the room.*)

Samir: But not that way.

Cleda *indifferent and without answering walks up to the beds. As she passes by* **Valva,** *the latter grabs her arm.*

Valva: Give it back.

Cleda: Leave me alone. It's nothing to do with you. (*She turns to* **Cluc** *who is making the trip over to his suitcase again with a plate.*) Let's see that plate.

Cluc (*half hiding it and pointing to the shelves with the other hand*): There are more over there if you want them. (*The girl goes over there while* **Cacansa,** *taking advantage of her back being turned, goes up to the suitcase to get the lipstick.* **Samir** *returns to* **Valva**'s *side.*)

Cleda: What sort of plates are these? (*She examines one.*) They're only good for one thing. (*She drops it on the floor where it shatters. She goes to pick up another but at that moment the* **Landlady's Voice** *is heard again. She stays near the piece of furniture looking at her nails, while* **Cluc** *hastily goes back to his bed, and* **Cacansa,** *who has the lipstick again, goes over to the mirror.*)

Landlady's Voice: Peace and quiet are the first priorities in this rooming house. If we add impeccable service and a room which must please you, you'll understand how right the decision was that brought you to our door. You'll find suitable companions here to share a time which I'm sure will seem short to you. Come in, come in and let me take you to the room which has been prepared for you, and whose refined comforts I'm sure you'll appreciate. (*Noise of bolts, locks, etc., until the door gives way to* **Belet,** *dressed in a blue undershirt and laden with the usual suitcase.*) Delight your eyes, and rest your tiredness, in this atmosphere of repose, where I wish you a long and entirely fruitful life. So be it. (*The door shuts as usual.* **Belet** *drops the suitcase at his feet, takes a handkerchief from his pocket and wipes his forehead and hands. Right away he moves over to the first bed and sits beside* **Valva.**)

Samir: Let me make the introductions. This is Valva, and I'm Samir.

Belet: Fantastic!

Samir: Did you say fantastic?

Belet: Well, after all it is fantastic.

Valva (*as* **Cluc** *goes over once again to the shelves, and* **Cleda**

examines a second plate): Are you very tired?

Belet (*taciturn*): Leave me alone, honey!

Samir: She asked you a civil question.

Belet: Shut up. (*But he gets up immediately because* **Cleda** *has dropped the second plate on the floor.*) What's that? (*He goes up to the shelves.*)

Cleda (*indifferent*): Plates. They're called plates.

Belet: And why do you have to break them?

Cleda: That's a good one. Because I felt like it.

Belet (*looking at her meaningfully*): Well, you're a girl with a mind of her own. Do you hear? I like you. (*He turns towards* **Cluc,** *who having picked up a deck of cards is about to go over to his own suitcase.*) Hey, you, what's that?

Cluc: Cards.

Belet (*holding out his hand*): Let's see them.

Cluc: They're mine.

Belet: Let's see them, I said.

Samir (*coming over to join them*): Don't talk in that tone of voice.

Belet: You're looking for trouble, aren't you?

Samir: Looks more like you are. Up to now everything has gone smooth as silk, or almost . . .

Belet: Go back to your bed. Come to think of it, we might as well do things right and look into this bed business. (**Cluc** *takes advantage of the fact that his attention has been diverted, to go away with his cards to his suitcase.*) The way I see it, there're only two.

Samir: That's right. I'm glad to see you're reasonable, and talking about something I've been giving some thought to.

Belet (*pushing him away*): Get out of the way. (*He moves towards the first bed.*)

Samir (*following him*): I think it'd be fairest to share.

Belet (*turning towards him*): Once and for all, will you shut up? (*He touches the bed with his hand, and then sits down to find out how comfortable it is. Immediately he goes over to the other bed, still accompanied by* **Samir** *and* **Cleda. Cacansa,** *who has finished tidying herself, goes over to her own suitcase, where she leaves the lipstick, and she and* **Cluc** *exchange a few words in a low voice as* **Belet** *continues.*) I think I prefer this one.

Samir: They look the same to me.

Belet: No. (*To* **Valva.**) Get up. I'll have this one.

Samir: What d'you mean, you'll have this one?

Belet: Just that, that you can find yourself another.

Samir: But . . .

Belet: You find yourself another.

Samir (*sitting down on the bed*): Certainly not.

Belet: No? (*He pulls him by the arm. To* **Cleda,** *while* **Samir** *resists.*) Let's see if you can get this one for me.

Cleda: Okay. (*Pushes* **Valva** *away.*) Get away. Haven't you heard that the bed is ours?

Samir (*obstinately trying to get back to the bed*): I won't allow it.

Valva: Leave off, Samir. (*She pushes him towards* **Cluc***'s bed.*)

Belet (*sitting on the bed he has won*): They don't understand anything!

Cleda (*by his side*): No.

Belet: You say that as if you *did* understand.

Cleda (*smiling*): Yes. Didn't I help you?

Belet: I saw right away that you and I would see eye to eye. (**Cluc** *and* **Cacansa** *stand up and together move away from the suitcases. They cross over to the shelves.*)

Cluc: Between the two of us, we'll always have more things.

Cacansa: Do you mean to say that they'll belong to both of us?

Cluc: Yes, that's it. Aren't you pleased?

Cacansa: Yes. (*Having reached the shelves.*) What shall we take now?

Cluc: Whatever appeals to you most.

Belet (*who has been watching them*): Take a good look and mind you don't touch much.

Cluc (*turns round*): Are you saying that to us?

Belet: Yes, precisely to you two.

Cacansa: It's not yours.

Cluc: It belongs to the first to grab it.

Belet (*leaping over to the shelves*): Get out of here. Are you dumb, for heaven's sake! (*Turning towards* **Cleda.**) You, bring the suitcase. (*The girl obeys.*) If anything is left after we've taken our pick, you can have it. Is that understood?

Cluc: That's not fair! We've all got the same right.

Belet: You just try to touch anything.

Samir: Cluc's right, and it's not because I personally claim anything . . .

Cleda (*who has opened the suitcase interrupts him with a cry*): My lipstick!

Belet: What's up?

Cleda (*excited*): I had a lipstick and somebody's taken it.

Belet (*steps back a little to face them all*): Who was it?

Valva: It was never hers.

Belet (*goes up to her*): What d'you know about it?

Valva: It was mine, and I gave it to Cacansa.

Belet: Who's Cacansa?

Samir: If you'd been paying attention to the introductions, you wouldn't need to ask us that.

Belet (*tapping with his foot*): I said, who's Cacansa?

Cacansa: That's me.

Belet (*approaching the girl*): Where is it?

Cacansa (*pointing to* **Cleda**): She stole it!

Belet (*getting hold of her by the hair*): Where is it?

Cluc: Let her go at once!

Belet: The lipstick!

Cacansa: I haven't got it.

Belet (*letting go of her*): We'll search the cases.

Cacansa: No. (*She runs up to her own and sits down on it. They all get behind her except* **Valva,** *who remains where she is.*) I won't let you take it away from me!

Belet (*turning round to* **Cluc**): Make her see reason, if you don't want me to do so.

Cluc: The lipstick's hers. We won't allow force . . . Right, Samir?

Samir: No, we won't allow it.

Belet (*looking at them attentively*): Two to one, is that it? (*He laughs.*) Fools! (*He goes away unhurriedly towards the shelves, and they all follow him with their glances, but* **Valva** *jumps up, and gets hold of the knife which is among the other objects.*)

Valva: Is this what you were looking for? (*Showing it to him.*)

Belet, *without answering, rapidly takes hold of a jersey hanging in the foreground, and throws it in her face. Then he falls on top of her, and grabs the knife, giving her a push to make her fall.*

Belet (*scornfully*): Amateurs!

Samir (*runs up to the girl*): Valva, Valva. (*He helps her to get up.*) Did he hurt you?

Valva: No, it was nothing.

Samir (*facing* **Belet**): You're, you're . . .

Belet (*opening the knife and threatening him*): Don't strain yourself. (*He goes up to the others.*) Get out of here, for goodness sake! (*But at that moment the* **Landlady's Voice** *is heard again, and they all stop what they are doing. Afterwards* **Belet** *and* **Cleda** *go to their bed and sit down, the former putting down the knife.* **Cluc** *and* **Cacansa** *remain on top of their suitcases.*)

Landlady's Voice: You are very welcome as you enter this house, where you'll be given all the attentions you deserve. We've always been distinguished for the affectionate and family-like treatment we give our guests, and which you'll enjoy from now on. I've no doubt that you'll appreciate it, as is only right and proper, and that like all your companions you'll behave in a worthy and honest way. I've prepared a room for you, the best one in the house, where many days of happiness await you. You'll find everything you need there. (*Noise of locks, etc., and the door opens on* **Alona,** *a girl clad in simple pyjamas. Naturally she too carries her suitcase.*) Here it is. You can't deny that it has everything that even the most demanding person could wish for. Up to now all our guests have always been happy, and I'm sure you won't be an exception. I wish you a pleasant stay. (*Appropriate noises as the door shuts.*)

Alona (*with her suitcase in her hand, makes a timid greeting*): Good morning.

Everyone (*except* **Belet** *and* **Cleda**): Good morning . . .

Alona: I'm Alona . . .

Cluc: We . . .

Belet (*getting up, cuts across the conversation*): Cut the small talk! Don't think that all that's going to make us forget the matter of the lipstick. (*He goes over to the suitcases, followed by* **Cleda.**)

Alona (*pointing to the knife, which he gets out again*): What's that?

Belet: Don't interfere, if you don't want to get . . .

Valva: Come here, Alona . . .

The girl leaves her suitcase and obeys while **Belet** *faces the other two.*

Belet: Let's get it over with.

Cluc: We won't give it to you.

Belet (*he leans forward, grabs* **Cluc** *by the lapels, and braces him, at the same time pointing the blade of the knife at the pit of his stomach*): The lipstick.

Cacansa: Don't kill him! (*She gets up from the suitcase.*) I'll give it to you.

Belet: Get moving, then!

Cacansa: First of all, let go of him.

While **Belet** *seems to be thinking about it sceptically, the other three watch him from the bed adjacent to the shelves.*

Alona: What's the matter with him?

Valva: He's a thug, who wants to grab things that aren't his.

Samir: He's a danger to everyone. Something'll have to be done.

Alona: I'm frightened.

Belet (*letting go of* **Cluc** *while* **Valva** *hugs* **Alona** *to her*): Okay. (**Cacansa** *opens the suitcase, takes out the lipstick and hands it over to* **Belet.**)

Cacansa: Here it is.

Cluc: You'll pay for this . . .

Belet (*scornfully*): How, when, and in what way? (*To* **Cleda,** *handing her the lipstick.*) Take it. (*To the other two.*) And as for you, get out of here; I don't want to see you any more around here. (**Cluc** *and* **Cacansa** *go off to their own bed, while he speaks to* **Cleda** *again.*) Bring both the cases; we're going to get some things. (*He walks over to the shelves, where* **Cleda** *follows him with the suitcase.*)

Cluc (*to* **Valva, Alona,** *and* **Samir,** *who are on his bed*): What are you doing here?

Samir: We have to find a spot, where we can . . .

Cluc (*bad-temperedly*): It's my bed. I don't want anyone else there.

Samir: But, what if there is no other!

Cluc: There's nothing I can do about it. Get out.

Samir (*standing up and facing him*): So you want to act the big shot too, is that it?

Valva (*getting up as well and catching hold of his arm*): Leave him alone, Samir.

Samir (*as* **Alona** *moves over to the other bed, where she sits down*): I can't agree to that. Where can we go?

Valva: It's all the same to me. Anywhere's good enough for me. (*She grabs him by the hand to drag him away.*)

Samir (*resisting*): It's a big bed. There's room for us all. A short while each . . .

Cacansa: Let them stay there, Cluc . . .

Cluc: No way. They had one before and let someone take it away from them. Let them win it back, if they like.

Samir: From that madman?

Belet (*turns round*): You talking about me? You watch what you say.

Samir: That's the only thing you can't take away from me, the right to say what I feel. You've taken advantage of your strength . . .

Valva: Be quiet, Samir. Be quiet!

Belet: Listen to what she says, because I'm beginning to lose my patience. (*He notices that* **Alona** *is sitting on his bed.*) Hey, you! (*He goes up to the bed.*) Who's given you permission to make yourself at home here?

Alona: I . . . I thought . . .

Belet: Don't think anything, then. Get out. (*But when* **Alona** *stands up he stretches out his hand.*) One moment. Just one moment. (*He holds her arm.*) Let's see. Turn round. (**Alona** *hesitates.*) Turn round, I said. (*And he himself forces her to give a half turn.*)

Samir: Always the same good manners, I see.

Valva: Let him alone, Samir. (*She pushes him up to the side of the table, but both of them turn towards the scene which is taking place beside* **Belet**'s *bed.* **Alona** *has just finished turning round slowly.*)

Belet: Fine. Fine . . . You're pretty, honey.

Cleda (*rushing over to the bed*): Belet!

Belet: Don't interfere. (*To* **Alona**.) Perhaps I was a bit offhand; after all, the bed is wide . . .

Cleda: I won't allow it!

Belet: Shut up! There's more than enough room for all three of us . . .

Samir: What a brute! (*He sits down on the little table.*)

Cleda: Either she goes, or I go.

Alona *starts to go away, but* **Belet** *stops her.*

Belet: No, stay here. Sit down. (*He forces her to sit down and sits down beside her himself. He turns to* **Cleda**.) You come too.

Cleda (*turning towards the shelves*): You'd better believe it!

Belet: You won't, then? (*He gets up and follows* **Cleda** *after saying to* **Alona**.) Don't move away from here.

Cacansa: What a man, for heaven's sake!

Cluc (*annoyed*): You seem to admire him!

Cacansa (*smiling*): No. No, not really. Only . . . it was just a way of speaking.

Belet (*who has caught up with* **Cleda,** *grabs her by the arm*): You think you're someone special, is that it?

Cleda: Of course, someone with a different opinion. The bed's too narrow for so many people.

Belet: Daring as ever. (*He tries to put his arms round her.*)

Cleda: Leave me alone. Don't think that with flattery . . .

Belet: The trouble with you is that you don't know her well. I'm sure that both of you would get on better that way . . .

Cleda: I said no; either her or me.

Belet (*irritated again*): That's enough. (*He takes hold of her violently.*) Come here, once and for all. (*He leads her over to the bed.*)

Cacansa: How he bosses them!

Samir: What things one has to put up with. (*He puts his hands in his pockets.*) I haven't any cigarettes . . .

Valva: Wait a minute . . . I've seen some. (*She crosses over to the shelves, where she picks up a packet, a box of matches, and also a bottle of whisky and two glasses.*)

Belet (*to* **Cleda** *who is still struggling*): Sit down beside her. I want you to be friends.

Alona (*to* **Cleda** *shyly*): As far as I'm concerned . . .

On hearing her voice **Cleda** *turns round and gives her a slap.*

Belet (*holding her down*): Keep your hands to yourself. I'm the one who'll do the slapping around here.

Cleda: I'll scratch you . . .

Belet (*suddenly won over*): Pussy cat. (*Wordless scene, during which she defends herself more or less, but without success, because he keeps cutting off her escape, until he finally makes her fall on to the bed.*)

Cluc (*who has noticed that* **Valva** *is taking things from the shelves, to* **Cacansa**): Come here, you . . .

Cacansa: Where?

Cluc (*pointing to the shelves*): We could make the most of it . . . Let's fill the cases.

Cacansa: What if they see us?

Cluc: No. We'll be careful. We'll do it little by little.

Valva crosses over to **Samir** *while* **Cluc** *and* **Cacansa** *begin to rout around in the shelves.*

Valva: Cigarettes . . .

Samir: So you really think we've any right to them? They belong to everyone.

Valva (*smiling at him*): Of course. We won't refuse to give them to anyone who asks for them. (*Referring to the bottle.*) I've brought that too. Do you want some?

Samir: Good . . .

While **Valva** *opens the bottle and fills the glasses,* **Samir** *lights a cigarette, and* **Cluc** *and* **Cacansa** *make their first trip over to the* *suitcases. He takes a folder of sheets of paper, and she some clothes pegs.*

Cleda: Don't think you can bribe me so easily . . .

Belet: I'm only helping. A girl alone . . . Look at her, you can't possibly feel jealous . . .

Cleda: But you said she was pretty . . .

Belet: I had to say something.

Cleda: But not pretty.

Belet: Quit nagging! You'd have liked being without a bed, I suppose.

Cleda: I'd have found one soon enough, don't you worry.

Belet (*grabbing her violently by the shoulder*): Just say that again, and you'll see what happens!

Cleda: I'll say what I please. You won't get anywhere with threats. (*Pause.*) Get that through your head!

Alona (*gets up*): No need. I'm going.

Belet: Sit down!

But **Alona** *pays no attention to him and crosses in front of him while* **Cacansa** *and* **Cluc** *return to the shelves where they pick out more things.*

Belet (*taking hold of* **Alona** *and brutally making her go back to the bed*): Sit down, I said!

Alona: I don't want to.

Belet: The only one who can say 'I want to' or 'I don't want to' is me. (*Threateningly to the two girls.*) Make friends at once!

Samir (*with the glass in his hand*): There we are. This guy doesn't stop at threats.

Belet (*turning round to him*): I don't want to hear another word out of you!

Samir (*going up to the bed, after putting down the glass*): I've already told you that you can't take away from me the right to say what I think.

Belet: Oh, I can't, eh? (*He notices* **Cacansa** *and* **Cluc** *returning to their suitcases, the former with a bottle, the latter with a pencil.*) One moment. What's that you're carrying?

Cluc (*as* **Valva** *unobtrusively approaches the shelves, where she picks up the handcuffs, and then returns to the table hiding them in the pocket of her skirt*): Nothing.

Belet (*pointing to the objects*): And that?

Cluc: Nothing of any importance. A pencil to write with . . .

Belet (*as* **Cleda** *removes* **Alona** *from the bed, after looking at* *her askance for a few minutes*): Don't you know that you can't touch anything without my permission?

Cluc: But just these trifles . . .

Belet (*vehemently*): Nothing at all, I said. Put it back in its place.

Samir: Haven't you ever thought that one day someone may catch you looking the other way?

Belet (*scornfully*): It won't be you in any case . . . (*To the others.*) Oh, forget it! (*He follows them over to the shelves and then turns to* **Cleda.**) You — come here! (*He notices that she is alone on the bed.*) What have you done with her, with the other girl?

Cleda (*looking straight at* **Alona** *who has escaped to the corner where the suitcases are*): I've got rid of her.

Belet (*after a moment's hesitation begins to laugh*): That's fine. You're like me. (*He shakes his head.*) It seems I can't get angry with you. (*More seriously.*) Here, come over here, the other thing's more important.

Cleda (*obeying him*): Do you want to fill up the cases?

Belet: Yes. (*He examines the shelves.*) It seems to me that there're many things missing from here. (*To* **Cluc** *and* **Cacansa.**) Have you taken them?

Cluc (*with a wink at* **Cacansa** *and showing the objects with which they've been caught*): Only these . . .

Belet: We'll see. Don't move away from here. (*He and* **Cleda** *begin to fill the suitcase, where first of all they put the·jersey which had fallen at the foot of the bed.*)

Samir (*who has stepped back to* **Valva**): We mustn't let him do it. He's robbing us of everything.

Valva: One day we'll get it all back. Look. (*She points out the handcuffs.*)

Samir: We'd have to tie them all up together, and that's not easy. I know that Cluc is not a bad fellow, and if he has pushed us out, it's only because he felt humiliated; but basically he hasn't any courage . . . (*He drinks a little more whisky.*) Before they take it away from us . . .

Valva: Yes. (*She also fills her glass.*) Shall we drink a toast?

Samir: To what?

Valva: To a better future.

Samir: All right. (*Touching* **Valva**'*s glass with his.*) To a better future.

Belet (*having heard the clink of glasses, turns round*): What's that?

Samir (*picks up the bottle and shows it*): Do you want some?

Belet (*while* **Cleda** *goes on putting things into the case*): Bring that bottle here.

53

Samir: It's yours, since you're the strongest. But you have to come and fetch it.

Belet: You're asking for trouble.

Valva: Don't try him too far, Samir.

Samir (*as* **Belet** *approaches*): Allow me to refill your glasses. (*He does so.*)

Belet (*snatching the bottle away*): You're squawking too much for my taste.

Samir (*turning to* **Valva**): And now, what shall we drink to?

Valva: The same as always — to a better future.

Cleda (*from the shelves*): That's it, Belet.

Belet (*with a backward glance at the other two*): Okay, I'm coming.

Cleda (*picking up the wheel of a bicycle*): But I don't know what to do with this wheel. It won't go in. Perhaps we should leave it . . .

Belet (*taking hold of it*): We're not leaving anything.

Cleda: There's nowhere to put it.

Belet: That doesn't matter. (*He points to the cases.*) Shut them up and come over to the other side. We'll pay a visit to the cases of these two. (*To* **Cluc** *and* **Cacansa.**)

Cluc: But we don't have anything! Things of no interest to you . . .

Belet: We'll see that right now. Come on, lets get on with it. (*He pushes them, but* **Cacansa** *smiles as she looks at him. He notices it.*) So you're a bit impressed, is that it, little one?

Cluc: Cacansa! (*He grabs her, looking at her reproachfully.*)

Cacansa: You're hurting me.

Belet *smiles as they all cross the stage,* **Cleda** *last of all, after having shut the suitcases.*

Samir (*to* **Valva**): Did you notice?

Valva: Yes, I did.

Samir: Poor Cluc.

Belet (*having reached the cases, to* **Alona**): Number two falls to you. (**Alona** *gets up and, frightened, goes over to the middle of the stage, but finally retires to the side of the empty shelves. To the other two.*) Open up the cases.

Cluc: But . . .

Belet (*raising a hand*): Have I got to repeat it?

Cluc *hurries to obey, as* **Cacansa** *smiles at* **Belet,** *who touches her chin, caressing her.*

Cleda (*behind them*): Belet!

Belet: What? What's that? Open up the suitcase; we'll put every-thing in there. (*He leaves the wheel on one side and himself proceeds to transfer the objects from* **Cluc**'s *suitcase to his own.*) You'd better watch the others.

Cleda (*obeying*): There isn't anything . . .

Belet: Fine then. We've finished. (*He goes to shut the suitcase but thinks again, takes out a bottle and glasses, and carries them over to the little table.*) Come here. (*The others go over to him except* **Alona.**) Okay, everyone fill his own. (*All of them obey.*) Whom shall we toast?

Cleda: Ourselves.

Belet: Yes, that's a good idea. To ourselves and a long future as wonderful as the present! (*He and* **Cleda** *touch glasses.*)

Cleda: To a long future as wonderful as the present!

Belet (*seeing that the others are not drinking*): Well? (*They all watch him indecisively.*) Or maybe you'd like me to swallow the glasses as well?

Cluc and **Cacansa** (*unenthusiastically*): To a long future as . . . wonderful as the present.

Belet (*satisfied*): Okay! (*To* **Samir** *and* **Valva.**) Now, you two.

Samir (*putting the glass down*): No.

Belet: Did you say no? (*He puts down the glass, and takes out the knife, with which he threatens them.*) Make up your mind!

Valva: Let's drink the toast, Samir . . .

Samir (*after a long hesitation*): Okay. (*He picks up his glass again and* **Valva** *toasts with him.*) To a long future as wonderful as the present . . . (*He drinks it down in one gulp, but immediately throws the glass on the ground and hides his face in his hands.*)

ACT 2

As the curtain goes up the position of the characters is as follows: **Cluc** is sitting or kneeling in front of the table writing on a sheet of paper. Behind him, in the foreground, is the bicycle wheel. **Samir,** sitting on the ground in front of the shelves, dressed in a jacket but no shirt, is holding some pieces of wood, and with the aid of a hammer and nails is trying to make a box. **Valva,** near him, is sewing his shirt for him. **Cacansa** sitting on her bed is reading a book. **Alona,** with a duster in her hand, is dusting the suitcases *and putting them in order.* **Belet,** *who has put on the jersey, and* **Cleda** *are sitting on the bed where they have been resting.*

Belet (*stretching himself and yawning*): Ay . . . (*He watches what the others are doing.*) That's nice. Everything neat and tidy, and everyone in his own place. (*Pointing to* **Cluc.**) Intellectual work. (*Pointing to* **Samir.**) Manual work, and (*pointing to himself*) someone to enjoy all these things. (*He yawns again, more discreetly, takes the pack of cards out of his pocket and goes up to the table. To* **Cluc.**) You, get out of here!

Cluc: I'm writing.

Belet: You can do that somewhere else. I want to play solitaire. (*Seeing that the other man cannot make up his mind.*) Get out, I said.

Cluc *leaves the table, looks for a place to settle down, and finally gets hold of a suitcase, sits on the ground in front of it, and goes on writing.* **Belet** *arranges the cards on the table as* **Cleda** *approaches.*

Belet (*after a moment*): Stop making dust.

Alona: Don't you want it neat and tidy . . .

Belet: Clean the other side now.

Alona *obeys, and moves over to the shelves with her duster.*

Valva (*to* **Samir**): How's it coming?

Samir: Slow but sure . . . though it's not as if it were ours. One works without enthusiasm, because it doesn't really seem worthwhile. (*He leaves his tools and takes out a packet of cigarettes with only one left in it. He puts the packet down again, empty, and divides the cigarette, handing half to* **Valva.**) Here you are. (*They light up.*)

Cleda (*showing a card to* **Belet**): This one.

Belet: I saw it already. You're always butting in.

Valva (*to* **Alona** *who is busy dusting*): Alona, we're here you know.

Alona: He told me to clean the other side.

Samir: That guy only thinks of his own convenience.

Alona: What am I to do, then? (*Bending over* **Samir.**) Are you making a box?

Samir: I am trying to make one, which is not the same thing at all.

Alona (*squatting at his side*): How I'd like to know how to make things like that!

56

Cleda (*who has turned round*): Alona, get to work!

Alona: Okay, okay. (*She returns to her work.*)

Cluc (*stopping writing, to* **Belet**): You'll have to give me another sheet of paper.

Belet: What, again?

Cluc: You haven't given me one since yesterday.

Belet: Since yesterday! Do you really intend to mess one up each day?

Cluc: That remains to be seen. It depends on the inspiration.

Belet: Have you written on the other side?

Cluc: Of course I have. Both sides are full.

Belet (*stretching out his hand*): Let's see. I can't trust any of you, and you, less than anybody. An artist . . .

Cluc: So you like my writing.

Belet: Everything in its right place. I like everything in its right place. (*He takes the paper the other hands to him and examines it on all sides.*)

Cleda (*bending over him*): He could write smaller.

Belet (*hitting the paper*): You're right. You'd make better use of the sheets of paper then.

Cluc: And then you'd complain that you don't understand it.

Belet: Don't think you've got the answer to everything. From now on, let's see. (*He counts the lines.*) Yes, from now on, six lines more per page . . . and another thing, don't cross out so much — that uses up paper too.

Cluc: You can't expect everything to come out perfectly with the first stroke of the pen!

Belet: Of course I do! You've got into bad habits.

Samir (*to himself*): We've all got into bad habits. It's gone on too long. (**Valva** *touches him on the shoulder to calm him down. He ends up agreeing, holding out his hand towards hers, and they stay like that for a moment looking at one another with love and understanding, until both of them return to their work.*)

Belet (*returning the paper to* **Cluc**): Here you are. That's enough for today.

Cluc: Don't you want me to write any more?

Belet: Not now. On the whole your things bore me.

Cluc: There was no need for you to read them if you didn't want to, but as far as I am concerned I feel like writing . . . I just need another sheet of paper! . . .

Belet: Tomorrow . . . the day after tomorrow . . . another day! Leave me in peace. I want to finish this game.

Cluc: Just a sheet of paper . . . that's not asking too much . . .

Belet: You always say the same. And you say it about everything. Perhaps you'd like me to ruin myself for all of you? One moment, it's a book so that your girlfriend can read . . .

Cluc: You didn't give it to her. You only lent it.

Belet: So what? Doesn't it get worn and lose its value? Then it's a cigarette, because smoking helps you to work . . .

Cluc: But I earn it!

Belet: If you really had a vocation, you'd write for nothing.

Cluc: I do anyway. A cigarette now and then can hardly be called fair payment . . .

Belet (*annoyed*): Is that so? But what did you think? Get out of here, if you don't want a knock on the head. (*To* **Cleda.**) He never does anything useful!

Cleda: I don't know how you ever put up with him . . . You're too generous.

Belet: Sometimes he amuses me. (*To* **Cluc,** *seeing that he hasn't gone away.*) So you're still here?

Cluc: I need a sheet of paper.

Belet: Well you won't get it! Not even half a sheet! You won't get it . . . (*He breaks off and changes expression and tone.*) That's to say: what would you be prepared to do to get it?

Cluc: I don't know . . . any old thing.

Belet (*gathering up the cards*): Let's see if we can amuse ourselves . . . (*Sitting down at the table.*) Get down on all fours.

Cluc (*surprised*): Man, I . . .

Cleda: You said you would do any old thing, didn't you?

Cluc *appears to hesitate, while they all watch him except his girlfriend, who goes on reading, oblivious to everything. Then slowly he squats down.*

Samir (*shouting*): No, Cluc!

Cluc (*stopping halfway*): Did you say, no?

Samir: Don't lower yourself in that way . . .

Belet (*leaving the table*): And why are you interfering? You'll be coming to ask me for cigarettes afterwards, maybe.

Samir: I haven't ever asked for anything. (*He points to the wood of the box he's trying to make.*) It's one thing in exchange for another. A simple exchange, by which, what's more, you're exploiting me.

Valva: Don't get excited . . .

Samir: I merely call a spade a spade.

Belet: You keep that up, and you'll go far. Right now, you've earned that: from now on you won't get more than one cigarette a day, half what you earned before.

Samir (*throwing the tools to one side*): Then do it yourself.

Belet (*without batting an eyelid*): Tomorrow when you come and ask me to work again the deal'll be different: half a cigarette. (*Turning to* **Cluc.**) You'd better get on with it, if you want to earn a sheet of paper.

Cluc: No, not now: Samir's right.

Belet: He is, is he? (*Pointing to the ground.*) On all fours, I said!

Cluc (*slightly childishly*): I won't do it, even if I can't write any more.

Belet (*takes out the knife*): If I've got to say it again, I'll say it with that. (**Cluc,** *resigned, kneels down and puts his hands on the ground.*)

Belet: That's what I like to see. Say: 'miau.' (**Belet** *and* **Cleda** *laugh loudly.*)

Cluc (*plaintively*): Miau! (**Belet** *and* **Cleda** *laugh loudly.*)

Belet: It's amusing, is it?

Cleda: Yes, let him do it again.

Belet: You heard, didn't you?

Cluc: Miau!

Belet, *this time without laughing, puts away the knife and goes over behind the table. He picks up the cards and without more ado lays them out again.* **Cluc** *gets up, flicking the dust off his knees, then goes straight over to the bed.*

Alona: Poor fellow!

Cleda (*without looking at her because she has returned to* **Belet**'*s side*): Alona, I don't want to hear you!

Alona: Yes, Ma'am.

Valva (*to* **Samir,** *pointing to* **Cluc**): Now perhaps would be the moment to speak about it.

Samir: I don't know if we can trust him.

Valva: After what's just happened? I'm sure we can.

Samir: Okay. Let's put it to the test.

Valva (*dropping the shirt on the ground*): Afterwards I'll finish sewing that for you.

While they get up, **Cluc,** *who has sat down beside* **Cacansa,** *takes the book and closes it.*

Cluc: Naturally, you didn't hear anything.

Cacansa: Hear anything? It's such an interesting book. (*She wipes her forehead with her hand.*) How come you're not writing?

Samir: Cluc. (*The other looks at them vacantly.*) We'd like to talk to you.

Cluc: I don't want to talk to anyone.

Valva: It's important.

Cluc: At the moment nothing is important.

Samir: Not even writing? (**Cluc** *doesn't answer.*) I know a way in which you can always go on writing without having to ask for sheets of paper.

Cluc (*getting interested*): How?

Samir (*pointing to the bed*): If you'll allow us . . .

Cacansa: Oh yes, of course, I should have said that.

They all sit down very close together and begin to talk in a low voice.

Cleda (*at* **Belet**'*s side*): This card. You're absentminded . . .

Belet: Yes. Maybe I just don't feel like it anymore.

Cleda: Leave it to me.

Belet (*letting her have the cards*): It's all mixed up.

Cleda: That's exactly when I enjoy it.

Belet *lights a cigarette, takes a few steps into the centre of the stage, and stares at* **Alona.**

Valva (*who has seen him leave the little table*): One moment. Before going on let's get together on what to say. If he comes closer, we'll pretend to be talking about the respective merits of manual work and intellectual work.

Samir: He won't come closer.

Cluc: But she's right. It's better to be safe than sorry. You were talking about some handcuffs . . .

Samir: Yes, we've got some. I've got them in my pocket, but I can't show them to you now.

Cluc: No, there's no need . . .

They go on talking as **Belet** *comes to a halt by* **Alona.**

Belet: Don't you feel like resting a bit?

Alona: Resting, no.

Belet: I know you're saying that so that I'd have something to scold you for.

Alona (*unsure*): No . . . I like working.

Belet: But not all that much either. (*Caressing her arm.*) There's a time for everything, right?

Alona: Yes, yes, of course.

Belet: And also a time for getting to know one another and talking. You hardly say anything.

Alona: What d'you want me to say?

Belet: I don't know. That's exactly the point. (*He takes out the packet of cigarettes.*) Wouldn't you like to smoke one?

Alona: I don't know.

Belet: Here you are, take one. (*He gives her one and lights it with his own.*) Put down the duster. (*He takes it from her and he himself puts it down on one of the shelves.*) Come on.

Alona (*with a glance at* **Cleda**): I don't know whether . . .

Belet: Don't worry. (*He leads her over to the bed.*) Sit down for a while. You can take off your shoes.

Alona: I'm not wearing any.

Belet: Your slippers, then.

Alona: No. I prefer . . .

Belet: Or undo your pyjamas. It's hot.

Alona: I'm not hot.

Belet: But it is hot all the same. Just a couple of buttons . . .

Alona: It's that . . . underneath I'm not wearing anything.

Belet (*glancing at* **Cleda** *and throwing away the cigarette*): All the better . . . I mean, of course, it's more comfortable.

Alona: Yes . . .

Belet (*caressing her arm again*): Even if at times I've shouted at you, you know that I didn't really mean anything. On the contrary, perhaps it was really a cover-up. You do understand, don't you?

Alona (*somewhat frightened*): I don't know . . .

Belet: You remember that when you arrived I wanted to keep you a share of the bed, don't you?

Alona (*agreeing with a nod of her head*): Yes, yes.

Belet: Circumstances made it impossible, but after all, I'm still the same person.

Alona: Yes.

Belet (*moving his hand up to her shoulder still caressing her*): That's why it seems as if I owed you something, you know?

Alona (*trying to draw back*): No. Perhaps it'd be better if I went back to work . . .

Belet (*slightly impatiently*): Forget your work! I don't frighten you, do I?

Alona (*very unsure*): No . . .

Belet: You see I haven't really got anything against you. You're a girl on your own, and a girl on her own needs someone to help her, to defend her . . .

Alona: Samir and Valva are always very kind to me.

Belet: But that's not the same. And what's more, they can't give you anything.

Alona: I don't need anything.

Belet: You think you don't. (*He plays with her ear.*) There are always things which please us . . .

Alona: Leave me alone . . .

Belet (*putting his arm round her neck*): There's no need to be shy. Hug me. (*He makes her drop her cigarette and forces her to put her arms round him.* **Alona**'s *fingers come up against the knife which is sticking out of his thigh pocket, and she pulls it out without his noticing.*) You and I should . . .

Cleda (*from the table*): It's coming out now. (*She raises her eyes.*) Belet!

Belet (*he disengages himself quickly*): What're you yelling about?

Cleda (*going over to the bed*): Why don't you leave her alone? (*She raises her hands to attack him.*)

Belet (*holds her down, while* **Alona,** *having hidden the knife leaves the bed and goes back to the shelves*): You're a beast. (*He has stood up too and both of them stare at each other very closely.*) That must be why I like you so much.

Cleda: Don't give me that — you like 'em all!

Belet (*half laughing, pleased*): Jealous, so that's it, is it?

Cleda: Me, jealous? (*She struggles to free herself from his hands.*) Let me go.

Belet (*while the group on the other bed separates with meaningful smiles, and* **Samir** *and* **Valva** *return to their respective tasks*): Don't you believe it. (*He tries to hug her.*)

Cleda (*rebuffing him*): You're a nobody, a ne'er-do-well . . .

Belet: Hey, come off it!

Cleda: Aren't I woman enough for you? D'you have to chase this one as well?

Belet: I wasn't chasing anyone. The poor girl was tired and . . .

Cleda: And that's why you were hugging her, is that it? So she could get her strength back? I'll get my own back one of these days.

Belet (*changing his tone*): That'll do! I don't like threats! (*He hears* **Samir** *driving in a nail and turns round.*) Look, he's begun to work again . . .

Cleda: We weren't talking about that.

Belet: Shut up, once and for all. D'you think that because I act nice to you, you can lay down the law to me? (*Throwing her on to the bed.*) Lie down and go to sleep! I've had enough of your scenes for now . . .

Cleda: One day you'll pay for all this . . .

Belet (*turning his back on her and going up to* **Samir**): Looks as though we've thought again, right? (*The other doesn't answer.*) Don't you hear me? When I ask a question I want an answer.

Samir (*raising his eyes*): Why? Isn't that a good enough answer for you?

Belet: You know the conditions. Half a cigarette.

Samir (*placidly*): Yes, I know that you're a slave-driver.

Belet (*surprised*): What's the matter with you? You've never insulted me in such a resigned way . . .

Samir: Times change.

Belet: So I see. You almost disillusion me. (*He awaits a reply without getting one and then turns round.*) Stuff and nonsense. What's it matter after all?

Cluc (*leaving the bed and following him*): Now, if you don't mind, you can give me that sheet of paper . . .

Belet: Which sheet of paper?

Cluc: The one you promised me.

Belet: I didn't promise anything, that I know of.

Cluc: Yes, when you made me kneel down and miau.

Belet: You said you didn't want it.

Cluc: But now I do want it. I'm very anxious to write.

Belet (*indecisively as* **Cacansa** *leaves the bed*): Very well. But it's got to do you for the whole of tomorrow.

Cluc (*as* **Cacansa** *goes up to the side of the table*): I'll do what I can.

Belet (*severely*): Leave out the 'what you can.' I've said that it's to do for the whole of today and tomorrow.

Cluc: Very well.

Belet *goes over to the suitcases, where he opens his own to look for a sheet of paper.* **Cluc, Cacansa, Samir** *and* **Valva** *exchange glances across the room.*

Cacansa (*to* **Cluc**): It's some time since you've done a card trick for us.

Cluc: Probably because I didn't want to.

Cacansa: I remember how we used to enjoy ourselves.

Belet (*standing up with the sheet of paper*): What was that that you enjoyed so much?

Cacansa: The card tricks he did.

Belet (*surprised*): Does he really know how to do some?

Cacansa: A lot. But now he doesn't want to.

Cluc: I haven't any cards now, nor am I in the mood. (*He stretches out his hand for the sheet of paper.*)

Belet: Don't be in such a hurry . . . You never said you knew how to do them.

Cluc: I expect I didn't remember . . . It was a long time ago, before you came . . .

Belet (*gathering up the cards*): Try it. I like card tricks too.

Cluc: No . . .

Belet: Where did you get that bad habit of always saying 'no'? If you don't do the card tricks, you don't get the sheet of paper.

Cacansa: Yes, Cluc, go on, do some.

Cluc: I'm out of practice, and if they don't come out well . . .

Cacansa: Of course they'll come out. Go on man, get going!

Cluc: Okay, if you really want me to . . . (*He picks up the pack of cards.*)

Cacansa (*to the others*): Come on, the rest of you, Cluc is going to do some card tricks for us.

All, except **Cleda,** *who continues brooding over her ills, draw up to the table.*

Valva (*giving the shirt to* **Samir**): Here you are, I've sewn it. (*He puts it on while the action continues.*)

Cacansa: Which one are you going to begin with?

Cluc: I'll do the four kings. (*To* **Belet.**) Do you know it?

Belet: No.

Cluc (*as he looks for the cards*): First of all, we'll find the four kings, to convince you that they're here, and so that everyone can see them.

Valva (*to* **Samir**): I think this is going to be interesting.

Belet: Shut up!

Cluc (*as he gets all the kings together*): No, they don't disturb me.

Belet: But they do me.

Cluc: Okay, here they are. One, two, three, four. (*He shows them, making each one of them stick out a little further than the previous one, away from the other cards.*) Have you all seen them?

Everyone: Yes, yes.

Cluc: Perfect. Now, I'll place them on the pack thus. (*He does so.*) And then I'll start separating them. (*He takes up the first card and places it in the middle.*) One. (*He takes up the next card and* *repeats the manoeuvre.*) This one in another place . . . and this one . . . and the last one . . . all four are well separated, but they don't like it, because during the short time we had them all together they got fond of one another. So they take advantage of the slightest possibility of getting together again . . .

Belet: Not so many words.

Cluc: Okay, I'll make it brief. (*He leaves the pack on the table.*) One of you now cuts. (**Cacansa** *puts out her hand but* **Belet** *stops her.*)

Belet: Just a minute. I want to be sure there's no cheating. I'll cut. (*He divides the pile into two parts and then puts the bottom part on top.*)

Cluc (*taking up the pack*): That's all. All you have to do now is prove that I've not cheated you. (*He separates the cards as they all watch his expectantly.*) Here they are. One, two, three, and four. (*He shows them.*)

Samir (*to* **Valva**): He really does know how to do them!

Belet (*scratching his head*): I don't understand. You separated them.

Cluc: Of course, you all saw it.

Belet: You must explain the trick to me.

Cluc: It's a professional secret.

Belet: There's no secret that's worth keeping. I want to know how you do it.

Cluc (*resigned*): You're the boss. (*Showing him in practice, as he explains.*) As I took up the four kings I was careful to keep four cards behind them, then when I put them on top of the pile to shuffle them, the ones I really shuffled in were those other cards. The kings remained together the whole time. You see, it's simple . . .

Belet: Yes, it is, but a good trick all the same. Do another one.

Cacansa: The one where the card changes.

Cluc: No, that's too difficult.

Belet: All the better.

Valva: Yes, do that one.

Cluc: It's a long time . . .

Belet: Cut out the excuses. You either do it, or you don't get your sheet of paper.

Samir (*to* **Valva**): Always the same convincing arguments . . .

Belet: Shut up! Let's see if we can amuse ourselves honestly. (*To* **Cluc**.) You get on with it.

Cluc: For this trick I need someone . . . you yourself will do, for me to convince you that things are above board.

65

Belet: What've I got to do?

Cluc: You'll see right away. (*He separates one card from the pile.*) Look at this card. (*He shows it so that they all see it.*)

Belet: It's the five of spades. (*Or whatever it is.*)

Cluc: Right, then you put your hands behind your back, tightly clasped, with the card in the palms. When I tell you, unclasp your hands and look at the card. It'll be a different one, and you can do that as many times as you like.

Belet: Do you mean to say that I won't even feel you touching it?

Cluc: Exactly; there's no way I'll be touching it.

Belet: I don't believe it.

Cluc: I'll convince you, and so as to make it more difficult I'll even say that when I tell you to look at it, you yourself will tell me which card you want to find in your hands, and that will be the one you'll find.

Belet: That's impossible.

Cluc (*holding out the card he has separated*): Now, you'll see.

Belet: That's it. Now I'll see. (*He takes the card and joins both hands in front of him.*)

Cluc: Not like that. Your hands behind your back.

Belet: Isn't it the same?

Cluc: No.

Belet: Surely the important thing is to hold the card in one's hand, isn't it?

Cluc: Yes, but you mustn't see your hands.

Belet: I can't see why not!

Cluc: You'll see afterwards.

Belet: I'll shut my eyes.

Cluc: No, not at all. You can do what you like in everything else, but not in that. You must understand that a trick can't come out right if it isn't done properly.

Samir (*ironically*): If he's giving the orders, I don't know why not. Give me the card and I'll do it.

Belet: Nobody will do anything. (*Putting his hands behind his back, palms together.*) It that the way?

Cluc: Yes. (**Samir** *takes out the handcuffs.*) When I tell you the omelette . . . I mean the card, will have changed. (**Samir** *starts to put on the handcuffs.*) Now you'll see what a surprise awaits you!

Cleda (*who has seen the trick jumps off the bed*): Belet, it's a trick!

Belet (*dropping the card and unclasping his hands just as* **Samir** *is about to handcuff him*): A trick?

Cleda: Look, they've got some handcuffs!

Belet (*looking round*): Handcuffs! (*He grabs them with a claw-*

like gesture.) So that was the trick. (*He laughs.*) Sleight of hand, eh? ... You were certainly right about that. (*Threateningly to* **Samir.**) I suppose the idea was yours?

Samir: What of it?

Belet: I might have known. (*Turning to* **Cleda.**) If it hadn't been for you, sweetie . . .

Cleda (*turns scornfully*): It wasn't because you deserved it.

Belet (*as all the others draw back towards the side where the shelves are*): I'll reward you for it, Cleda, you can be sure. I've never liked to owe anybody anything. (*He notices that the others are moving away.*) Hi, you, where d'you think you're going?

Samir: Not far away, unfortunately.

Belet: Come here. (*They all obey slowly, in a demoralised way. To* **Samir.**) Hold out your hands. (**Samir** *hesitates.*) Have I got to say everything twice over? Hold out your hands, at once!

Alona (*as* **Samir** *is about to obey*): Don't take any notice of him. (*They all stare at her, surprised, even* **Belet** *himself.*)

Belet (*reacting*): Where d'you think you're getting with that? Get on with your dusting. (*Without saying a word* **Alona** *goes off to look for her duster.*) That's that dealt with. (*To* **Samir.**) Hey, you, give me your hands.

Alona (*picking up the duster*): Don't you obey.

Belet: Do you want me to slap you, you big mouth?

Alona (*going back towards him and holding out the duster*): Here you are, take it.

Belet: Me, take it! . . . (*With a flick of his hand he makes it fall.*)

Valva: Alona, have you lost your senses?

Alona (*without taking any notice of her, to* **Belet**): Pick it up!

Belet (*very indignant*): But who d'you think you are? Pick it up at once, or . . . (*He empties his pockets.*)

Alona: Are you looking for the knife, perhaps?

Belet (*without listening to her, emptying his pockets more hurriedly*): Where could I have put it?

Alona (*shows it to him*): Is this it, maybe?

Belet (*rushing at her*): Give me that.

Alona (*threatening him*): Be careful. It cuts. (**Belet** *stops.*) Pick up the duster.

Belet (*furious*): I . . . I . . .

Alona: The duster. If you want to save your skin.

Belet (*bends down to pick up the duster*): This isn't the end of it.

Alona: Come on, dust the shelves now.

Cleda *laughs and* **Belet** *turns round in a fury, half advancing.*

Alona (*still with seeming calm*): The shelves, Belet. (*He hesitates, looks at the knife, and then without a word, goes up to the shelves which he dusts unwillingly, all the time looking sideways at the others.*)

Valva (*as they all surround* **Alona** *full of admiration*): But Alona, we didn't think you could be like that, so courageous . . .

Alona: I'm not. I don't know how it was. (*She drops the knife and passes a hand across her face, swaying as if she were going to fall. The others, except* **Samir,** *who picks up the knife, hasten to support her.*)

Valva: Alona, Alona, what's the matter?

Cluc: I think she's fainted.

Cacansa: Bring her here on to the bed.

Valva: It must be the nervous tension. (*They drag her by her arms to* **Cluc**'s *bed, where they lay her down.* **Cacansa** *on one side and* **Valva** *on the other rub her wrists, while the two men stand together at the foot of the same bed.*)

Cluc: We should think of the other one now. (*With a gesture.*) Of Cleda.

Samir: On her own she's not dangerous.

Cluc: But she's always sided with him. She should be punished somehow.

Samir: What d'you want to do to her? She's a woman.

Cluc: I've an idea. I remember seeing a mask among the things on the shelves. Why don't we make her wear it? It would be a sort of punishment, and it has something romantic about it too.

Samir: Perhaps. Yes, it isn't such a bad idea. (*Both of them go over to the suitcases to look for the mask.*)

Valva (*still at* **Alona**'s *side*): I think she's coming round. Her lips are moving.

Cacansa: A drop of whisky would do her good.

Valva: There's some in the suitcases. I'll go and look for it.

Samir (*who has just found the mask*): Here it is (*They both look at it.*) Yes, that was an excellent idea of yours. It'll be a fine punishment.

Valva (*on her way to get the whisky*): What are you doing with that?

Cluc: We want to give Cleda a new face. (*He takes the mask out of* **Samir**'s *hands.*) Don't you think that would look nice on her?

Valva (*laughs*): Yes, I'm sure it would. (*She opens the suitcase to take out the whisky and the other two go up to* **Cleda** *who is still beside the bed.*)

Samir: We've brought something for you.

68

Cleda: Leave me alone.

Cluc: Yes, after a little ceremony. We've condemned you to wear this mask from now on.

Cleda: Condemned me? Why? What've I done to you?

Samir: You've always sided with Belet, right from the first moment, and as if that wasn't enough, because of you we were on the point of failing in our efforts.

Cluc (*holding out the mask to her*): Put it on.

Cleda: And, what if I refuse?

Samir (*showing the knife*): Then we'll be forced to resort to other more persuasive arguments. For your own good, we'd advise you not to push us too far.

Cleda *takes hold of the mask, looks it over, and finally decides to put it on.*

Valva (*who is back again beside the bed and has raised* **Alona**'s *head with* **Cacansa**'s *help, so as to make her drink a drop of whisky*): A little more. All of it. It'll do you good.

Cluc (*to* **Cleda**): What's more, from now on you'll give up this bed, which you took by force. It belongs to Samir.

Cleda, *without answering, goes over to the mirror to look at herself while* **Samir** *laughs without conviction.*

Cluc (*pointing to* **Cleda**): Very becoming, isn't it?

Samir (*shaking his head*): No, that's not it. It just occurred to me that it's only right that you, who once made me get off your bed, should now give me a . . .

Cluc (*slightly embarrassed*): You must understand . . . I shouldn't have done it, I know, but at that time I wasn't the same . . .

Samir: Don't make excuses. The past is the past.

Cluc: You know that when circumstances are against us, we become selfish.

Samir: You'd do better to shut up. You'll only make matters worse.

He walks over to the bed where **Alona** *is and* **Cluc** *follows him.* **Cleda,** *on the other hand, after looking at herself has shrunk back into a corner, near the table.*

Valva (*hearing the two men approach*): She's come to now.

Alona: Yes, I'm all right now.

Samir: I'd like to thank you on behalf of us all. Without your opportune intervention things would have been worse than ever. We failed through stupidity, despite our careful planning.

Alona (*sits up*): You had to fail.

Cluc: Why did we have to fail?

Alona: I didn't understand until afterwards and I suppose that was what gave me the courage to threaten him with the knife.

Samir: What did you understand?

Alona: That you were going to accept him, however much against your will. That's why I had to do it, as I was the only one who didn't drink the toast. (*They all look at one another, bewildered and ashamed.*) I knew I would succeed.

Samir: You're right. We weren't worthy.

Alona: I don't know if that's it. He made you do it and forgot all about me. If not, I too would've had to do it. Probably even before the rest of you, because I'm weaker and more easily frightened . . .

Valva: When you stood up with the knife, you didn't seem to be!

Alona: No, for a few seconds I managed to forget myself. In my normal state, I couldn't have done it. Now, I can hardly believe it.

Cluc: Well, it's true, Thanks to you, perhaps we can begin another kind of existence with more justice and more peace. (*She is about to get up.*) No, don't get up.

Alona: But I'm all right now.

Cluc: But from now on, this is your bed.

Alona: No, no.

Cluc: Yes, yes it is. We'll let you have it with the greatest of pleasure, isn't that right, Cacansa?

Cacansa (*not very convinced*): Yes, of course. Now that we can take a good look at it, it's a wide enough bed to hold three . . .

Cluc: Cacansa!

Cacansa: What do you want? One gets used to comfort and it's difficult . . .

Cluc: I knew you'd spoil it all.

Alona: Don't quarrel on my account. (*She tries to move away from the bed.*)

Cluc (*holds her*): No, no. I insist. (*To* **Cacansa.**) Aren't you ashamed?

Cacansa: Okay, as you wish, but where are we to go?

Cluc: To the place where Samir and Valva have lived up to now.

Samir: There's no need. With a little goodwill, we can fix it to the satisfaction of everyone. We can take turns. Things well shared . . . Of course, speaking of that; we've got to divide out the things in the suitcases belonging to those two.

Cluc (*cheering up*): Oh, yes. The sheets of paper for me.
Samir: Of course.

They all leave the bedside but then stop again because **Belet** *has left his task and is now smoking a cigarette and leaning against the shelves.*

Samir: Hi, what's that you're doing?
Belet (*calmly*): I'm smoking.
Samir: You seem to be taking things very calmly, don't you?
Belet: That bother you?
Samir: No, but you'd do well to go on dusting.
Belet: Dusting what? I've never seen such clean shelves.
Cluc: It doesn't matter. We want to see you busy.
Valva: Perhaps we'd do well to handcuff him while we share out the contents of the suitcase . . .
Cluc: Do you mean to say that he might think up something?
Valva: I don't know. But just to be sure . . .
Samir (*takes out the handcuffs*): It's no trouble, you're right. (*He approaches* **Belet**.) Let's see your hand. (**Belet** *looks scornfully at him without obeying.*)
Cluc (*advancing*): He said your hand. (*He takes hold of it and* **Samir** *puts the handcuff round it and fastens the other to the shelves.*)
Belet (*scornfully*): And what's the point of all that?
Samir: To show that we don't trust you far. (*Turning to the others.*) Let's get on with the work. (*They all go over to the other side where the suitcases are.*)
Cacansa (*pauses as she reaches the little table and points at* **Cleda**): Oh, look at her! I hadn't noticed . . . (**Cleda** *turns her back.*)
Alona: Did she put that on?
Cluc (*facetiously*): No, we've condemned her to an eternal carnival.
Samir (*to* **Cleda**): You go with your friend. Here you're only a nuisance. (**Cleda** *obeys.*)
Valva (*amazed*): That's not at all like she usually is, obeying so easily, and without protest. She seems another person.
Samir: She is. We'd all be different if we had different faces, that's why we shouldn't allow her ever to take off the mask. But come on, let's get on with it!
Cluc (*while* **Cleda**, *who has rejoined* **Belet**, *sits at his feet*): How shall we go about it?

Samir: We'd better bring all the suitcases here, open them up and share it all out equally, don't you think?

Cluc: That's fine by me. Here we are. (*Followed by* **Cacansa** *and* **Alona** *he goes to fetch the suitcases.*)

Valva: Remember that before we didn't want anything . . .

Samir: But we were wrong because we didn't understand this world. Here things are necessary.

Valva (*sighs*): Unfortunately . . .

Samir (*while the others return with the two suitcases each*): The only thing we can do is try to make the best use of them.

Valva: And that's difficult . . .

Samir (*going away to get the last suitcase*): Yes, very. (*They all put the suitcases in front of them in the foreground and open them.*)

Cluc: There's only one full one, Cleda's.

Samir (*coming back*): Leave it on the table. This one's Belet's. (*He leaves it to one side while* **Cluc** *obeys the instructions which have been given to him.*)

Cacansa: How shall we divide it up? Without taking account of personal preference?

Samir: No, as far as possible, we'll try to please everyone.

Cluc: One moment, we have to pick up all the other stuff.

He goes to get the hammer, pieces of wood, and nails which are still on the ground.

Valva: I'm going to get the bottle. (*She goes away to get it together with the glass which she left near the bed when* **Alona** *was drinking. She also picks up* **Cacansa***'s book.*)

Cacansa (*looking around her*): Have we left anything?

Samir: I don't think so.

He puts his hands in the suitcase, routing around, and the others return with the objects they have gone to get. They leave everything on the table.

Cluc: Now we can begin.

Samir (*showing them*): Two books and two empty boxes. I think they belong by rights to you, Cluc, especially the boxes. (*Everybody laughs.*)

Cluc (*also laughing as he takes them*): Yes, I think so.

Samir: A bar of soap, a comb, an alarm clock. (*He looks at them questioningly.*)

Alona: I'd like them.

Samir (*seeing that nobody else objects*): They're yours then. (**Alona** *takes them and just as* **Cluc** *has done, and as the others will all do, goes to put them in her own suitcase.*) A packet of cigarettes . . . matches . . . I could keep those. (*He puts them into his pocket.*) A bottle . . . two glasses . . . What about these, Cacansa?

Cacansa: Yes. (*She takes them.*)

Samir: And for you Valva there's a fan and an iron.

Valva (*picking them up*): They're useful things.

Samir (*who is putting his hand in the suitcase again*): Aha, and the lipstick! I'm sure Cacansa would like that . . .

Alona: I would too.

Cacansa: It was mine before.

Valva: It's not that I want to decide anything, but I think because of what's happened, Alona should have preference . . .

Cacansa: We've given her the bed. No need to overdo things!

Valva: Give it to the one who draws the highest card . . .

Samir: A good idea. (*He picks up the pack of cards and gives it to the two girls.*) The one who draws the highest card has the lipstick. (*Both of them, one after the other, draw a card. They look at it and show it.*)

Cacansa (*unwillingly*): Okay, she's won.

Samir (*giving the lipstick to* **Alona**): Here you are . . . Let's go to the other one. (*He puts the suitcase on the ground, and puts the other one on the table.*) Let's see what surprises this one has for us . . . (*He opens it.*) A book and a tie. Perhaps I'll keep those . . . (*The others nod their heads in agreement and he leaves them on one side.*) Two pencils and a packet of paper . . . nobody takes those from you, isn't that right, Cluc? (*He hands them to him.*) An ashtray . . . (*He looks at them all.*) How about leaving that as common property?

Valva: An excellent idea.

Samir: A key-ring, six plates . . . they're suitable for a hardworking girl, Alona.

Alona: Yes, give them to me.

Samir: Two bottles, three glasses, a saw . . .

Valva: I'd like the saw . . .

Samir: Since Cacansa had the other bottle and the glasses, you could take the lot.

Valva: Yes, give them to me. (*She takes them.*)

Samir: There's still a box and a pack of cigarettes . . . For you, Cacansa, since you haven't had anything from this case yet. (*He* *hands over the objects to the girl, shuts the suitcase, and leaves it on the ground.*) There are some other things left yet . . . A box of thread, needles, etc. I think they should go to Valva.

Cacansa: Yes.

Samir (*gives them to her*): A pack of cards. Cluc has earned those . . . Another bottle and another glass. For you, Alona.

Alona: Thank you.

Samir: A hammer, nails, pieces of wood . . .

Cluc: That's all yours, Samir. They're your tools.

Samir: Okay, there's nothing else then.

They all shut the suitcases and he himself places the objects which have fallen to his lot in his own suitcase.

Belet (*from beside the shelves*): And us, what about us?

Samir (*turning towards him*): We haven't forgotten you. For you, the duster, the mask and the handcuffs, and if necessary (*showing him*) this knife. Oh! And there's one other thing. (*He moves over behind the little table.*) This bicycle wheel. (*He rolls it up to the shelves while all the others laugh discreetly, as they pick up their suitcases.*)

ACT 3

As the curtain goes up **Belet,** *without handcuffs, seated in front of the shelves, tries to build the same box on which* **Samir** *was working during the second act. He has taken off his jersey, now left on a shelf.* **Cleda** *at his side, also seated on the ground, has her head in her arms, as if she were sleeping. Of course, she is wearing her mask.* **Valva, Alona** *and* **Cluc,** *sitting on suitcases round the table, play cards. On one side they have a bottle and three glasses.* **Cacansa,** *in front of the mirror, is slowly combing her hair like a person who knows she has lots of time.* **Samir** *is walking up and down the room, a cigarette in his mouth.*

Belet (*touching* **Cleda** *on the arm*): Are you asleep?

Cleda: No.

Belet: You could easily do it.

Cleda: What, sleep?

Belet: No, the other thing I spoke to you about.

Cleda: Samir's incorruptible.

Belet: He was, perhaps, but times have changed.

Cleda: He loves Valva . . .

Belet: Perhaps not as much as we think. Anyway, that hasn't anything to do with love. We don't ask him to love you, but merely to forget himself sufficiently for a moment, so that I can catch him unawares and take the knife away from him.

Cleda: It won't work.

Belet: Goddam mask! You're only speaking like that because you're wearing the mask. If you weren't wearing it, you yourself would have thought of doing it . . .

Cleda: No. It's just that . . . I don't know . . .

Belet: Take it off a minute.

Cleda: I can't. He would see me.

Belet: When he turns his back.

Cleda: But why?

Belet: You'll see. So that you'll become yourself again.

Cleda: That's no use either. I couldn't approach him and try to seduce him without the mask.

Belet: Of course, you could. We'll find a way. (**Samir** *stops close to the cardplayers.*) Look now . . . Quickly. Take off the mask. (*She does so and* **Belet** *looks at her for a few moments.*) I'd almost forgotten what you looked like . . .

Cleda (*with a hard smile*): Me too. I think we'll do it. Listen . . . I'll find an excuse to drag him over to the bed and I'll play on him the same trick that Alona played on you.

Belet: No, he'll catch on. He wouldn't have it in the same pocket; we'll have to search him. All I want you to do is to distract him a few moments, when all the others are far away, as they are now. (*Pointing to the table.*) You hold him down . . .

Cleda (*interrupting him*): I know what to do. Look. (*She leans over close to his ear, and as she speaks,* **Belet** *agrees.*)

Valva (*raises her head from the game and turns to* **Samir**): Why don't you play for a bit too?

Samir: No, it's boring. Later on, there's enough of you playing now.

Alona: Take my place. I'm a bit tired and I'd like to rest. I think I'll lie down for a while on the bed. (*She gets up to do so.*)

Cluc (*to* **Samir**): Sit down.

Samir: No, I don't want to.

Cluc (*glancing over to the other side*): What about you, Cacansa, don't you want to play for a bit?

Cacansa: Yes. Why not? (*She shrugs her shoulders.*) One has to do something.

Cluc: Yes, one has to do something. And always working's no good either.

Valva (*half laughing*): But you never write now.

Cluc (*picking up the cards and shuffling them*): Yes, you're right. I don't. Perhaps because now I'm free to do it my own way.

Samir: The fact is that one way and another we're all a little demoralised . . .

Cluc: There's nothing strange about that. Before we had an immediate objective to fight for. Now, on the other hand . . . (*He shrugs his shoulders and deals out the cards.*)

Valva: You wouldn't say, however, that you miss the old days . . .

Cluc: Miss them, no. We've managed to recover our human dignity.

Samir: I'm not so sure of that. Sometimes I wonder whether there wasn't more dignity in our past efforts than in our present inertia.

Cluc: Man, I wouldn't put it so strong as inertia . . . Of course, obstacles are an incentive.

Samir: It depends. They have to be in proportion to our strength. If they're more or less than we can handle, they either overwhelm us or we ignore them . . .

Cluc: And now you're saying that we're suffering from the latter.

Samir: Possibly.

Cluc: If you only observe . . .

Samir: Well, I'll observe . . . It's a sort of theoretical knowledge, up to a certain point unworkable.

Cluc: In any case we've made a lot of progress . . . Are you going to play, Cacansa?

Cacansa: Yes. (**Samir** *moves off.*)

Belet: Put on your mask.

Cleda (*obeying*): Agreed then.

Belet: Completely. After all, this seems to me to be the opportune moment. Where've you left the duster?

Cleda: Here, as usual. (*She gets up to get it but stands rooted to the spot on hearing* **Alona**'s *shout.*)

Alona (*from the bed*): Valva! Cacansa!

Landlady's Voice (*with a certain note of urgency*): Alona, get ready to leave . . . get ready to leave . . .

Valva and **Cacansa** (*now getting up hurriedly and running over to the bed*): What's up, Alona? (*They lean over her while* **Cluc** *and* **Samir** *also approach more slowly.*)

Cacansa: What's that?

Valva: That voice . . .

Alona: I've got to go now . . .

Valva: But why?

Alona (*weakly*): My suitcase please . . .

Landlady's Voice: Alona, get ready to leave . . . get ready to leave . . . (**Samir** *rushes to fetch her suitcase while the other two girls half embrace the girl.*)

Valva: Alona . . . it's not fair . . .

Alona: I don't know . . .

Cacansa: After all you've done for us . . .

Cluc (*to himself*): Now she remembers of her own accord.

Samir (*leaving it on the bed*): The suitcase.

Alona: Thank you, Samir. Open it up. (**Samir** *obeys.*) I'll leave the lipstick to Cacansa and all the rest . . . all the rest to Valva.

Valva: But, Alona. (*She covers her face with her hands.*) It can't be true, it can't be true!

Alona (*as* **Samir** *hastily empties the suitcase*): Yes, it is.

Cacansa: But so suddenly . . .

Landlady's Voice: You're urgently required . . . your time has come . . . (**Alona** *slowly gets up, grabs the suitcase, and looks at the others.*)

Alona: Good-bye, friends . . .

Cluc: Good-bye . . .

Samir: Alona . . .

Cacansa and **Valva** (*they repeat as they half take hold of her*): Alona, Alona. (*They help her to walk over to the door on the right side. On reaching it, the girl half turns round.*) I . . . (*But she bends her head, leans on the door, which gives way to the other side, and immediately she disappears with her case. The door shuts again.*)

Valva (*overcome with amazement*): But . . . it can't be true!

Cluc *and* **Samir** *turn to the two girls and they each put an arm round the shoulders of their girlfriends, leading them back towards the front of the stage.*

Belet (*to* **Cleda**): Tough luck for us. Let's see how long we'll have to wait for another chance . . . (*He sets to work while* **Cleda** *sits down again at his side.*)

Cluc (*to* **Cacansa**): Come now, don't take it like that . . .

Samir (*to* **Valva**): It was inevitable . . . It's inevitable for everyone . . .

Valva: But why? Why?

Samir: Don't ask me . . . I'm not the one who has established this order or disorder. (*Searching through his pockets.*) Here, have a cigarette.

Cluc (*to* **Cacansa,** *leading her over to the table*): Here, sit down . . .

Cacansa *follows him, but just as she is going to sit down she breaks free.*

Cacansa: The lipstick, I forget about it. (*She goes over to the bed to collect it.*)

Samir (*who has lit* **Valva**'s *cigarette*): That'll calm you down a bit.

Valva: Yes, but I just can't understand . . .

Samir: No one can. When we came in nobody told us that one day we'd be thrown out. That's what gets me.

Cacansa (*from the bed*): Everything of yours is here, Valva.

Valva (*as* **Cluc** *sits down at the table and drinks some whisky*): If there's anything you want to keep, keep it.

Cacansa (*looking at the objects*): The fan, perhaps, if you don't mind.

Valva: No, you can take it.

Cacansa *takes it and goes to put it with the lipstick in her own case.*

Valva (*who follows her with her glance, to* **Samir**): So you see, that's that. She's already forgotten her. It's as if she'd never lived with us . . .

Samir: Up to a certain point she never did really live here. If it weren't for that moment of courage she had . . .

Valva: But she did have it. And that counts. It must count.

Cluc (*from the table*): Don't you want to play again?

Valva (*turning round almost indignantly*): Play?

Cacansa (*who comes back after leaving the objects and putting her suitcase near the table where* **Alona**'s *had been*): He said it with the best of intentions, Valva.

Samir: Yes, however unfair, sad, or horrible it is, the sooner we forget the better. Or perhaps, that's exactly why we must forget, because it is sad, unfair, and horrible. Unpardonable. (*He pauses.*) Come here. (*He leads her over to the table where* **Cacansa** *has already sat down.*)

Cluc: After all, we only knew her very slightly . . . hardly at all in fact . . . Perhaps because of the way she was, so reserved and modest . . .

Samir: No. We all know each other very little. We'll leave . . . we'll leave, without expressing ourselves . . .

Cluc: Don't speak for me, as I've spent half my life writing!

Samir: That doesn't matter. Because if expressing oneself is to have any meaning, there must be someone capable of understanding . . . and we don't understand . . . (*With a disheartened gesture he starts pacing up and down again.*)

Cluc (*as he shuffles the cards*): It's affected him more than one'd imagine. That's why he's saying things which might seem profound to us.

Valva: It's affected us all. (*She pours a trace of whisky into the glass.*)

Cluc: But it's over now, it's over . . . Let's play.

Belet (*to* **Cleda**): Everything seems to be working out better than I expected. You can try it now . . .

Cleda: I don't know whether it's the right moment. He can't be in the mood for such tricks.

Belet: On the contrary. We're all easier to seduce in moments of instability, when grief or joy overcome us . . . Try it. (**Cleda** *gets up, collects the duster and goes over to the bed where she begins to dust. Suddenly she pulls off the elastic which keeps the mask on.*)

Cluc: Your turn, Cacansa. You're always asleep.

Cacansa: I was thinking that Valva hadn't collected all the things Alona left her.

Valva: There's no hurry.

Cleda (*taking advantage of the fact that* **Samir** *reaches the bed, sits down with the mask in her hand*): Oh! (*She raises her eyes.*) Samir . . .

Samir (*looking at her*): What are you doing without your mask? Don't you realize you've got to wear it always?

Cleda: Yes, I do.

Samir: Then, why've you taken it off?

Cleda: The elastic's broken . . . I don't know . . . I dropped it.

Samir (*drawing closer*): Let's see . . .

Cleda: Perhaps you could fix it . . . (*She smiles at him in a coquettish manner, as he sits down beside her.*) You've got such skilful hands . . .

Samir (*examing the mask*): It hasn't broken; it's slipped out.

Cleda: You don't know how pleased I am.

Samir (*as he tries to put the elastic through the hole which holds it*): I can imagine.

Cleda: Oh, no! It's not for the reason you think . . . (*Getting as* *close to him as she can.*) I was so anxious to speak to you . . .

Samir: I don't know that we've anything to say to one another.

Cleda: Yes, I have for one . . . (*Shamming an embarrassed smile.*) That's to say, if I dare . . . (**Belet** *gets up silently and advances carefully towards the bed.*)

Samir: Then it's better if you don't dare to.

Cleda (*putting her hand on his shoulder*): It's that you don't notice . . . of course, as I was wearing this mask you couldn't see how I was looking at you, how . . . I was getting interested in you, Samir . . .

Samir (*without brusqueness*): Leave me alone, Cleda. You don't know what you're saying.

Cleda: Yes, I do. Or, perhaps not . . . Sometimes, a woman . . . Oh, Samir! (*Embracing him just as* **Belet** *throws himself on top of them.*)

Samir (*struggling desperately as he sees the trick*): So that was it! I should have known it . . . (*He succeeds in pushing off* **Belet** *and takes out the knife but the other man attacks him again.*)

Cleda (*alarmed*): Belet!

The noise seems to startle the three players, who look towards the bed and immediately get up.

Cluc: He's attacked him! (*He rushes over to the bed.*)

Landlady's Voice (*excited*): Get ready, Belet, get ready to leave!

Cleda (*covering her face*): Oh!

Samir *succeeds in freeing his arm, which the other man was holding down, and at the very moment that* **Cluc** *is going to intervene, he plunges the knife into his stomach.* **Belet** *draws back, swaying.*

Cacansa: He's stabbed him!

They all separate almost respectfully to let him go by. **Belet** *advances with his hands on the wound, his step unsure.*

Landlady's Voice: The time's come, Belet. We're waiting for you, we're waiting for you.

All except **Cleda,** *who is sobbing on the bed, advance behind* **Belet** *who is walking to the door. On the way he picks up his suitcase.*

Samir (*looking at his hands*): I've killed him . . .

Cluc: It's not your fault. He attacked you.

Belet *leans against the door, which gives way to swallow him up, and shuts again.*

Samir (*turning to the table*): Now I too need a drink.

Cleda (*from the bed*): Murderers . . . Murderers . . .

Cluc: Don't let's exaggerate. Put your mask on.

Samir (*turning round*): No. Leave it . . . (*He drinks.*)

Cluc: After what they were trying to do to us?

Samir: We're all to blame.

Valva: But that's the second time she's tried to double-cross us. And the first one would have worked, if it hadn't been for Alona.

Samir: Despite that, the blame is ours. We've never thought about her, we've kept her on the outside . . .

Cluc: She chose the side she thought was best for her.

Samir: But it was our duty to try and rescue her. We could have done so, instead of punishing her. (*Thoughtful.*) I wonder if there's still time . . . (*He crosses over to the bed, followed by the others.*) Cleda . . .

Cleda: Go away, go away! . . .

Samir: We wanted to talk to you. I know it's a bit late . . .

Cleda: Late? Of course it is!

Samir: Try and understand. From the first moment you sided with Belet, you've always been against us. We had to defend ourselves . . .

Cluc: But it's not right! You're the one who's giving them explanations!

Samir: Perhaps we owe it to them. We've never respected their dignity.

Cluc: And, what've they done — have they respected ours? Don't you remember when you had to work for half a cigarette, when I had to suffer all their whims, just to obtain one sheet of paper?

Samir: Yes, I remember. But what's the point of building up a whole series of grudges? Somebody has to make the first step to break it.

Cluc: And must it be just now? And does it have to be us?

Samir: Yes, because we're the ones on top and for that reason we're to blame.

Cleda: On top of what? Have you ever been able to make us do what you wanted, to make me do what you wanted?

Valva: Yes, while you were wearing the mask.

Cluc: It's hard for me to understand. It could be that I've been shut up in my ivory tower and lost contact with the realities of the outside world, but you said we were to blame . . . What for? For

81

defending ourselves?

Cacansa: I understand.

Cluc (*slightly scornful*): You of all people? You?

Cacansa: It's not difficult. We began to be guilty at the very moment our defense became an attack.

Samir: Yes, and that's why we're no better than them . . . than her. (*To* **Cleda.**) You have to understand that we're acting with the best will in the world.

Cleda: Leave me alone! Do you think I'm not strong enough to live without the rest of you?

Samir: I'm sure you can't.

Cleda: You're right. Not without you all, but against you.

Valva: That's called hate!

Cleda: No. Why? It's just a matter of obeying a different law.

Samir: There's only one law.

Valva: Then, perhaps you haven't understood what Alona's and Belet's departure meant?

Cluc: Of course you haven't understood! Nobody can understand that. That's why it seemed so terrible to us. (*To* **Samir.**) You yourself said it was unpardonable . . .

Samir: And it was. But we're the ones who must make it unpardonable. We've got to have something more than a desire to dominate, which does its best to crush all those around us. We've got to have some respect.

Cleda: You're not sincere.

Samir: I've never been more so.

Cluc: Then you must have changed. First of all you spoke of obstacles, which act as an incentive and without which it's impossible to be anything . . .

Samir: Many things have happened since then, Cluc. Enough things anyway for us to be able to see that we ourselves are the obstacle, a sizeable obstacle, neither impossible, nor too easy.

Cluc: But that obstacle must always have been there. Maybe we didn't notice it, but we must have felt it.

Samir: We were too busy watching each other, fostering our grudges and dislikes.

Cleda: If only I could believe you . . .

Samir: You can believe me, and I'll give you the proof. (*He holds out the knife.*) Take it.

Cluc: No, not that! (*He goes over towards the table, where he drinks again.*)

Cleda (*stretching out her hand as if she were going to take hold of the knife but stopping at the gesture*): No . . .

Samir: Yes, you can take it.

Cleda: Haven't you thought that I could take my revenge?

Samir: Not from the moment you said: 'if only I could believe . . . Here, take it.

Cleda: No.

Samir: Then, I don't need it either. (*He throws it to one side of the bed.*)

Cleda: I've been stupid. (*She takes hold of the mask and puts it on.*)

Valva: What are you doing now?

Cleda: Can't you see?

Valva: But it's not necessary! None of us want to or can punish you now.

Cleda: Yes, I can.

Samir: I don't want to force my point of view on you, but it seems wrong to me.

Cleda: Why?

Samir: That voluntary act of humiliation still cuts you off from us.

Cluc (*from the table drinking*): He knows everything!

Cacansa: Take it off, Cleda. If not, you'll make us wish that there were masks for all of us.

Cluc: She too knows everything. (*Drinks again, fills the glass up, and picking it up, gets up.*)

Cleda: I'll only wear it a short while . . .

Samir: In that case, it'll be a hypocritical act. Yet one more way of cutting you off from us.

Cluc (*who has advanced as far as the bed*): Well, what do you want? You want us all to look as alike as drops of water?

Samir: Drops of water don't look alike.

Cacansa: Don't drink any more, Cluc.

Cluc: They all look alike to me.

Samir: But they're not. If they were aware of themselves, they would be able to see the differences. It's only we who confuse them, as the landlady must confuse us, for whom we've only a name she could give to anyone.

Cluc (*raising his glass*): To the landlady, then! (*He looks at it disappointed.*) It's empty. (*He goes back to the table to refill it.*)

Valva: How can he be so stupid?

Cacansa: It's not that. It's repulsive to him that things can be the way Samir says, the way we all think.

Samir: In our hearts, we all find it a bit repulsive.

Cacansa (*going over to the table where **Cluc** is drinking again*): You're drinking too much . . .

Cluc: Too much? Since when?

Cacansa: Since now.

Cluc (*raising his glass*): To the Landlady! (*He drinks.*)

Landlady's Voice: Cluc, get ready to leave ... get ready to leave ...

Samir and **Valva:** It's not possible! (*They rush over to* **Cluc** *as he lets his arms fall on to the table.*)

Cacansa (*hugging him*): Cluc, Cluc!

Cluc: The case. (**Cacansa** *and* **Valva** *between them get him to his feet and* **Samir** *empties out the contents of the suitcase.*)

Cleda (*who also draws close to the table*): He's probably only drunk.

Samir: Didn't you hear the Landlady's Voice?

Landlady's Voice: Now's the time, Cluc. You're urgently required ...

Cacansa: No, no.

Samir *helps* **Cluc,** *carrying his case for him, and accompanies him to the door, near which he gives it to him. They all follow as usual.*

Cluc (*weakly*): Forgive me, all of you ... (*He pushes the door and disappears.*)

Samir (*looking at the others*): You see how simple it is ...

Cacansa *runs over to the table where she helps herself to a large glass of whisky.*

Valva (*behind her*): Don't be so silly, Cacansa. Put down that glass! (*She takes it from her.*)

Cacansa (*almost begging*): I want to drink, I want to drink a lot ...

The other girl hugs her, makes her sit down and remains at her side.

Samir (*turning to the bed where he sits down*): Always beginning, always ending ...

Cleda (*standing beside him*): You're depressed, aren't you?

Samir: Yes.

Cleda: But all those things you said at first ...

Samir: I don't believe them.

Cleda: You believed them a moment ago.

Samir: No, I didn't. I don't think I've ever believed anything.

84

Cleda: And yet you gave me the knife . . .

Samir: Yes . . .

Cleda: But if you didn't believe what you said, you couldn't be sure I wouldn't do you any harm.

Samir: Perhaps it was that I wanted you to do it, wanted you to finish us all off, once and for all. (*Looking at her.*) In fact you're the only one who's strong.

Cleda: Me? Why?

Samir: You stood up against us all, siding with Belet, you overcame his treachery when he tried to seduce Alona, you helped him even when we were going to overcome him . . . in reality you're the only one worthy of living in this room . . . That's to say, you were.

Cleda: You're wrong, I am now.

Samir (*sarcastically*): All the same, it's strange that you can be successful preaching what you don't believe! Was it really so convincing to you?

Cleda: Yes, and I still find it so.

Samir: Even after I've told you how false it is?

Cleda: It's not false to me. Perhaps it is to you, because each person must have his own version of the truth. You gave me mine, perhaps without realising it.

Samir (*laughs*): It's all nonsense! (*To the two women.*) Come here, listen!

Valva: What's the matter, Samir?

Samir (*pointing to* **Cleda**): She believed it all!

Valva: All what?

Samir: All those long words which meant nothing . . .

Valva (*leaving* **Cacansa**): Samir. (*Hugging him as she reaches his side.*) The death of your friend has turned your head . . .

Samir: He wasn't my friend. We never were friends.

Valva: But Samir . . .

Samir: And I don't want anyone to come and comfort me, because I'm not unhappy! Go back to Cacansa, as she probably does need you . . .

Valva: My duty is at your side!

Samir: What duty? (*He stands up with a flourish.*) There's no such thing as duties! Nor rights either. Leave me alone!

Valva: Samir, Samir, what are you going to do?

He, without answering, escapes into the foreground while the girls gather near the little table and contemplate him as he paces back and forth.

Samir (*after he's gone back and forth twice*): What are you looking at?

Cleda: You're not being reasonable, Samir . . .

Samir: And why should I be? Is there anything that's reasonable?

Cleda: Everthing could be if we made up our minds that it should be.

Samir (*pointing to the door*): Even that? Those urgent cries which drive us out of the room?

Valva: Perhaps . . .

Samir: Not at all! If they were reasonable they wouldn't affect us in that way. Look, look at us, what do you think we look like for God's sake! Four drowning men, waiting for their wave to overcome them . . .

Valva (*going up to him*): No, Samir, no. We'll struggle! Just as drowning men struggle . . .

Samir (*sarcastically*): To see if some ship'll pick us up? Is that it?

Cleda: Don't take away our hope after you've given it to us . . .

Samir: I haven't given you anything! Nobody can give anybody anything, because nobody has anything. It's not having anything possessing these few objects. (*He runs over to the suitcase and starts emptying it on to the bed.*) And what's more, we don't possess these things either, because things which can be taken away from us are not ours.

Cleda: But while we have them they're ours. If that wasn't true, we couldn't refuse them or give them away.

Cacansa: That's true. We give them away freely.

Samir (*pointing to the objects which came out of* **Cluc**'s *suitcase*): Okay then, get on with it. Dispose of these! Fill a suitcase which sooner or later you'll have to empty.

Cacansa: We don't know.

Samir: Haven't you got any eyes? Don't you see that they're going one after another . . .

Cacansa: But nobody says that we'll have to go too.

Samir (*sarcastically*): Of course. Each person thinks he's an exception . . . Ah, that's enough. I'm fed up! (*He sits on the bed and covers his face with his hands.*)

Valva (*getting nearer to him as* **Cacansa** *picks up the objects and leaves them in her own suitcase, and* **Cleda** *sits down at the table*): Samir . . .

Samir: Go away, Valva. Go away . . .

Valva: Don't push me off, Samir . . .

Samir: Leave me alone. Go away and play cards.

Valva (*hugging him*): No, Samir. I love you . . .

Samir: Shut up! (*He disentangles himself from her arms and stands up.*) To love . . . (*He is about to take a step then falls full length on the floor.*)

Landlady's Voice: Get ready to leave, Samir, get ready to leave . . .

Valva (*letting herself fall down beside him as the other women run to join her*): No, Samir, no, no, no . . .

Samir (*stretching out a hand to take* **Valva**'s): Yes, it was inevitable . . .

Valva: But I don't want you to . . .

Samir: It's nothing . . . (*He tries to smile.*) I love you, Valva . . .

Landlady's Voice: Get ready, Samir, your time is drawing to an end . . .

Cleda (*to* **Cacansa**): One more . . .

Samir: Good-bye, Valva . . . Help me . . . All of you help me . . .

Between them all they help him stand up and pick up his case. Afterwards, they go towards the door, **Valva** *crying.*

Cleda (*moving away from them towards the little table*): Now I don't know what to think.

She pours a little whisky into a glass and drinks while the other two girls stay with **Samir** *by the door.*

Valva (*just as* **Samir** *disappears over to the other side*): Beloved . . . Beloved . . . (*She hides her face in her hands.* **Cacansa** *hugs her, but she disentangles herself after a minute.*) There's no need. I'm okay. (*She walks away from the girl towards the foreground, while the other girl sits down at the foot of the bed. She looks around her and finally goes over to pick up the suitcase. She carries it near to the shelves, where she empties it. She closes it again and walks over to the door.*)

Cacansa (*vaguely alarmed*): Where are you going?

Valva: Nowhere. (*She gets nearer the door.*)

Landlady's Voice (*excited*): Now's the time, Valva, now . . .

Cacansa and **Cleda** (*both getting up*): No! (*But* **Valva** *has already pushed the door and disappears. The other two girls look at each other overcome with amazement.*)

Cacansa: She's done it of her own free will!

Cleda: Yes. (*She walks about the room, as* **Cacansa** *draws near the door, and then goes back to the table where she sits down on her own suitcase.*)

Cacansa: I couldn't ...

Cleda (*takes a cigarette and lights it*): Sometimes, it seems one way, and sometimes it seems another ... Of course, it's because we change.

Cacansa: What's that you're saying?

Cleda: I don't know. (*She sits down at the foot of the bed.*) I don't even know myself ...

Cacansa: We're the only ones left ...

Cleda: One of us two will still have to remain longer ... after ... not for long, of course ...

Cacansa: Don't say that!

Cleda: As you like. (*She pauses.*) If it were possible to decide, to make a choice ... but when it seems as though you have got something ... (*She shakes her head.*) No.

Cacansa (*anxiously*): I don't understand what you mean, Cleda!

Cleda: Never mind. It's not worth the effort.

Cacansa: You seem so serious that you almost frighten me.

Cleda: Perhaps in a moment I'll laugh or ... I don't know. We can't even be sure of the immediate future. We don't know what'll happen to us, perhaps because we are living in a kind of vacuum without any substance ... Haven't you noticed that nothing is as it should be?

Cacansa: How should it be?

Cleda: As it should have been, because for us two ... never mind ... Don't you know?

Cacansa (*nervous*): But what are you trying to say?

Cleda (*getting up from the bed and beginning to walk about between the little table and the shelves*): Nothing. I've gone beyond my role, like all of us, or almost all of us ... and we don't even know if that's all right, or if it'll be punished ... (*Looking around her.*) I remember when I entered this room ... it seemed to be all mine ... right until later when you all forced me to put on the mask. (*She goes to fetch it and puts it on holding it with her hand.*) The mask ... Now I wouldn't mind at all wearing it.

Cacansa: No, Cleda ...

Cleda (*takes it off*): No, I know that. It's useless and not worth the trouble. (*She goes to leave it on the shelves in front of which she remains.*) I don't feel anything.

Cacansa: Nor do I.

Cleda: I was violent and full of ambition, without scruples, because I wanted to have the best and have it quickly ... perhaps it was that I knew something. (*She turns.*) I couldn't, however, know more than I do now, and now (*with a depressed gesture*), now I don't want anything . . .

Cacansa: Because they've all gone . . .

Cleda: Because they've all gone. Or only because the first one has gone. We've all changed then. But in any case, we've never been what we should have been, what each one of us hoped for himself. Why not?

Cacansa: I don't know.

Cleda: Of course . . . only Valva and Belet could have come at all near to being themselves, because they went when they wanted to, and in the way they wanted . . .

Cacansa: Belet didn't.

Cleda: Yes, he did. He couldn't hope for anything more. He couldn't wish for anything more, but that's not important either because the door through which they left us is the same. And the worst of it is, not to know whether it's fair or whether it's unfair, not to know anything. (*She pauses and crosses to* **Cacansa**'*s side, takes the bottle and drinks a drop of whisky thoughtfully.*) Not to know anything. (*She drinks and leaves the glass. Immediately she goes to get her suitcase and sits down near* **Cacansa.**) You and I alone, Cacansa, the last of our generation. Any moment now we'll hear the voice calling out to us . . .

Cacansa: Be quiet, Cleda . . .

Cleda (*imperturbable*): And we'll wonder what we've done. Not you, nor me, but us, all of us. What have we done? (*Touching her elbow.*) What will you be able to answer?

Cacansa: Perhaps we weren't meant to do anything.

Cleda: Perhaps not. (*She gets up.*) Don't let's get things out of proportion. It isn't anything more than the room of a boarding house where chance has brought us together, equals, different and contradictory. Everything at once. We've loved. We've fought. We've hated. We've looked for explanations which we've given up in favour of other explanations, which were worthless too. We've let ourselves be influenced. We've also influenced others and finished up being different, but of all that, nothing's left.

Cacansa: Us two, still . . .

Cleda (*going to the foot of the bed where she sits down again*): Us two. Yes, for a few moments . . . Afterwards the empty room, as it was before we entered it in the first place, the impersonal room . . . (*She's silent and turns towards the objects spread out on the bed.*) And the impersonal objects too; the majority, useless. We've never had an opportunity of using them. Perhaps because they didn't fall into the kind of hands which needed them.

Cacansa: If you want anything you can have it now.

Cleda (*turns round and laughs*): I can have it. What would I do
with it?

Cacansa: I don't know. As you were saying . . .

Cleda: I was saying . . . yes, I was saying things. So as not to keep
completely silent, because if I were to remain silent the landlady
might feel tempted to fill my silence with her voice. And she only
talks to say one thing, to throw us out . . .

Cacansa: Do you think she'll send us to another room?

Cleda (*surprised*): Why?

Cacansa: A better room, if she's satisfied with our behaviour . . .

Cleda: She's unaware of our behaviour, because she's never bothered to look into it. And then what kind of behaviour? Have we
always behaved in the same way? Is there anything in common
between that selfish and ambitious Cleda of before and this different girl I've become? And which of the two is the authentic one?

Cacansa: This one, I imagine. Life in this room, the contact with
the others, has allowed you to develop, to show yourself as you
really are.

Cleda (*with sarcasm*): And I'm better than I thought, is that it?

Cacansa: Yes.

Cleda: And what about those that got worse because of the contacts they made, which were not the most suitable, nor the atmosphere of the room the most ideal? . . .

Cacansa: I don't know. (*She fills the glass with whisky and
drinks.*)

Cleda: If we are different it's natural that the same circumstances
are not equally suitable for everybody. And in that case, what
value does our behaviour have? In different circumstances we'd
have emerged differently. Look at me. If Samir had not lived in
this room he couldn't have said to me the words he did say, and as
a result of which I reacted. Without him, I'd have gone on being
the same Cleda who came into the room, I no longer wish to
remember how many years ago. You see that don't you, Cacansa?
(*Getting up and going over to the little table.*) It's thanks to the
others that we change with the constant rubbing up against one
another. And those others could be anybody . . .

Cacansa: I haven't changed.

Cleda: That's how it seems to you. Perhaps you haven't changed so
much, because your contacts have not been of the same kind.
Because there's another thing, each one of us establishes a different type of contact with the group which is best for us, or for
whom we are best. It depends on so many things. On the moment
you enter into a relationship, on the first person with whom you

speak, on the attitude with which all and each one receives you, don't you see?

Cacansa: Perhaps I do. (*She takes up the bottle again to drink some whisky.*)

Cleda (*intercepting her gesture*): Do you really want to drink?

Cacansa: No. (*Leaves the bottle.*) More than anything, it's just to do something. Suddenly it seems as though everything has been done . . .

Cleda: Yes.

Cacansa (*she gets up*): As if everything has always been done.

Cleda: Yes.

Cacansa (*she moves over to the door*): As if everything were reduced to one solitary act already completed on the day we entered the room . . .

Cleda: Yes. (*Turning round and seeing her near the door.*) What are you doing, do you want to copy Valva?

Cacansa: No. (*She returns to the table.*) You were right, we change. We change when we least expect it.

Cleda: You should have noticed it.

Cacansa: Perhaps I've never really been interested enough in anything, but now . . .

Cleda: But now what?

Cacansa: Now I'm interested against it all . . .

Cleda: Against it all? What do you mean?

Cacansa (*leaning over the table where she rests her hands*): Yes, against everything we are, against the room, the relationships we've established, against myself . . .

Cleda: I don't know if there's any point in that.

Cacansa (*shaking her head*): No, there isn't, but that's possible. What you said had no point to it either.

Cleda (*looking at her with a certain measure of reserve*): If you'd drunk more I would say that it was the liquor . . .

Cacansa: If you mean to say that I'm drunk, you're right. I am. But against . . .

Cleda (*impatient*): Don't you know how to say anything else?

Cacansa (*standing up*): The landlady's sleeping. She's let us talk too much. She's let you talk too much.

Cleda: Probably.

Cacansa (*as she moves away*): If she offered me another room now I wouldn't accept it. (*She turns.*) Listen . . .

Landlady's Voice (*cutting in*): Cleda, get ready to leave . . .

Cacansa (*surprised*): Did she say, Cleda?

Cleda: Yes.

Cacansa: But that's not possible, now that I'd so many things to tell you. (**Cleda** *gets up and goes to get her suitcase.*) No . . . Wait . . . (*She hurries.*)

Cleda: You're too late . . . and that's no use either.

Cacansa: Listen, but . . .

Landlady's Voice: Get ready, Cleda, because your hour has come . . .

Cleda (*taking a step towards the door*): Good-bye, Cacansa. I don't know whether to say I'm pleased to have known you . . .

Cacansa: Only one moment more. (*But then she gives up.*) Okay, Cleda, I know that you can't do anything. (*She bends to kiss her.*) Good-bye.

Landlady's Voice: We are waiting for you, Cleda. We are waiting. Leave . . .

Cleda (*looks at* **Cacansa** *and disentangles herself from her arms*): Good-bye. (*She pushes the door and disappears.* **Cacansa** *remains looking for a long while then comes back into the foreground.*)

Cacansa: I'd never have thought that I could be the last. (*She looks around her.*) But everything's coming to an end now. (*She goes over to her own suitcase, carries it to the side of the shelves where she begins to empty it, placing everything untidily. Then she goes to leave it near the door, steps back again and then begins to transfer to the shelves all the other objects scattered around the room, leaving until last the bottle and the glasses which are on the little table, beside which she pauses for a moment thoughtfully.*) I don't know why I'm doing it. (*But she picks it up too and carries it to the shelves.*) I don't think there's anything else now. (*She picks up the lipstick and a pencil and moves over in front of the mirror, where she begins to paint her lips; then she laughs and makes them larger until she makes them into a clown's mouth. Immediately with the pencil she underlines her eyebrows, making them extend right to her cheekbones. She laughs and goes back to pick up the lipstick, with which she draws two circles on her cheeks. Then with her hands she loosens her hair, and throws it over her face.*)

Landlady's Voice: Cacansa, now it's your turn . . . make yourself ready to leave the room . . .

Cacansa (*sarcastically*): Of course. You can see that I've prepared myself as is fitting. (*She paints her lips again with almost angry movements.*) When you wish. (*She turns to the room with her pencil and lipstick in her hand, and crosses over to the other side where she leaves both things on the shelves.*)

Landlady's Voice: We're waiting for you, Cacansa ... we're waiting for you ... you can leave.

Cacansa: Yes. (*She crosses over to the suitcase, picks it up, turns round and contemplates the room. Then she turns decisively and pushes the door, saying*): I'm here.

There's a moment's silence and then is heard once more:

Landlady's Voice (*welcoming as at first*): You've been lucky, young fellow. The room, as you see, is pleasant and contains all the comforts you could wish. We've taken care of your well-being, without sparing any efforts, and it is with pride that I can assure you that up till now our guests who have passed through this room have had no cause to make the slightest complaint. It's for that reason that we don't even have a complaints book. (*She is silent as the usual noise of bolts and chains is heard and then the door opens to let through a young man in shirt sleeves who is carrying a suitcase in his hand. The voice continues.*) Look and judge for yourself ... A room like a whole land, large and welcoming, where besides the indispensable things you'll find all those other superfluous objects which'll make you happy, as they have made those who preceded you happy. And you'll wish to stay a long time ... Make yourself at home. (*The door closes, with the same accompaniment of chains and bolts as the curtain begins to fall.*)

Young Fellow (*leaving his suitcase and looking around him*): Perfect.

CURTAIN

Full Circle

(Situació bis)

Manuel de Pedrolo

English version by Brian D. Steel

CHARACTERS

Melo
Pral
Orel
Nisal
Man with the sack
Man with the stick
Fila
Glada
Denta
Erna

The house lights go out and the curtain rises. Behind it, another curtain, semi-transparent, reveals moving shadow effects.

Noises, a few bars of music which turn into a murmur of voices above which another voice rises.

Voice: Man . . . Indeed, man . . . (*The voice is raised to be heard above the murmurs*). Someone wants to speak and no one listens to him! We must conquer the sea, the land . . . (*The murmuring voices gradually fade away.*) And let inspiration utter words as old as man himself . . .

Voice (*as a guitar is strummed, mockingly*): Baldness makes men prone to intellectual work. I'm sorry. Intellectual work makes men prone to . . . What intellectual work? What . . . Oh, yes . . . I'm sorry . . .

Voice (*still against a background of guitar music, now joined by other instruments*): One of the objects of modern biological science is to consider organisms from a collective point of view, according to their relationships with each other and with their surrounding environment . . . (1)

Voice: We know that man is an imperfect animal. Let us not be misled by those millennia that separate us from the beasts and from the trees in which we used to live, nor those millions of years which have elapsed since we received the first inspiration which opened up our path to freedom . . .

Voice (*as the music turns into the sound of waves breaking*): We have come to give you it in the name of what we hold most sacred: our respect for Homo sapiens (*piercing laughter*), you who tomorrow will decide between dignity and ignominy, between power and annihilation, between hunger . . . (*Loud roaring, above which another voice rises with difficulty.*)

Voice: Statistics show us that the standard of living tends to rise among peoples who are submissive to ancestral laws, who are orderly, voluntarily obedient to a code imposed on them and which the ruling class adapts to suit its own needs . . . (*Some shots ring out and a female voice wails and then slowly fades.*)

Voice: My brothers, one day there was a mingling of bloods because of a word and a sacrifice which, once and for all, destroyed falsehood and established truth . . . Man . . .

Voice (*accompanied by a volley of rifle shots which ceases abruptly*): A body with paws! Limbs which are crippled by arthritis, adipose tissue which swells bellies, a growing cancer . . .

Voice (*against a chorus of wailing*): Two thousand three hundred and twenty-six products, registered and patented, have come from behind the desks where a tall man smokes cigarettes . . .

Voice: Life begins at ninety. (2)

Voice (*cheerful music*): Many famous people owe their success to astrology. If you have an accurate and sufficiently detailed horoscope you are no longer in the dark . . . (3)

Voice: We must face up to reality! (*Clash of cymbals.*) The people always have the last word and we humble representatives . . .

Voice: The crime rate has increased by 6.03 per cent in the last twelve months (*mocking guitar music*), and all the facts suggest that we have not seen the worst yet. We have strayed from the straight and narrow, my brothers . . .

Voice: The discoveries of genetics have enabled us to use the results obtained to improve the human race both physically and mentally . . . (1)

Voice: There has been a decrease of sixteen millions in the number of cinemagoers as compared with last year and it is believed that this is due to competition from television . . . (4)

Voice: Please note: husbands who wish to buy articles in this store are requested to produce permits signed by their wives. (5)

Voice (*over a background military march*): Man's future state will be absurd and desperate if he allows the remaining traces of totalitarianism to multiply with the excuse that no one subscribes to these ideas . . . (6)

Voice: There are, however, people who, in spite of receiving sufficient education, still have poor reasoning powers . . . (7)

Voice (*sad music*): Why are we reluctant to admit that man is a moral being?

Voice (*monotonous*): Mental cruelty. Physiological deficiencies . . . Carnivorous animals return from the war . . .

Voice (*background military march*): The last one, citizens, because the world is destined to be ours and the inferior races are already in retreat before the onslaught of our victorious soldiers . . .

Voice (*harsh*): Right face! Left face! About face! Ha–alt!

Child's Voice (*breaking a sudden silence*): Is Daddy with the angels now?

Voice: Love, brothers, love is the word, the love we shall win with our sacrifice and if necessary by force, since some hearts are closed to it and must be opened.

Voice: Gentlemen! (*A fist thumps a table.*) Let us not be afraid to face up to the truth: we are a race of old people. We must increase the birthrate, encourage marriage and set up production bonuses.

(*He clears his throat.*) I'm sorry, that belongs in the section which I shall come to later on our armaments position . . .

Voice (*over the singing of a crowd*): A person who has been trained in sociology can point out a pattern of cause and effect for any given phenomenon and he can predict the consequences . . . (7)

Female Voice (*soft sweet music*): Just the two of us alone . . . and a cottage . . . a cottage on the mountainside from where I shall see you coming home every evening. And you will give me children . . .

Voice (*accompanied by a single note, prolonged and repeated*): This time the victim of the sex killer comes from one of our most distinguished families of industrialists who . . .

Voice (*noise of gears and machinery*): A hundred and fifty hours a week at eleven coins per hour equals one thousand six hundred coins . . .

Voice (*over the clamor of an excited crowd*): Citizens, we are here to restore normal order and we just want to hear you shout, in a single voice: we are with you!

Child's Voice: I'm hungry . . .

Voice: Ignorance, that is, the inability to understand the meaning of events, can be the cause of countless suffering which man inflicts on his fellow beings . . . (7)

Voice (*sad*): No one in the whole world will be entirely free of sin . . .

Voice (*cheerful music*): Thinking is indestructible; it destroys baldness . . . I'm sorry. Baldness does not destroy thought neither does thinking destroy . . .

Voice (*pompous*): In other words, the voice of authority tends to weaken. But when superiority over the exploited classes is overwhelming, the gulf between those who command and those who obey becomes wider. (8)

Voice (*organ music*): Because it is written: the humble shall be richly rewarded . . . First we must learn generosity, to free our hearts of all passions . . . What an ideal for man, my friends, what an ideal!

Voice: The village was totally destroyed and its ruins levelled out. Its five hundred inhabitants were rounded up in the main square and were shot after receiving the Last Rites . . .

Voice: Progress demands specialization, but modern scientific theories, on the other hand, point out very forcefully the dangers of excessive specialization. Whole nations are faced with an impasse.

Voice (*bird song*): Earn money by breeding giant species and take advantage of our range of special cages . . . (3)

Voice (*pedantic*): In all human society there is a system of attraction which assumes in each member a consciousness of his own relationship to others and a desire to regulate his behavior according to this relationship . . . (1)

Voice (*military march*): One-two-one-two-one-two . . .

Voice: Emerging from the jungle did not solve all our problems. (*Speeches in the background.*) New needs arose or gathered strength and they could not be satisfied without uprooting ourselves from the primeval mud . . .

Voice (*vehemently*): There is no evidence in the whole of history to justify the belief that any benevolent dictator will remain benevolent for long . . . (9)

Voice (*sad and inspired*): I did not come into this world through the doors of the womb; my birth was a terrible struggle . . . (10) (*Howling of a storm.*)

Voice (*dictatorially*): Nothing less than the bending of the individual will to the collective will, the sacrifice of personal whims to common needs, can guarantee the stability of a government which represents . . .

Voice (*muddled*): The triumph of baldness . . . I'm sorry. Thinking predisposes to baldness and . . . I'm sorry.

Voice: The states of a person's conscience cannot be submitted to or controlled by the observation which scientific objectivity demands, and therefore cannot be measured. (1)

Voice (*over the crash of waves*): In recent months, three hundred and two families have chosen the solitary life on the islands; the price of land has increased considerably . . .

Voice: Don't let the right hand know what the left is doing . . .

Voice: The repression of antisocial attitudes is as fanciful as it is unacceptable as a principle. All individual acts are antisocial. (10)

Voice: Between the idea
And the reality
Between the motion
And the act
Falls the Shadow (11)

Voice: But the course of history has made it abundantly clear that a fundamental integrity exists, that man, man, man . . .

Woman's Voice (*impatient*): Stop it!

Voice: Man, man, man . . . (*and the word, fainter with each repetition, appears to vanish in the light that comes up while the curtain rises, or opens, and the action begins.*)

References

1. *Histoire de la science* (Gallimard).
2. Elsa Maxwell
3. Advertisements.
4. News item.
5. Notice in certain American department stores.
6. Barrows Dunham, *Man against Myth.*
7. Czeslaw Milosz, *The Captive Mind.*
8. Erich Fromm, *Escape from Freedom.*
9. Aldous Huxley, *Science, Liberty and Peace.*
10. Antonin Artaud, posthumous text and "Letter to doctors in charge of mental institutions."
11. T. S. Eliot, "The Hollow Men."

ACT 1

On the right, four doors, and four more on the left, close to each other and numbered one to four on each side starting from the front. Another, larger door at the back. The walls are black and the doors white, with the exception of the one at the back which is painted in vertical black and white stripes. The only object on the stage is a gigantic wastepaper basket.

When the curtain rises, all the doors, except the one at the back, are open and the stage is empty. After a moment, **Orel,** who occupies the room behind the second door on the right, pokes his head out cautiously, looks to left and right and then at the wastepaper basket; then he disappears from sight. Immediately, the same sequence is observed by **Denta,** fourth door on the left. Then **Pral,** first right, and **Fila,** second left, peep out simultaneously but both withdraw when they notice the other's presence in the other doorway. Finally, **Erna,** third left, goes through the same sequence, but instead of withdrawing as the others have done, she ventures out to the centre of the stage and stops beside the wastepaper basket. She looks at it, peeps inside and, disappointed at not finding anything there, returns to her room. **Melo,** fourth right, pokes his head out, watches the girl's movements and, when she disappears from view, comes out in his turn and also goes up to the wastepaper basket, which he examines carefully and contemptuously, even going as far as to lift it up and feel inside it. **Nisal,** third right, catches him examining it by creeping silently into the middle of the stage.

Nisal (*stopping behind* **Melo**): Anything there?

Melo (*quickly dropping the basket*): What? (*He turns round and recognises* **Nisal**.) Oh, it's you!

Nisal: Yes. Isn't there anything there?

Melo (*picking up the basket and turning it upside down*): See for yourself. Not a thing. (*He replaces it.*)

Nisal: Still, it's strange. It's so late . . .

Melo: Late?

Nisal: Yes, it ought to be full by this time.

Melo (*slightly surprised*): By what time? What do you mean?

Nisal: They always fill it at the same time. They have to.

Melo: Have to?

Nisal: Yes, by law.

Melo: Oh. (*He scratches his neck and looks from the basket to his companion.*) And how do you know it's late?

Nisal (*shrugging his shoulders*): I just do, I tell you.

Melo: I don't know.

Nisal: Yes you do. But you're afraid, like the rest of us. And you don't want to admit it.

Melo: No, it's not that. They always come when they feel like it.

Nisal: That's not true. They have to obey the law.

Melo (*laughing*): Why? Didn't they make the law?

Nisal: Yes, but for everybody.

Melo: I don't know about that. Besides, what law are you talking about? Has there ever been one?

Nisal: Course there has. You know that as well as me.

Melo: I've never seen any proof of it.

Nisal (*pointing*): The wastepaper basket. They fill it, we empty it.

Melo: But nothing's ever been laid down. Sometimes I ask myself: "What if they didn't fill it one day?"

Nisal: That's impossible.

Melo: Yes, impossible. But just suppose. Suppose it happened. What could we do?

Nisal (*a little uneasy*): Complain.

Melo: To whom? And how?

Nisal: We haven't been told how to do that, have we?

Melo: You see! In fact, we haven't been told anything. There's no way of getting in touch with them.

Nisal (*pointing to the basket*): Yes there is, the letters.

Melo: No. I've thought of them many times. Haven't you noticed that through the letters they can communicate with us but we can't communicate with them?

Nisal: Communicate? They've never tried to communicate with us.

Melo: How do we know? We think that all the correspondence goes into that basket, but that's an act of faith. We can't be sure of it.

Nisal: What are you getting at?

Melo: Just this. What if they *select* that correspondence? Or, even worse: what if they write the letters themselves?

Nisal: Why should they do that?

Melo: Don't you see? To have an even tighter control over us, to make us do what they want us to, according to what suits them.

Nisal: But they are only middlemen.

Melo: That's what we think. But what if they weren't? They might have tricked us from the start.

Nisal: But the letters come from outside.

Melo: The envelopes do. We don't know about the letters. They are opened letters. Anyone could have written them. I could have.

Nisal (*shaking his head and laughing*): You? Now I know you're joking. (*He becomes serious again and seizes* **Melo** *by the arm.*) Tell me you're joking!

Melo (*as* **Glada,** *first left, looks out and on seeing them talking, comes over towards the wastepaper basket*): Don't worry, I haven't got anything to do with them.

Nisal: Then why did you say you had?

Melo: I didn't. I wanted to make you understand that perhaps we're too gullible. We've never asked for any explanations.

Nisal: We can't.

Melo: Don't you think that's odd? (*He notices that* **Glada** *has come over to the basket and stares at her.*) No, there's nothing there.

Glada: They're late.

Melo: You too?

Glada: What do you mean, me too?

Melo: You all say they're late and . . . But what difference does it make? We are stupid. We know that there can't be anything there until the bell rings, and yet we still keep prowling around the basket.

Glada: They might forget one day.

Melo: What? To ring the bell?

Glada: Yes.

Melo: I'd like to see that happen!

Nisal: I wouldn't.

Melo: I would. Just think . . . we might find ourselves face to face!

Nisal (*apprehensively*): And what would happen?

Melo: Exactly! What *would* happen?

Glada: The law says that we would pay with our lives.

Melo: Yes, if they caught one of us. But what if we were all here?

Nisal (*after a short pause*): They'd still kill us.

Melo: But how? There's only two of them. We could stop them.

Nisal: By force, you mean?

Melo: Why not? We've never tried . . .

Nisal: I'm not going to listen to you . . . (*He moves off towards his room, but does not go inside.*)

Melo (*contemptuously*): I knew it . . . (*To* **Glada.**) What about you, are you going?

Glada: No.

Melo: Aren't you afraid of what I said?

Glada: I'm not afraid of words.

Melo: What if they were actions?

Glada: I don't know. I don't understand . . .

Melo: What don't you understand?

Glada: Everything, anything. Why things are this way. Why we wait for the letters; why they bring them.

Melo: Exactly. No one understands.

Glada: And what can we do about it?

Melo (*as* **Erna** *comes out of her room and walks towards the basket*): You or me, on our own, nothing. But the two of us and someone else . . . all together . . .

Glada: We might be left without any letters . . .

Erna (*alarmed at hearing this*): What's that, Glada? No more letters?

Melo: But it wouldn't be the end of the world. A few letters which aren't even addressed to us . . .

Glada: Yes they are!

Erna (*worried*): What are you talking about?

Melo (*taking no notice of her*): No they're not. They've got names on them. But not our names.

Glada: They are the names they give us.

Melo: We think they are the names they give us. No, wrong. We tell ourselves that to put our minds at ease. Do you ever look at the names, when the letters arrive?

Glada: No.

Erna: What's that?

Melo: No. You pick up as many as you can, whoever they're for.

Glada: Of course we do, because none of us knows which name is supposed to be his . . .

Melo: And do you think that's natural or right?

Erna: It's always been like that.

Melo: Here we go again! It's always been like that! (*He kicks the basket which rolls away. While the two girls rush after it,* **Pral** *and* **Orel** *come out of their respective rooms almost at the same time.*)

Orel (*seeing* **Nisal** *standing by his own door*): Nothing yet?

Nisal: No. Nothing.

Orel (*noticing the girls carrying the basket towards the centre*): What's going on?

Nisal (*shrugging his shoulders*): Melo . . .

Pral (*who has joined the other two men*): Is he up to his tricks?

Nisal: Yes. (*They lapse into silence as the other two resume their conversation.*)

Glada: You shouldn't be so bad-tempered.

Melo: I know, I know. It isn't the wastepaper basket's fault, right?

Glada: Right. And it isn't Erna's either. Or mine.

Melo: That's true. That is . . . (*He looks at the wastepaper basket and begins to walk round it, staring at it in a strange way.*) There's something we've never tried . . . (*He glances at the girls.*) What if I made it disappear?

Glada: How?

Simultaneously.

Erna: No!

Melo (*slightly amused*): Yes. I could take it away, get rid of it and . . .

Glada: Where would they leave the letters then?

Melo: That's what I was wondering: What would they do with the letters? (*He leans forward and picks up the basket.*)

Erna (*quickly holding him back*): No!

Melo (*struggling*): Let go of me!

Erna: Glada, help me! (*To the others.*) All of you, help me!

Nisal (*coming forward with his companions*): What's going on now?

Erna (*anxiously*): He wants to get rid of the basket.

Pral (*as they all rush forward*): Oh no!

Nisal: Have you gone mad or something?

Orel: Put the basket down.

Melo (*giving in*): All right. If you can't take a joke . . .

Nisal: We've had enough of your jokes for one day. (*They put the basket back in its proper place.* **Melo** *moves a few paces away from them, rubbing his hands with a handkerchief that he has taken out of his pocket.*)

105

Orel: He gets worse every day.

Nisal: Let's leave him alone. The least said the better.

Glada: I've got an idea you're wrong . . .

Pral (*as the rest turn on the girl*): What, have you got bright ideas too?

Glada (*retreating a little, timidly*): No. But it's true we've never tried anything . . . not a single thing.

Pral (*moving towards her with the others*): Quiet! Don't make things more difficult for us. (**Melo** *turns round and moves nimbly to the watepaper basket and seizes it.*) Do you think they . . . ?

Erna (*who has not moved*): The wastepaper basket! (*They all turn round and on seeing* **Melo** *carrying it towards his room, they rush over and bar his way just as he is about to succeed in his plan. There is a brief struggle which they finally win after dragging* **Melo** *back to the centre of the stage.* **Fila** *and* **Denta,** *attracted by the scuffle, come out of their rooms.*)

Pral (*clutching the basket*): What were you up to?

Melo (*straightening his clothes*): Nothing. We just don't see eye to eye.

Nisal: Perhaps you'd like to see us cut off.

Melo: I just want things to happen.

Orel: They do already. Every day. Twice a day.

Nisal: When they bring us the correspondence.

Melo (*sarcastically*): What things? (*The others look embarrassed by the question.*)

Nisal: Well . . .

Melo: Can't you explain what things you mean?

Nisal: I admit it's difficult.

Melo (*to the others*): Can the rest of you explain them? (*No one says a word.*)

Melo (*to the girls*): Perhaps you . . .

Glada: No, you're right. Nothing happens. (*Thoughtfully.*) That's why it's even more strange that we're always so eager for them to come.

Melo: Yes, isn't it?

Glada: And that we never feel completely cheated.

Melo: That's because they play on our hope. We always tell ourselves: tomorrow perhaps, the day after tomorrow . . . (*He looks at them all.*) Isn't that true?

Pral: What if it is? What are you trying to prove?

Melo: You always ask me the same question. Just this: that if we don't provoke them, it will go on like this forever, as it always has done.

106

Pral (*anxiously*): Let's not listen to him.

Melo: Does it bother you?

Pral: You're a troublemaker, a malcontent. If they . . . (*A bell rings shrilly. They all glance towards the door at the back and begin to rush around.*)

Fila: It's them.

Erna: Come on, quickly.

Denta: Let's get out of sight . . . (**Melo** and **Glada** *are left alone, one on either side of the wastepaper basket.*)

Glada: Aren't you going inside, Melo?

Melo: Are you?

Glada: We can't do anything, just the two of us.

Melo: You're right. Especially without planning it.

Glada: Another time.

Melo: Can I rely on you, then, Glada?

Glada: Yes. We'll talk about it later. Now get out of here.

Melo: You too.

Glada: Both of us. (*They go off towards their rooms, but halfway there* **Glada** *stops and turns to look at* **Melo,** *who disappears just as the door at the back opens to reveal two* **Men,** *one of them carrying a sack, the other armed with a stick.*)

Man with the Sack (*to his companion, when* **Glada** *begins to move*): Get her! (*The* **Man** *with the stick rushes over to the rooms to cut the girl off. She desperately runs to the other side.*)

Man with the Stick (*to his companion*): Get round the other side of her. (*The* **Man** *with the sack drops his load and moves forward with the intention of stopping the girl.*)

Glada (*anxiously*): Melo! Melo! (*All the doors close, as* **Melo** *rushes out of his room and comes right into the middle of the stage.*)

Melo: Glada! (*The two* **Men** *stop the chase in surprise, and* **Glada** *seizes the opportunity to slip away.* **Melo** *and the* **Men** *stare at each other without saying a word. The* **Man** *with the stick comes slowly forward in order to cut off his retreat and* **Melo** *moves slowly towards the back. Gradually the two* **Men** *force him into a corner. There is a moment of tension as they all stop moving.*)

Melo: Come on, what are you waiting for?

Glada (*watching from her doorway*): Melo . . .

Melo (*without turning round*): Don't come out. I can deal with both of them.

Man with the Stick: Oh, can you? (*He hits him and* **Melo** *quickly grabs the other end of the weapon; they struggle for a* moment but **Melo** is overcome by the intervention of the **Man** with the sack.)

Melo (as he struggles): Damn you!

Glada (moves towards the **Men** and tackles the one with the sack from behind): Cowards, cowards! (For a moment there is a hand to hand struggle, with the **Man** with the sack and the girl on one side and the **Man** with the stick and **Melo** on the other. **Melo** manages to overcome his attacker and gets him on the floor; he rushes to the aid of the girl, whom the other **Man** is trying to strangle. The **Man** with the sack releases her when he feels himself being attacked.)

Melo (to **Glada**): Quick, get away.

Glada: What about you?

Melo: Don't worry. Get away, quick! (The girl obeys hesitantly, and staggers around the stage. Then the **Man** with the stick, still on the floor, but recovering his senses, seizes **Melo**'s leg and brings him down beside him. The **Man** with the sack jumps on top of **Melo** and, sitting on his stomach, rains blows on him.)

Glada: No! (She comes back but the **Man** with the stick, who has just got to his feet, seizes her. She struggles, tries to get free, succeeds and runs desperately towards her room with the other at her heels. They both vanish into the room and immediately the girl's voice is heard). No, no, no . . . (With an effort, **Melo** throws off the **Man** sitting on top of him but the latter immediately regains his position on top. He has just managed to get his hands round **Melo**'s throat when the **Man** with the stick comes running out of **Glada**'s room, in a panic.)

Man with the Stick: Let's get out of here!

Man with the Sack (panting): Let me finish this one off.

Man with the Stick (frantically): But I've killed her!

Man with the Sack (sitting up): Killed her? Inside her room?

Man with the Stick: Yes.

Man with the Sack: You fool!

Man with the Stick: Let's get going! (The **Man** with the sack rapidly empties the letters into the wastepaper basket.) Quickly, quickly!

Man with the Sack: Right. (They both run towards the door at the back.)

Man with the Stick (stopping): The stick! (He hurries back to pick it up beside **Melo**'s body but the latter is just beginning to get up. The **Man** hits him on the head and runs back to the door, through which he vanishes behind his companion. **Melo** remains motionless, unconscious, as the bell is quickly rung twice.

Immediately the doors are opened and everyone rushes out of the rooms and races towards the wastepaper basket.)

All: The letters! The letters! (*Greedily, they delve into the basket with both hands, picking up all the papers they can. Finally they tip the basket up and everything is strewn over the floor from which they pick up the letters, snatching them from each other's hands. They then go back towards their rooms, clutching their treasure tightly.*)

Pral (*noticing* **Melo**'s *body on the floor and stopping*): Melo! (*The others stop too and look towards him.*)

Fila (*coming up to him*): Have they killed him? (*They all look at one another, and after a momentary hesitation, they all rush off to their rooms where they deposit the letters they have picked up and then come out again to see* **Melo**.)

Nisal (*kneeling beside him and putting his ear to* **Melo's** *chest to listen to his heart, while the others form a circle around him*): I think he's breathing.

Pral (*feeling* **Melo**'s *pulse*): Yes, he's alive.

Denta: He can't be! They've always killed them . . .

Pral: Not this time . . . (*He gently slaps* **Melo's** *cheeks.*) Melo, Melo . . .

Nisal (*bending over him again*): His heartbeat is getting stronger. (**Melo** *stirs.*)

Erna: He's coming to.

Pral: Melo. (*He and* **Nisal** *help* **Melo** *to sit up while they support him.*) Melo, what happened?

Melo (*looking around him*): Glada?

Pral (*also looking around*): Glada! (*On failing to see her he shouts louder towards her room.*) Glada!

Fila: She must be going through her letters.

Denta: Glada! (*Getting to her feet and going over to the girl's room.*)

Pral (*to* **Melo** *again*): You were lucky. What happened?

Melo (*coming to his senses*): They caught us and we had to defend ourselves.

Orel: It's queer they didn't finish you off. They never leave anyone alive.

Melo: I don't know why they left me. Glada and I . . . Where is Glada?

Pral: Now, now . . .

Denta (*coming out of the room with an expression of horror on her face*): Oh, Pral! Orel!

Pral (*leaving the injured man and getting to his feet*): What's the matter?

Denta (*pointing to the room*): There . . . Glada . . .

Pral: What?

Denta: She's dead.

All: Dead?

Pral (*coming up to the girl and shaking her arm*): Are you sure?

Denta: Yes. No. I don't know. I saw her on the floor . . .

Nisal: It's not possible. They wouldn't have dared, inside the room. (*While they all stare at one another in astonishment,* **Melo** *struggles to his feet like a drunken man and lurches towards the room. The others follow him. On reaching the doorway,* **Melo** *hesitates but finally takes a step into the room.*)

Pral (*stopping him*): Do you think . . .?

Melo: Yes.

Nisal: It may be dangerous.

Melo: I know. (**Pral** *lets him pass and* **Melo** *disappears inside. The rest crowd round the door.*)

Melo's Voice: Glada.

Orel (*optimistically*): Perhaps she's just unconscious.

Melo's Voice: She's not moving or breathing. Glada!

Denta: Is she dead then?

Melo's Voice: There are still fingermarks round her throat. They've strangled her . . .

Pral (*indignantly*): The murderers! (*They all stand aside to let* **Melo** *through as he comes out with the girl in his arms. Gently, he lays her on the floor. They all bend over her.*)

Nisal (*softly*): They've killed her.

Erna: They've never dared to do it inside before.

Pral: They've broken the law!

Nisal (*who has gone over to the door at the back, shouting outside*): Murderers, butchers! (*He shakes his fist.*)

Melo (*straightening up, now completely recovered, and looking at the others*): Right, now what?

Pral: This is all so unexpected.

Melo: They went into her room to kill her. They knew they weren't allowed to.

Orel: Perhaps they were, but we didn't know it.

Melo: No, there's a law. You've always said there was a law.

Pral: That's true. Melo's right. There is a law which we've always obeyed. All those who have broken it have paid with their lives. And we've never said anything, we've never protested. It was the law . . . for us and for them.

Melo: But now they've broken it, it doesn't hold any more. The contract, if it was a contract, has been broken . . .

Fila: We can't be sure. Perhaps they attacked her out here and as she was dying . . .

Melo (*vehemently*): No! You're just saying that because you're afraid to face the truth. They have deliberately committed a criminal act — and they've got away.

Nisal: Got away? Do you mean they won't come back?

Melo: I don't know. Perhaps not. Perhaps they are getting scared.

Denta: And we shan't get any letters . . .

Melo (*contemptuously*): Letters! Can't you think of anything else but . . . (*He breaks off, looking towards the wastepaper basket. He points at it.*) Didn't they bring any?

Pral: Yes. As usual.

Melo: Well, where are they?

Orel: In our rooms. We left them to help you.

Melo (*in surprise*): What? You left the letters? For me?

Pral: Yes, Melo.

Melo: But weren't they more important to you than anything else? Weren't you dying to read them?

Erna: Yes, and we are still impatient to . . .

Melo: That's not true! Friends, just think carefully and answer this: Hadn't you forgotten all about them?

Pral: Well . . . maybe.

Orel: Only for a moment.

Melo (*who bursts out laughing*): Only for a moment. But just tell me, how many times has that ever happened to you before?

Orel (*uncertain*): I don't know. Never.

Melo (*triumphantly*): Never! And it hasn't ever happened to the rest of you either! The point is, you suddenly realized that there were more important things . . .

Pral: The law . . .

Melo: Yes, the law. The same law that cannot be restored until the offenders have been punished.

Nisal: But how, Melo? No provision was made for . . .

Melo: No provisions have been made for anything, Nisal. No punishments, no rewards . . .

Nisal: I don't see how we can inflict punishment in this case.

Melo: But we can. By putting right the defects or omissions in that law.

Pral: By making another one?

Melo: Not necessarily. By making those who thought of it complete it. Then we will decide whether the law is just.

Orel (*dubiously*): But we would have to argue, protest.

Melo: That's just what we'll do.

Nisal: How?

Melo: We'll talk to them when they come back, if they do come back. (*The others exchange glances, slightly alarmed.*) Are you afraid?

Pral: Yes. But although we're afraid . . .

Melo (*anxiously*): What?

Pral: I can't decide for the rest, but I'm with you.

Denta: Me too. (*The others say nothing.*)

Melo: And you, Nisal?

Nisal: I don't know . . . of course, if the majority wants to . . . I . . . well . . .

Melo: Yes or no?

Nisal: Well . . . yes.

Melo: That makes four of us.

Fila: And me, five.

Erna: Six.

Melo (*to* **Orel**): What about you?

Orel: If you all agree . . . I can't stay on my own.

Melo: That's more like it. All together! We should always have been together.

Pral: We always have.

Melo: No. And perhaps we aren't even now.

Nisal: What do you mean?

Melo: There's a barrier between them and us now. So we have to do something to make this clear to them.

Pral: Yes, ask for justice.

Melo: More than that. Because they won't discuss things with us if we don't teach them to respect us. And the only way we can achieve that is by an act of protest.

Orel: What do you suggest?

Pral: What act?

Melo: The letters.

All (*not understanding him*): The letters?

Melo: Yes, we'll put them back in the basket.

Denta: Oh no, not that!

Erna: We can't give up the letters.

Melo: You mean we can't give up anything else, because that's all we've got. You can only give up what you have or what you are pretty sure of getting . . .

Pral: But the letters . . .

Melo: When they see the letters they will realize that the matter is serious and not a silly game.

112

Nisal: But what about the present, while we're waiting? What will we do without the letters?

Melo: The same as we're doing now. Or something better: learn to do without them. Win a victory at the same time over ourselves . . .

Denta: We won't be able to.

Melo (*firmly*): We shall, we shall! For years the letters haven't told us anything of importance or contained a single personal, useful message . . .

Erna: What if they did today?

Melo: That would impress them even more. (*Nodding towards the door at the back.*) And that's what we have to do, impress them. (**Nisal** *nods his head and goes towards his room.*)

Denta: What if we don't achieve anything with all this?

Melo (*pointing to* **Glada**'s *body*): We've already achieved something: a martyr. (**Denta** *looks at him and then goes off towards her room.*)

Orel: We weren't looking for one. After all, it was an accident.

Melo: Not for her. She died because she tried to fight on my side. She had just discovered the meaning of solidarity . . . (**Orel** *goes to his room.*)

Fila: What do you mean? Love, maybe?

Melo: Right, Fila, love. (**Fila** *goes to her room.*)

Erna: It was a pretty fruitless sort of love, since she's dead.

Melo: Because she's dead, it's the most fruitful of all: she has made it possible for us to respect one another. (**Erna,** *convinced, goes towards her room.*)

Pral: But love . . . I would have said that you were preaching hatred . . .

Melo: No, Pral; love.

Pral (*jerking his head in the direction of the door at the back*): What about them?

Melo: They are an obstacle. They have always been a sort of barrier keeping us apart. Something you don't hate when you've just discovered love, but which you fight with all your strength. (*All the others begin to bring their letters out and put them in the wastepaper basket.*)

Pral: Do you forgive them for killing Glada?

Melo: More than that. I'm grateful to them.

Pral: But you loved her, too . . .

Melo: That's just it. If I hadn't it wouldn't have mattered, she would have been no one. But because we love her, we have a duty to her dead body. She makes real what you all thought was an abstract idea. You can see the others have all understood this. (*He points to the others who are still piling up the letters in the basket. Silently* **Pral** *nods and as he too walks towards his room the curtain falls.*)

ACT 2

The same scene as before. A few hours have passed and **Glada**'*s body has been removed.* **Fila, Erna** *and* **Orel** *are standing in a group, back right; another group consisting of* **Pral, Nisal** *and* **Melo,** *is talking, front left.* **Denta** *is slowly walking across the stage on her own, away from both groups.*

Nisal: Allowing for the expected delay, they can't be much longer.
Melo: Don't get impatient; we must keep calm.
Pral: Providing they do come!
Melo: I'm sure they will.
Pral: What makes you so sure?
Melo: Something very simple: the fact that basically they despise us.
Nisal: Do you mean they think we'll put up with anything?
Melo: Yes. They know we've never made any fuss.
Fila (*talking to the other group*): Are you sure it will turn out all right?
Orel: I'm not sure of anything. But Melo's right; we must give it a try.
Erna: I only hope he does the talking because for my part . . .
Orel: You're not going to back out now, are you?
Erna: Of course not.
Melo (*to his group*): We must present a united front. We must make it clear to them that we will defend any of us who is attacked.
Pral: They won't dare attack anyone.
Melo: That's what I believe too. Basically, they are cowards. Above all, we must cut off their retreat.
Pral: I'll see to that.
Orel (*to the other group*): What he asks of us isn't much: just to be here, to make sure no one is attacked.
Erna: Melo has always been waiting for a moment like this.
Fila: He's the only one who's ever had doubts about the legitimacy of the situation.

114

Orel (*as* **Denta** *stops beside the paper basket*): Him and Glada.

Fila: And they very nearly both paid for it with their lives! (**Denta** *stretches out her hand towards the basket, but immediately withdraws it.*)

Melo (*shouting*): Denta! What are you doing?

Denta (*as they all look at her*): Me?

Melo: Yes, you.

Denta: Nothing.

Melo (*accusingly*): You were going to take a letter . . .

Denta: No . . .

Melo: I saw you reaching out your hand.

Pral: It's true; so did I.

Melo: Do you want to let us down, now?

Denta: No, Melo.

Melo: Don't you remember we have promised not to touch any of the letters again?

Denta: I didn't want to touch one. I was just making the movement . . .

Pral: But why?

Denta: I don't know. I said to myself that perhaps I wouldn't ever be able to do it again.

Erna: What do you mean, Denta?

Denta: Perhaps they'll take the paper basket away from us.

Melo: They can't take it away if we don't want them to.

Denta: They'll do what they like.

Melo: They will do what is decided after we've all had a discussion.

Denta: Perhaps not. They may make promises, if we frighten them. But how do we know they'll keep their promises?

Fila: She's right. How can we be sure they'll keep them?

Melo: They won't be in a position to do anything else. We will show them that they can't trick us twice.

Denta: What if they go away and never come back again when they see we're questioning their power?

Melo: They won't.

Pral: We don't know that, Melo. Denta may have guessed . . .

Melo: Denta can't guess anything. It's not a question of guessing. Can't you see that, in one way or another, they need us? What would they do without us?

Nisal: I've never had that impression. That they needed us, I mean.

Melo: Because you haven't thought about it. Why do you think they bring the letters?

Nisal: I don't know. Because it has been arranged.

Melo: Well, they have arranged it themselves. And why?

115

Nisal: I don't know. (*Angrily.*) Don't ask so many questions!

Melo: I wouldn't have to if you gave me satisfactory answers.

Nisal (*piqued*): I suppose you can give them, then?

Melo: Perhaps I can. Some. To start with, none of us has ever made any agreement with them. They're the ones who decided on a line of action and have subjected us to it.

Nisal: Perhaps because it was the best thing to do.

Melo: Best for who?

Nisal: For them and for us.

Melo: For them perhaps. But we can hardly be sure if it's best for us until we've been given a chance to choose.

Orel: But we know nothing! How could we choose, in those conditions?

Melo: We know all we need to for now; that the law is unjust as long as they can break it and get away with it.

Pral: They can't get away with it. That's why we're here.

Melo: For that and for something else. Have you forgotten already what we agreed to do? Or do I have to stand up to them on my own?

Pral: No, we gave our word and we won't let you down. (*The bell rings and they all stop talking, looking at the door at the back.*)

Denta: They're here! (*She rushes off towards her room and* **Fila** *and* **Erna** *follow her example.*)

Melo: Wait a minute. (*They stop.*) We have to know if you are ready to back us up . . .

Pral: You said you would.

The Three Girls (*unenthusiastically*): Yes, yes.

Melo: Well, with so many objections, I was beginning to wonder.

Nisal: We'll do it, Melo.

Melo: All right, then. You remember what you must do . . .

Pral: Yes. Come on, let's go to our rooms. (*Each one moves towards his respective room. A moment later, the door at the back is opened and the* **Man** *with the sack and the* **Man** *with the stick come in. They look around and leave the door ajar.*)

Man with the Sack: Everything looks quiet — as usual.

Man with the Stick: Of course. I don't know what you were afraid of.

Man with the Sack: You weren't too happy yourself!

Man with the Stick (*as his companion comes over to the wastepaper basket*): Perhaps not, at first . . . But after all . . .

Man with the Sack (*stopping abruptly as if hit by something*): Look!

Man with the Stick: What is it?

Man with the Sack: The wastepaper basket! All the letters are still in it!

Man with the Stick: They can't be. (*They both approach the basket, and stand beside it.*) You're right.

Man with the Sack (*anxiously*): This isn't natural.

Man with the Stick: They must've been afraid of coming out.

Man with the Sack (*not completely convinced*): Perhaps. But what do we do now?

Man with the Stick: The same as usual. Tip them in.

Man with the Sack: With the others there?

Man with the Stick (*as the seven characters come out of their rooms and fan out towards the door at the back, forming a semicircle around the two men*): Why not?

Man with the Sack: We've never done that before.

Man with the Stick: So what? Many things haven't been done before but that isn't a reason for not doing them some time.

Man with the Sack: You have to say that to justify what you did in the first place.

Man with the Stick: I don't have to justify anything. It's just that the consequences could show me to be wrong and you can see . . . (*He stops talking as he sees the others surrounding them.*) What's this?

Man with the Sack (*about to empty the sack*): What do you mean?

Man with the Stick (*in a whisper*): Look around you. (*The* **Man** *with the stick takes two or three steps towards the door, raising his weapon threateningly over his head. The others do not move.*) Clear the way! (*No one moves.*) Let me past, I said!

Melo (*calmly*): Put your stick down.

Man with the Stick (*as if unable to believe his ears*): What?

Melo: Put your stick down.

Man with the Stick: I'll bring it down on your back! (*He goes towards* **Melo** *to strike him but* **Nisal** *and* **Orel** *move towards their companion with the unmistakable intention of protecting him.*)

Melo (*still calm*): Put your stick down.

Man with the Stick (*halting, prudently*): What are you trying to do?

Melo: Get this business sorted out.

Man with the Stick: What business?

Melo: You killed someone. Inside her room. You have broken the law.

Man with the Sack (*intervening for the first time*): And you haven't collected the correspondence. You've broken it too!

Melo: That isn't true. The law was no longer valid because your act had cancelled it.

Man with the Stick: We've always been allowed to defend ourselves.

Melo: No one was attacking you. No one has ever attacked you.

Man with the Stick: It is an offence to our dignity for you to be out of your rooms while we do our job.

Melo: Glada was inside her room.

Man with the Stick: Not all the time she wasn't.

Melo: You have violated our right to sanctuary inside the rooms.

Man with the Stick: We don't have to give you explanations.

Melo: Then you are abolishing the law yourselves.

Man with the Sack: It's our law, after all.

Melo: That's exactly why we've had enough of it. From now on you'll have to deal with us . . .

Man with the Stick (*to his companion, slightly mocking*): Did you hear him?

Man with the Sack: I heard him but I can't believe it.

Melo: Well, we've only just started. You won't leave here until you give us guarantees of good will. And before you do, we'll decide on what the new law will be or how to modify the old one.

Man with the Sack (*incredulously*): We'll discuss it?

Man with the Stick: With blows we will.

Melo (*coolly defiant*): Just try it.

Man with the Sack (*to the others*): We assume he is speaking for himself . . .

Pral: No, he's speaking for all of us.

Man with the Sack: You realize we can leave you with no letters?

Pral: We don't care.

Man with the Sack: Don't you? (*He begins to pick up the ones in the basket and puts them in the sack with the other.*)

Denta: No!

Man with the Stick (*with a nasty laugh*): I thought so!

Man with the Sack (*leaving the letters*): Don't you agree with your friends?

Denta (*uncertain*): I . . .

Pral: Denta!

Man with the Stick: All those who disown these wretches will have their ration increased. (**Denta** and **Erna** *take a step forward, then stop.*)

Man with the Sack: Come on, be brave!

Nisal: Denta! Erna! Remember your promise.

Melo: There will be letters for everyone if we still want them, after we've decided on the future of the law.

Man with the Stick: You won't get anything.

Melo: Maybe not. But then neither will you, in that case.

Man with the Sack: Let's get things straight. Who is with us, for order, for the preservation of the old values and of all that is worthy of preserving? (*No one moves.*) Denta? Erna?

Pral (*to the two girls*): Keep still.

Man with the Stick: Keep quiet. We will not permit coercion.

Melo: And what are you doing if it isn't coercing us with your empty promises?

Man with the Stick (*threateningly*): Be quiet or I'll hit you.

Melo: Threats only weaken your position.

Man with the Sack (*to his companion*): Leave them alone. No threats or pleas . . .

Melo: Only a frank discussion can clarify things.

Man with the Stick: Why am I listening to all this? (*At a signal from* **Melo,** *the men advance but the girls seem more hesitant; they all form a closer circle around the two men.*)

Man with the Sack: What are you going to do?

Man with the Stick: Get back!

Melo: It seems you only understand one language . . . (*After a brief struggle,* **Nisal** *and he grab the* **Man** *with the sack;* **Pral** *and* **Orel** *do likewise to the* **Man** *with the stick. They finally overpower them.*)

Man with the Stick: You'll pay for this!

Pral (*seizing the stick*): Shut up!

Man with the Stick: No. (**Pral** *hits him and the* **Man** *lets go and falls to the floor.*)

Melo (*sharply, to the* **Man** *with the sack*): You see . . . Perhaps that will teach you to be more reasonable.

Man with the Sack: But exactly what do you propose to do?

Melo: We already told you: discuss things.

Man with the Sack: There's nothing to discuss.

Melo: Is that your final word?

Man with the Sack: It is. (**Melo** *gestures to* **Pral** *and* **Orel** *who take hold of the* **Man** *with the stick and carry him off to* **Glada**'*s room.*) What are you going to do?

Melo: You'll soon see, or to be more correct, you'll feel it . . .

Man with the Sack: You're murderers!

Melo: You started the killings.

Man with the Sack: You're making things awkward for yourselves. You'll be sorry.

Melo: Neither of you two will get away. (*A loud scream is heard from* **Glada**'s *room. The three girls cover their ears with their hands.*)

Man with the Sack (*anxiously*): What are they doing to him? (*The* **Man** *with the stick screams again.*)

Denta: It's horrible!

Melo (*turning to her*): They killed Glada, remember.

Denta: It's still horrible. (*More screams which terminate in a moan of agony.*)

Melo: That's that.

Erna: Oh! (*She runs off to hide in her room.* **Pral** *and* **Orel** *come out of* **Glada**'s *room.*)

Denta: This is horrible!

Melo (*to the* **Man** *with the sack*): Have you changed your mind?

Man with the Sack: Well . . .

Pral: Shall we take him away?

Melo: In a minute.

Man with the Sack (*making up his mind*): That won't be necessary. We can talk.

Melo: That's more like it. Sit down.

Man with the Sack (*looking around*): Where?

Nisal (*laughing*): In the paper basket, of course.

Man with the Sack: You're joking.

Pral (*seriously*): He said in the paper basket.

Man with the Sack (*seeing their threatening look*): All right . . . All right . . . (*He sits in the wastepaper basket and half disappears from sight.*)

Nisal: Is it comfortable in there?

Man with the Sack: Let's get to the point.

Melo (*sitting down on the sack of letters*): Yes, let's get to the point. My friends and I think that it wouldn't be a bad idea to revise the law.

Man with the Sack: That's difficult.

Melo: Why?

Man with the Sack: It is too simple a law to allow modifications.

Pral: Too simple?

Melo: Then it can be changed. We are ready to begin all over again.

Man with the Sack: That's impossible. You don't realize what you're saying. There is a tradition . . .

Melo: We'll make another one.

Man with the Sack: You can't make traditions as easily as that.

Pral: Someone has to start them.

Man with the Sack: But you never start out with the intention of making them. It's something, a way of doing things, of behaving, which gradually becomes a custom. You can't just improvise.

Melo: If we have to, we can for once.

Man with the Sack: You won't have my consent.

Nisal: You aren't giving us a chance.

Man with the Sack: No. Why should I? Hundreds of generations have gradually devolved a type of organization, which is reflected in what we call the law. They have perfected it. They are still perfecting it. And you, without any experience, want to throw it all away . . .

Melo: Without any experience?

Man with the Sack: Yes, that's what I said: without any experience.

Melo: We've got just as much as you have. Those generations you talk about are common to us as well.

Man with the Sack: But time has separated them from you. Now they are the most experienced, the most familiar with that age-old spirit . . .

Orel: You say that because chance has put you among the legislators.

Fila: And besides, how can we be sure that you have put the right interpretation on that tradition which you are defending?

Melo: That's it, Fila. I'm proud of you!

Man with the Sack (*petulantly*): If you're going to take that attitude, there is nothing further to say. (*He attempts to get up.*)

Pral: Sit down! (*The **Man** with the sack quickly seizes the wastepaper basket and uses it as a weapon to attack his enemies who, momentarily disconcerted, retreat; the **Man** takes advantage of this and rushes towards the door at the back, but **Fila** reacts more quickly than the others and grabs at him. He pushes her back and throws the paper basket at the others who are now coming to get him. He takes advantage of the resulting confusion and opens the door but they all come after him and **Nisal** manages to close it, catching the **Man**'s arm between frame and the door.*)

Nisal (*laughing*): I've got him!

Melo (*who has not left the sack, gets up and goes over to him*): You don't seem to have been very successful, do you?

Pral (*pulling his arm and knocking him to the ground*): What were you trying to do, eh?

Man with the Sack: Don't touch me! Don't touch me, I tell you!

Pral: You hear that? Because he says so. Our lord and master!

Melo: Hold him. (**Pral** and **Nisal** obey, although the **Man** resists.)

Nisal: What do you want us to do with him now?

Melo: He has decided his own fate. Let him join his friend.

Man with the Sack: No, not that!

Pral (dragging him): Come over here . . .

Man with the Sack (struggling, to **Melo**): Tell them to stop. We can still talk things over . . .

Melo: No, it's too late for that.

Man with the Sack: Yes we can. It's never too late. Before you do something you'll regret . . .

Melo: I couldn't trust you any more. You have shown us that you are completely untrustworthy.

Man with the Sack: But it'll be different this time. I swear it will. We'll change the law as you suggest.

Melo: You only say that because you're scared.

Orel: But it wouldn't hurt to listen to what he has to say, Melo.

Melo: It's useless, because he has nothing to say. And besides, once he got away from us, he would take it all back.

Nisal: Maybe not.

Melo: Yes, he belongs to the race of traitors. I'm surprised I hadn't realized that till now.

Pral: What do you mean?

Melo: That there are some people who are basically traitors to all that is best, most noble and perfect in the human character . . . They are those who have tasted power.

Man with the Sack: It's not true. It's not true. And we don't have power either.

Melo: What do you have then?

Man with the Sack: Hardly a delegation of that power even. A middleman's job.

Melo: Worse still, since although you possess nothing of your own you betray everything in the name of something which is foreign to you.

Man with the Sack: You don't understand.

Melo: I understand much more than you think. I understand so well that I realize that you do not even have any authority to discuss things. You cannot make any decisions on your own.

Man with the Sack: I certainly can. Power has been unconditionally delegated to me.

Melo: Then you are responsible for law and order . . . and for the

122

infringements of that law which you have been a party to. (*To the others.*) You see what I mean?

Pral: Yes. He serves something he does not know and he justifies his actions with a convenient principle.

Nisal: And he denies responsibility for them.

Melo: You decide yourselves. What can be done with someone like that?

Pral: He is only fit to die.

Denta: But a life . . .

Melo: One single life against all of ours.

Man with the Sack (*anxiously*): Don't be hasty. I can explain to you . . .

Melo: Don't strain yourself. You can't explain anything. The law has been nothing but your personal wishes.

Man with the Sack (*anxiously*): But just suppose you're right. If you are trying to rearrange things in a more just way, you can't allow yourselves to fight my personal wishes with your own.

Melo: We are prompted by a more primitive instinct, that of self-defence: Don't you see that if we set you free we shall continue to be slaves?

Man with the Sack: You always will be. We all are. If not the slaves of someone else, then of ourselves.

Melo: We shall be able to find out if that is true. But right now, you are in our way. (*To the others.*) Take him away. (**Pral** and **Nisal** *seize him and drag him towards* **Glada***'s room.*)

Man with the Sack: Why do you listen to him? Can't you see that you are only changing one master for another?

Pral (*hitting him*): You were told to shut up, weren't you? We don't like prophets. (*They force him into* **Glada***'s room. The others, led by* **Melo**, *go over and, without entering, watch the action inside the room. Suddenly the* **Man** *with the sack, who has managed to free himself, breaks through the group.*)

Nisal's Voice: The swine!

Pral's Voice: Stop him! (*They have all surrounded him and they overpower him. While he struggles they drag him off again to the room, into which they all disappear. From inside come sounds of a scuffle.*)

Man with the Sack's Voice (*hoarsely*): No, no . . . no . . . I . . .

Melo's Voice: Get it over with. (*The struggle stops and a moment later, they all come back on stage with their heads slightly bowed.* **Denta** *covers her face with her hands.* **Erna** *comes out of her room and stands staring at them without realizing what is going on.* **Melo** *leads the others forward to the sack of letters*

123

and stops beside it. The rest spread out around him.)

Pral: That's that.

Melo: Yes; that's that.

Orel: There won't be any more letters . . .

Nisal: There won't be anything else . . .

Orel: We'll be left on our own.

Melo: Are you complaining? Do you regret what you've done?

Nisal: Not exactly, Melo. But now . . .

Melo: Now what?

Orel: What I'm trying to say is that we now have nothing but our own resources.

Melo: That's fine. Now no one can make us the victims of his own personal interests.

Orel: But drifting along at the mercy of chance, in no particular direction, isn't very pleasant either.

Melo: We will find our own direction.

Orel: How?

Melo (*nodding towards the room in which they have murdered the other two*): By taking their places.

Pral: Do you think we can?

Melo: Yes.

Nisal: But who will take their places?

Melo: We will. Not all of us, of course . . .

Nisal: Well, I don't know . . .

Melo: Yes. The situation hasn't caught me unawares. I've thought it out very carefully.

Orel: What do you suggest?

Melo: Simply this: we must nominate two of us to take the place of those two.

Pral: But are we ready to take on such a responsibility?

Melo: Time will tell. But it's the only way.

Orel: And who will the two be?

Melo: We'll decide amongst ourselves. Those we can trust most.

Nisal: Shall we vote on it?

Melo: That would be the best idea.

Nisal (*to the others*): What do you say about it?

Pral: We can try it.

Orel: Rather that than nothing.

Melo (*to the girls*): What do you say about it?

Denta: Obviously someone must take charge of the letters . . .

Melo: So you all agree? We will elect two people who will then carry out the duties of Man with the sack and Man with the stick. They will study the conditions under which we live and as soon as possible they will proceed to set up a more just law, valid for everyone . . .

Pral: Yes, I like the idea.

Melo: Who are our candidates then?

Pral: In my opinion you're the most suitable person. You were able to unite us, you gave the signal for throwing off our chains.

Nisal: Yes, Melo must be one of the two, but who can be the other one?

Fila: I think Pral.

Orel: All right. But we must think seriously about it. Melo may have a perfect right to it but this isn't true of the rest.

Pral: Do you want to be nominated, then?

Orel: I didn't say that. The majority will decide. But a hasty decision . . .

Nisal: Yes, we had better discuss it calmly.

Pral: So you oppose Fila's candidate?

Nisal: We don't oppose anything. But we have a right to express our opinion.

Pral: Express it, then. The sooner we finish, the better.

Nisal: Speaking objectively . . . er, I would just like to remind you that I have always been on Melo's side. I wasn't one of those who were won over at the last minute.

Pral: I think that I was the first to help him . . .

Orel: I don't know what you're talking about. I'm sorry to have to point this out but he has always been able to count on me, for moral support at least.

Denta (*bursting out laughing*): The three of them all want to be nominated! (*To her female companions.*) And wouldn't you like to be nominated too?

Erna: It might be nice.

Pral: It isn't a question of being nice, but of carrying out a duty.

Denta: A duty which is beginning to look attractive . . .

Pral: Quite the opposite, it's full of responsibilities. That's why you need someone with a clear head and an idea of how things must be done.

Nisal: I don't want to appear conceited, but my whole behavior until now . . .

Denta: Why don't we do it another way?

The Three Men: How?

Denta: We elected Melo unanimously, didn't we?

Pral: That's correct.

Denta: All right then. Why doesn't he choose his companion himself?

125

Melo (*evading this responsibility*): I would regard it as abusing the authority which you have all just given me.

Denta: But if we leave it to them, they'll never finish . . .

Melo: You three vote then.

Denta: Yes, of course. (*To the men.*) Do you agree?

Pral (*glancing at the other two men*): It's all right with me . . . (*The others nod their heads and shrug their shoulders.*)

Denta: Good. I vote for Nisal.

Fila: Pral.

Simultaneously.

Erna: Orel.

Denta (*laughing*): That leaves us where we started.

Melo: There's another way. And a more amusing one.

Denta: What's that?

Melo: You and your two friends decide amongst yourselves on a number, then I'll start to count amongst the three of them and when I reach the number you've decided on, you sing out; that's it!

Fila: Oh, yes, what a good idea!

Nisal (*sceptically*): If that's the only way to solve the problem . . .

Melo: Do you promise to abide by the decision?

Pral (*whilst the girls whisper to one another*): I do.

Orel and **Nisal:** Me too.

Denta (*to* **Melo**): You can begin.

Melo (*beginning with* **Orel,** *then* **Nisal** *and then* **Pral**): One, two, three, four, five, six, seven, eight, nine, ten, eleven, twelve, thirteen, fourteen, fifteen . . .

The Girls: That's it.

Melo: Pral wins.

Denta: Hurray for Melo. Hurray for Pral.

All (*the two unsuccessful men rather unenthusiastically*): Hurray!

Melo: Thank you for your kindness and for your trust. I'm sure we won't let you down. And now, Pral, to work.

Pral (*slightly bewildered*): Where do we start?

Melo: By taking our places on the other side of the door. (*He leads him over to the door at the back, opens the door whilst the others watch expectantly, and then turns round*). A new era is beginning today, don't forget that . . . (*He looks at the wastepaper basket.*) Oh, the sack.

Pral: I'll empty it. (*He goes forward, picks it up and empties it,*

126

scattering the letters around him. All the rest rush forward to pick them up with loud shouts of joy, as the curtain falls.)

ACT 3

The scene is the same as for the previous acts. A few hours have passed, the letters have been picked up and the inmates are awaiting the next delivery. All five of them are onstage when the curtain rises. **Fila** *and* **Denta** *are lounging in the doorway of their rooms;* **Orel** *and* **Nisal** *are walking up and down at the front of the stage;* **Erna** *is standing beside the empty wastepaper basket.*

Orel: They're very late. This never happened with the others.

Nisal: Let's be fair. These are abnormal circumstances and we helped to make them so; it's natural we should be inconvenienced, for the time being. Besides, Melo and Pral are new to the job. We can't expect . . .

Orel: Why not? The organization hasn't broken down; we have simply replaced two people.

Nisal: But we are expecting a radical change to come out of it and that will be a question of time. I should imagine that working out the new law isn't all that easy. I don't envy them.

Orel: Neither do I, in fact. But still there are some basic needs which must be satisfied even in a changeover period . . .

Denta (*to* **Fila**): I don't know if I shall be able to stand this much longer.

Fila (*as* **Erna** *goes over to the door*): We're all suffering but I'm sure they haven't forgotten us.

Denta: All the same, they are not showing the concern for us which we have a right to expect . . .

Fila: You must realize that . . . (*She breaks off and points to* **Erna** *who has stopped by the door and is putting her ear to it.*) Look at her!

Denta: What's she doing?

Fila: Listening.

Denta: But that's not allowed! Nisal! Orel! (*The two men turn round and she points to the girl who is now trying to peep through the keyhole. Both of the men run over to her.*)

Nisal: Hey, you mustn't do that! (*The girl pays no attention to him but goes on looking or trying to look.*)

Orel (*gripping her arm and forcing her to stand up*): What are you doing, you little fool?

Erna: Me? I don't know . . . They're so late . . .

Orel: But we mustn't look or listen.

Nisal: The law doesn't allow it.

Erna: Law? What law? Didn't we replace those men in order to change it?

Nisal: Yes, but nothing has been decided yet. And until it is . . . (*He stops speaking, suddenly confused*). Well, I hadn't thought about that . . . (*To the others.*) What *is* the position in the meantime?

Orel: I took it for granted that, for the moment, for the sake of order, the law was still in force . . .

Nisal: So did I. But now that she questions it . . .

Denta (*coming forward, followed by* **Fila**): We should have mentioned it before Melo and Pral went away. It's annoying not knowing what to do.

Fila: Perhaps we don't know what to do because we don't want to.

Orel (*as they all stare at her*): What do you mean by that?

Fila: I mean that Melo and Pral are like us. They could only make the same decision as we would make.

Orel: So what?

Fila: So that makes things easier. From now on we can do as we like. We are the law.

Nisal (*scratching his head*): I don't think it's as simple as that. We can't see everything from here. There are higher interests which we do not know but which exist and to which something must be sacrificed.

Fila: What?

Nisal: Don't ask me. But that's why we must discuss it with Melo and Pral when they come, because now they are in a position to judge.

Orel: You mean we should put ourselves unconditionally in their hands? If so, the change was a waste of time.

Nisal: No it wasn't. They will explain everything to us so that we too can appreciate these higher interests. And then we can all decide on the future, bearing them in mind.

Fila: They'll explain it all to us! How do we know? They'll explain whatever they choose and no more.

Denta: But we can't start to mistrust them.

Fila: All right, but suppose they do explain how things really are. Will we be able to understand what they're talking about when we are still where we were before?

Nisal: Obviously it may be more complicated than we thought.

But we can trust their judgment even when we can't understand what they are saying.

Erna: And in the meantime we can trust our own judgment. So I feel perfectly entitled to look and listen through the keyhole.

Denta: There's only one objection to that: it's futile. And, in fact, there's no point in sticking our necks out by making a personal decision if we don't gain anything by it.

Erna: We don't know yet whether there is anything to gain or not.

Nisal: We don't, perhaps, but you do. Did you see anything; did you hear anything?

Erna: No, not yet.

Nisal: Then it would be wiser not to carry on.

Erna: If that's your attitude, it would have been wiser to leave things as they were.

Orel: No, that's not true. We only replaced those people because we hoped it would benefit us in some way.

Erna: And because of this hope we have put ourselves in the hands of strangers.

Nisal: No we haven't, stupid! Melo and Pral are not strangers to us.

Erna: Aren't they? Each of us is a stranger to himself. Did you ever imagine you would be brave enough to kill those two?

Nisal: That's not fair. A person may be forced . . . None of us liked killing them . . . We were forced to do it. (*At that moment the bell rings stridently; the conversation stops.*)

Denta: The bell, run! (*They all rush towards their rooms, but* **Nisal,** *who has also begun to run, suddenly stops.*)

Nisal: Just a moment! (*They all stop.*) Don't be silly, where are you going?

Denta: To our rooms.

Nisal: Why?

Erna: We always do, don't we?

Nisal: We did in the past. Don't you remember that we are waiting for Melo and Pral?

Erna: What difference does that make?

Nisal: They are our friends, our companions . . .

Denta: But didn't you say yourself that, for the moment, we should abide by the law!

Nisal: Yes, but maybe we don't have to be so careful about it!

Orel: I think Denta's right. Do it properly or don't do it at all.

Nisal: Besides, we've got to talk to them.

Orel: They'll call us if they want us.

Nisal: I don't agree. If we hide away it's . . . it's as if we weren't being fair to them.

Fila: That's true. We can't treat them as strangers, can we?

Nisal: No. They'll be pleased to find us waiting for them.

Orel: I wish I were as sure of that as you are. (*The door at the back opens and* **Melo** *and* **Pral** *come in, the former as* **Man** *with the stick, the latter as* **Man** *with the sack.*)

Denta: Well, it's too late now. Here they are. (**Melo,** *who has come in behind* **Pral,** *closes the door and stands facing them.* **Pral,** *too, has stopped a yard in front of him. There is a moment's silence, as both groups stare at each other.*)

Melo (*harshly*): What are you doing here?

Nisal: Waiting for you. You seem to have taken a long time . . .

Melo: Don't you know what you should do?

Nisal: What we should do? You mean . . . ?

Melo: Yes, I mean exactly that. You have always waited for the letters in your rooms.

Nisal: Yes, we know, but now things have changed.

Orel: Perhaps not as much as we thought, Nisal.

Melo (*ignoring this*): The law is still in force.

Erna (*to the others*): I told you we should have gone.

Nisal (*apologetically*): In view of the changeover, we thought . . .

Melo (*curtly*): You are not supposed to think.

Nisal: But still . . .

Melo: The law was broken once by your guardians. Now you're breaking it.

Nisal: Do you mean we've done wrong?

Melo: Yes, you have.

Nisal (*to* **Pral,** *who has not said a word yet*): Is that what you think, Pral?

Pral: Of course it is. Replacement is not an excuse for anarchy. (*To all of them.*) Don't you see the awkward position you are putting us in?

Fila: What position?

Pral: Have you forgotten the penalty for anyone who leaves his room?

Denta: Do you mean nothing has changed?

Melo: Everything has changed. If it hadn't, we would be chasing you now in order to punish you. That's what Pral means. It would be our duty and we are not doing it.

Orel: But will you do it next time?

Melo: We shall have no alternative.

Orel: And you call that a change?

Melo: Yes. We are showing a tolerance which has never been shown you before. But as you will realize, this cannot happen

130

again.

Fila: What if it does? The new law must be drawn up with the unanimous consent of all concerned.

Melo: No one is denying that. That has already been done and it has been decided . . .

Nisal: But we haven't decided anything yet! We haven't had a chance.

Pral: You appointed us to take over these matters.

Nisal: No, that isn't quite correct.

Orel: In fact, it's very far from the truth.

Pral: You elected us to take over the positions of responsibility.

Orel: Yes, because somebody had to make sure that everything worked. But it was always understood that we would have a say in the new organization.

Melo: You do, through us.

Denta: What do you mean, through you?

Pral: It's quite obvious. We are merely your spokesmen but we now have full authority.

Nisal: Our spokesmen! Have you ever put over our point of view?

Melo: We know what you want. Don't forget that we were like you . . .

Fila: You wouldn't think so!

Pral: Perhaps it's because, in our present position, we are able to see more clearly what is good for you.

Melo: Now we are part of your world and also of the world which our duties have led us into. You can't deny that that allows us to . . .

Orel: Continue the unfair treatment!

Melo: Orel! We cannot tolerate such language!

Orel: At the moment it's the only sort I can use.

Denta: Careful, Orel, you're sticking your neck out.

Orel: Maybe I am. But not so long ago, someone (*shooting a meaningful glance at* **Melo**) taught me something: that you have to be bold.

Nisal: Careful, Orel!

Melo: You didn't learn the lesson properly then. There's a time to be bold and a time to be quiet.

Orel: And this is the time to be quiet, eh?

Melo: Correct, this is the time to be quiet. Apart from the usual difficulties caused by replacements, you no longer live under the same conditions.

Orel: I'd like to know in what way they've changed.

Melo: I've already told you: you are in control.

Orel: We? You? Aren't you making a slight distinction?

Melo: Only a small one.

Orel: Yes, but it's still a distinction. You and I are no longer on the same side.

Melo: On the contrary, now we *are* on the same side. We weren't before because you didn't see the need, or the possibility if you like, of a change. Now this change has been brought about by our decision.

Fila: But what if this is not a decision by all of us?

Melo: It is. You can't now go back to the conditions you were in before.

Fila: But perhaps we want something more now and you are the obstacle preventing us from achieving it.

Orel: And you may have betrayed yourselves by betraying us.

Pral: Don't you see that we cannot betray ourselves because we represent your ambitions?

Melo: What more can you want? We have obtained power . . .

Orel: Not us, you!

Melo: I've already told you there is no difference between us.

Nisal: That's not true, Melo. As soon as an argument is possible, it shows that somehow or other a difference has arisen. We are in conflict.

Melo: It's the same conflict that is present within every person. The better part has won but the other part hasn't given in yet.

Orel: How can the better part have won if you reject that part?

Fila: We all feel you've identified yourselves with your role. And it was against that role that we rebelled.

Pral: No, we rebelled against the way of carrying it out.

Nisal: There's only one way to carry out one's role; when the way changes it's because the role is no longer the same.

Orel: Well said, Nisal! That chap's dying words were right.

Erna: Whose?

Orel: The Man with the sack. He told us we were only exchanging one lot of masters for another.

Melo (*haughtily*): Are you trying to insult us?

Orel: Take it as you like.

Pral (*to* **Melo**): Don't you think we've stood enough of this?

Melo: Yes.

Orel: You are using the sort of words your predecessors would have used.

Melo (*threateningly*): If you compare us with them, we shall be forced to act like them as well.

Orel: I see, so my actions or our actions determine your line of conduct!

Melo: Largely, yes.

Fila: But only when you want to oppress us, to subject us to rules which we have rejected. (*She goes up to him.*) You're just as bad as they were.

Melo (*slapping her*): Be quiet!

Fila (*turning round*): Did you see that?

Orel: We saw the coward. (*To the others.*) Are we going to let them get away with it?

Nisal: No.

Melo (*seeing that in spite of this no one makes a positive move*): Words! Come on, get back to your rooms! (**Fila** *stands still but the other two girls begin to move away.*)

Orel (*stopping them*): No! Stay here, all of you, we must stick together. (*The girls stop.*) We will not go back to our rooms; we will not obey any more orders.

Melo (*sarcastically*): I suppose you'll give them instead, will you?

Orel: Yes, we'll give them! Aren't you our representatives, don't you embody our demands?

Pral: That's just what we've been trying to make you understand, but you wouldn't listen.

Orel: All right, then. One of the things we want is to abolish the rooms.

Melo: Don't you mean that you personally want to? The others have never expressed any such desire.

Orel: They will now. (*To his companions.*) All those in favor of abolishing the rooms raise their hand.

Melo (*quickly as the hands begin to rise*): No!

Orel: What do you mean?

Melo: It won't do. This sort of voting is illegal.

Orel: I don't see why.

Melo: Because it's a matter of common concern affecting everyone.

Orel: Exactly!

Melo: Yes, but that's precisely why you elected us, so that on your behalf . . .

Orel (*furiously*): No, no, no! That was before, not now. We can see now that we made a mistake.

Pral: You seem to be forgetting, Orel, that we live in an adult world, not a children's one. We can't start a game and then leave it when we get tired of it . . .

Nisal: Why not? We all agree with Orel.

Pral: Even if you did, there are still rules.

Orel: All right, then we'll refuse to recognize them.

Melo: You can't do that.

Orel: You showed us yourself that it can be done.

Melo: That was another game.

Fila: Not for us.

Melo: For all of us.

Orel (*to his companions*): Why don't we shut them up?

Erna: Yes, why don't we shut them up for good? Why don't we go further and replace them?

Denta: Yes, let's replace them!

Orel: You see. We are all against you. Do you still dare to claim that you are our representatives, acting in our interests?

Melo: The long wait has made you forget things. When we've given out the correspondence you will think differently. You will see . . .

Nisal (*interrupting him*): The letters won't change anything. You yourself once advised us not to touch them, and we obeyed, showing we were capable of sacrifices. What makes you think the position is different now?

Melo: The fact that you're not dealing with enemies this time. The sacrifice would be pointless. We've thought of that too.

Orel (*to the others*): Did you hear him? They've thought of it! (*To the two men.*) You mean this situation doesn't take you by surprise, you were expecting it . . .

Melo: Nobody can know your weaknesses better than we do.

Nisal: We've noticed yours too, I might tell you.

Pral: We have no weaknesses. We are faithful servants of the law.

Orel: But which law? The one you fought against?

Melo: The eternal law. There is only one.

Orel: Supposing you're right, it can still be interpreted in more than one way.

Melo: We have been appointed to interpret it to you.

Orel: But you can't if we withdraw our permission to do it.

Melo: It is sufficient to have obtained the permission in the first place.

Nisal: You're wrong. You have to prove yourselves worthy of it every day.

Melo: But we don't have to put up with your changing moods.

Fila: Why do you accuse us of being fickle? You're the ones who have changed your tune, and we still don't understand why.

Orel: We understand perfectly. Power has corrupted them.

All: Yes, yes, power!

Orel: That is why we must now . . .

Melo (*resolutely*): That's enough! (*To* **Pral.**) Empty out the letters and let's go.

Orel (*defiantly*): If we let you go, you mean.

Melo: Didn't you admit that we have power? Well, we'll use it!

Orel: Correction: you did have it, but you don't any more.

Melo: Come on, Pral!

Pral (*hesitantly*): Shall I leave the letters?

Melo: Do as you like. On second thoughts, no. Until being without them makes them see reason . . .

Orel: That's more like it! You've thrown away the mask . . .

Melo (*to* **Pral,** *without paying any attention to* **Orel**): Let's go.

Orel (*quickly*): Nisal, Fila, the door! (*They quickly obey.*)

Melo (*raising the stick*): You'll get hurt.

Orel: That doesn't worry us. We are used to it, as you well know. Give me the stick!

Melo (*threateningly*): Come and get it.

Orel (*without moving*): Doesn't that remind you of anything, Melo? Doesn't it remind you that once you were on this side and you gave orders against another man who, like yourself, was also waving a stick about?

Melo: Then we were working for a noble cause.

Orel: We are still working for the same cause, Melo, and don't try to pretend otherwise. We are the same as we were, people with no possessions, tortured by fear, always scared and yearning . . . And therefore more to be feared.

Melo (*sarcastically*): To be feared?

Orel: Yes, Melo. We proved it that day and we can prove it again now.

Melo: But don't you realize that without me, without my example, you would not be able to talk as you're doing now?

Orel: Yes, I do, and that other Melo will always have a place in our hearts . . .

Pral: Don't let him speak to them like that, Melo.

Orel: He can't stop me. He can't stop anything. I am sure he can't be unaware that he is about to be sacrificed. (**Melo** *says nothing.*)

Pral (*in an anxious tone*): Is that true, Melo?

Melo: I don't know, Pral. Perhaps.

Orel (*in surprise*): Perhaps! Then why don't you give in? We are simple enough to forget all this if only you'll bring yourself to admit that you did not do your duty.

Melo: But I did. You just don't understand.

Orel: No, I don't. Neither do the others, I imagine.

Nisal (*turning back from the door*): No, I don't.

Fila: Neither do I. None of us does.

Denta: I don't.

Erna: Fila's right; none of us does.

Melo: None of you . . . Not even you, Pral?

Pral (*in surprise*): Me? Why me, exactly?

Melo: Because you too have done your duty.

Pral: I know.

Orel: No, he doesn't know. Neither of you knows.

Melo: I do.

Nisal: All right then, explain what you mean. If you convince us that we are wrong . . .

Orel: No. Nisal, don't give in to him. We don't need verbal proof, we need actions.

Fila: And the actions condemn him.

Melo: Perhaps they do at the present.

Orel: We are talking about the present. We are living in the present.

Melo: Perhaps that's why you can't see any further than the end of your nose.

Nisal: Are you trying to justify yourself by dragging in the future?

Melo: Exactly.

Nisal: And is that why we can't judge you?

Melo: Yes.

Orel: Wait a minute. We judged your predecessors by their present actions. Why shouldn't the same apply to you? If the law has not been modified and you claim it is valid for the future why wasn't this so before, since it was the same law?

Melo: Because it was not applied with the same purpose.

Orel: But since it's the same it would have had the same results in the long run . . .

Melo: No. The law depends on man, not man on the law.

Nisal (*shouting*): Can't you see you've just condemned yourself? Get him, friends! (*They all throw themselves on* **Melo** *and* **Pral,** *who struggle to escape from the hands and bodies which are holding them prisoners.* **Pral** *drops the sack on the floor.*)

Melo (*waving the stick at them*): Get back, you fools!

Pral: Let go of me. what do you think you're doing?

Orel: Hold on to them! (*He grabs* **Melo**'s *stick.*)

Fila: To the rooms, to the rooms!

Denta: To Glada's room. (*They drag them towards it.*)

Melo: You've gone crazy!

Pral (*uneasily*): You're not going to . . .

Orel: Come on, inside with them! (*They push them into the room* and all crowd in behind them, except **Orel** who stays outside.)

Nisal's Voice: Shall we cut off their heads?

Fila (*coming out of the room*): Hey, Orel!

Orel: What's the matter?

Fila: We can't kill them.

Orel: Why not?

Fila: Because then we would have to start all over again.

Orel: All right, we'll start again. It won't be the first time.

Fila: That's just it.

Orel: What do you mean?

Fila: We will have to elect two new replacements . . .

Orel (*impatiently*): What are you driving at?

Fila: They will be corrupted too.

Nisal's Voice: That's true.

Orel: They may not be. We must try it.

Fila: We have tried it already.

Nisal (*coming out*): Let's not fool ourselves, it's the system that's rotten, so it must be changed in the following way . . .

Orel: No; we would just make the same mistake all over again.

Fila: What mistake?

Orel: It's pointless to replace *people* when it's the system itself which corrupts them.

Nisal: He's right.

Fila: What can we do, then?

Nisal: Create a different system.

Denta's Voice: Hey, he's getting away!

Melo (*coming out and holding his arms in the air to stop the men who are about to pounce on him again*): We are not trying to escape, I assure you.

Orel (*hesitantly*): What do you want then?

Melo: Right now, just to talk to you.

Orel: Haven't we done enough talking already?

Melo: No, this time in private.

Orel: I don't see the point.

Melo: You will. (*Solemnly.*) From now on the law is changed.

All: Changed?

Melo: Yes. Isn't that what you wanted? But first of all there are a few formalities . . . Pral!

Pral (*coming out, followed by the two girls*): I'm here.

Melo (*taking Orel by the arm*): Come . . . (*He leads him to his room, followed by* **Pral.**)

Nisal (*to the girls*): Do you understand what's going on?

Fila: No.

Denta: He says the law is changed.

Nisal: He says . . . That's the trouble . . . And why does he come out with that so suddenly? (*No one answers. There is a brief silence.*)

Fila: I reckon they're planning another trick . . .

Nisal: What do you mean?

Fila: They will make Orel an offer and win him over to their side.

Nisal: Do you really think so?

Fila: Why should they want to talk to him in private otherwise?

Nisal (*perturbed*): Yes, it's strange.

Pral (*coming out of the room*): Nisal. Just a moment, please.

Nisal (*stepping forward*): You want to talk to me too!

Pral: To all of you.

Nisal: I warn you, you won't convince me easily.

Melo (*coming out of the room*): No, not in here; in your room, Nisal.

Nisal: As you like. (*The three of them go inside.*)

Fila: They're up to something.

Erna: I'm all on edge.

Nisal's Voice (*faintly*): Ah! . . .

Denta (*frightened*): Did you hear that? (*After a moment's hesitation the three girls run over to the room,* **Erna** *and* **Denta** *merely following their friend's lead.*)

Melo (*barring the way, with* **Pral**): Where are you going?

Fila: What has happened?

Melo: Nothing. Now we want to talk to you.

Fila: What have you done to them?

Melo: Come over to your room . . . (*He begins to lead the way.*)

Fila (*stubbornly*): No, I don't trust you. Let me go in there . . .

Pral (*blocking the doorway*): Where do you think you're going?

Fila: I want to see what you've done to them.

Pral: You're not going to see anything.

Melo: No, on second thoughts, let her see for herself. (**Fila** *steps up to the doorway and then, from behind,* **Melo** *pushes her into the room. He and* **Pral** *quickly move in after her.*)

Fila's Voice: They've killed him! They're going to kill us all! (**Erna** *and* **Denta,** *panic-stricken, look questioningly at each other and immediately run over to their respective rooms. The stage is empty.*) Murderers! Murderers!

Melo's Voice: Hurry up and twist her neck! The others were easier . . . (*A silence ensues and after a few moments* **Melo** *and* **Pral** *come out of the room. They look around the stage.*)

Pral: They're hiding. (*He takes a few steps towards* **Denta**'s *room.*)

Melo: Leave them.

Pral (*stopping*): But they are dangerous . . .

Melo: No, they are harmless. Besides, how could we perform our duties if there were no one left?

Pral: What shall we do, then?

Melo: Nothing. We've crushed the rebellion. (*He picks up the stick.*) Empty the letters out. Give them something to occupy their minds. (**Pral** *picks up the sack and obeys.*)

Melo (*gesturing to him to stop*): Wait. Don't tip them all out.

Pral: Not all of them?

Melo: No. We mustn't spoil them.

Pral (*tipping out a few more letters*): How's that? Enough?

Melo (*almost without looking*): Yes, that's fine. (**Pral** *does the sack up and throws it over his shoulder.*) Let's go. (*They walk over to the door and go out. When they are outside and the door is closed, the bell rings.* **Denta** *and* **Erna** *cautiously peep out and look all around them.*)

Erna: Do you think it's safe to come out?

Denta: Yes. The bell's rung.

Erna (*excitedly*): Yes . . . and there are letters in the basket!

Denta: And they're all for us!

Erna: Let's get on with it then! (*They both rush over to pick them up and as they scrabble about, each trying to pick up more than the other, the curtain falls.*)

The Ship

(La nau)

Josep Benet i Jornet

English version by George E. Wellwarth

CHARACTERS

Jove
Marso
Dan
Candia
Jana
Arbenet
Several Workers

Metallic structures. The noise of factory machines. Nine work-
ers — six men and three women — are seated at two formica-cov-
ered tables finishing their lunch and drinking wine, beer, and soft
drinks. They wear clean clothes under their work coats, and the
younger ones follow the current fashion in the way they wear their
hair, in their shoes, and in all other details of their appearance.

The following conversation is divided up among six of the work-
ers: four men and two women; the other three confine themselves
to following the words with gestures.

— My grandfather followed our line of work, but in those days they
made corks out of the real thing, and they made them by hand. He
liked his work. In those days a cork worker was respected. And he
used to act more as if he was going to a meeting of friends than as
if he was going to work. We, on the other hand, wish the day was
over practically as soon as it starts.

— Your grandfather probably had to do a lot of extra work at home.
We've got as far as the moon, and you still want corks to be made
by hand!

— The moon is all right for looking at.

— Well, at least it's Saturday tomorrow.

— I'll be lucky to get through a Saturday without having a fight with
my wife — the same old Saturday song!

— Your grandfather made corks by hand, but my grandson won't
have to work at all and he'll spend his weekends on Mars or
Venus. I'm saving up to buy a telescope.

— Television's gone to your head!

— Science, my friend, science! And a little imagination doesn't hurt
either. What do you think about while you're working?

— A piece of tail.

— I think up stories while I work. I've got it up to here with these
machines. Every day I think up a different story. A movie producer could get rich with me.

While they have been speaking, one of them has been picking up
bits of paper strewn over the tables and has made a spaceship out of
them.

— Here — a rocket. You can fly away in it and quit bothering me.
And take all the boneheads like you along as well.

143

— To the moon.

— Never mind the moon; that's too near. Try for the stars and see if you can't get lost.

— There's still plenty of people who know what to do with their lives; we wouldn't fit into your rocket. Wait a minute ... You've given me a terrific idea! Let's imagine a really huge rocket — an enormous one. (*He illustrates his actions with the paper plane.*) A ship that can hold an enormous number of people. And then imagine that man has already conquered space, colonized the planets — and now wants to get to the furthest stars.

— Oh boy, he's off again!

— The stars are far away, and any spaceship that's going to get there would have to travel years and years — centuries!

— The ones that start the journey won't be the same ones that end it when they get to the stars. That's why they'd have to build a really huge ship, nothing like any that were ever built before. Besides the crew, they'll take their wives and their children and doctors and people to manufacture food for them ... It'd be a little world all by itself, with, let's say, about a million people.

— Why not make it more while you're at it?

— Yes, a million. And it'll be a journey that'll last centuries. It'll be the most fabulous expedition in the history of mankind. And the ship's name will be Drudania, in memory of the land they left.

— Oh, so it'll leave from here!

— Yes. Because Drudania will be the centre of the world then.

— Boy, oh boy!

— Haven't you always said that imbeciles like me ought to fly off to the stars and lose themselves on the way? Well, then that'll be the plot of my story — the ship will get lost on the way.

— Why?

— After they've been on their voyage for many, many years the people on the ship will forget where they've come from and where they're going — and where they are.

— Don't they have enough sense to look out of the windows?

— There won't be any windows. Just try and put yourself in their place. All those poor devils will be working, eating, and making love without knowing that on the other side of the steel walls around them are the stars and infinite space.

— And what else?

— Nothing. Years and years will pass and everything will always be the same.

— Except that one day they'll find out again where they are, start navigating the ship, and, after a few more years, they'll get to the stars, and there you are . . .

— So you say.

— Well then? (*A bell rings.*)

— Interesting, isn't it?

— It's late. The cork machines are waiting. (*They put everything, including the tables and chairs, away.*)

— While I'm working I'll figure out the ending.

— He talks a lot, but nothing ever comes of it.

— I bet he never thought all that up by himself. Probably got it out of some novel.

— You're just jealous because I'm creative. I'll figure out an ending that'll make your hair stand on end.

— You go tell the ending to your aunt. I've got other things to do.

— Come on, own up — it's a damn good idea. Suppose you were a television producer and somebody came to you with that story. Think about it. What would you do? (*Truculently.*) The ship's name is Drudania and it left the Earth centuries ago, and the million men and women that live in it have forgotten the Earth. (*Calm again.*) Come on, how much would you pay for a plot like that? My mother's said it already — "I've got a boy worth millions."

They leave, carrying the tables and chairs. The sound of machines can be heard. The light starts to go down, fading to a spot on the ground where the paper airplane has been dropped. The sound of the factory machines changes gradually into the throbbing of a ship's motors. Only the paper airplane remains illuminated. But this light fades away too. After a moment of darkness, the back of the scene lights up.

I

The scene is now transformed into an enormous metallic structure which gives the impression of crouching over the various spaces beneath it. Whenever necessary, these spaces must be able to be united into a scenic whole. Light comes from the rear, but it is barely sufficient to illuminate the scene. A glowing light touches the heads of a group of people from which a woman with a veiled face stands out. This woman will take the part of **Candia** *in the following scene. A middle-aged man, with an open book from which he is reading, addresses this group. Next to him there is a medium-sized screen on which slides are projected to illustrate his words. These slides show stylized images, vaguely barbaric in manner. The sound of motors gradually fades away, disappearing altogether at the end of the scene.*

Jove: The first chapter of the *Book of Man's Fate*. Lend ear and listen. (*He reads.*) The Spirit created man at the beginning of time and placed him in a land of milk and honey called the Earth. The Earth was a vast and endless garden without walls so that one could walk a thousand days and a thousand nights without reaching unto its end, and the sight of man encountered no obstacles as it gazed into the distance. Nor was there aught above him, so that the soul of man rose up unto immeasurable distances where there were luminescences called stars which testified to the loving presence of the Spirit. Men covered the Earth from end to end and dominated it. But then, grown proud and headstrong, they raised their arms to the stars and said unto them: "You shall be ours too." And the Spirit answered them and said, "The Earth have I given unto you and no other thing. Stay there where you are now and seek no more, lest my wrath should make you lose the more." But the men listened not, and met among themselves saying, "The Spirit has made the Earth, but we will make the Ship, and with the Ship we will journey unto the stars. The stars are far, so far that their distance can be measured only in infinity. The voyage will be long and we must design the Ship to withstand it." And so, they built the Ship and fitted it with all that was needed for such a voyage. And in this Ship there was a place called the Hall of Machines, in which were placed the levers that guided the Ship in the direction of the stars. On the final day, the men drank until they were merry and called out, "Goodbye, Earth." Then they moved the levers and began their voyage. The number of the men was one million. And then the Spirit came and spoke with sadness and with anger, saying, "This day and all the days that shall come to pass shall be the days of my vengeance." Thus began the Diaspora. Within the Ship, the months passed, and the years, but the men were not happy; they were full of anxiety and cast their minds back to the Earth. Among them some who called themselves Technicians repented having entered into the Ship and determined to rise up among their fellows. And so they entered into the Hall of Machines and slew the Scientists, who had decided upon the voyage, and took control of the Ship. And they turned their countenances unto the Spirit and lamented and tore their hair and wailed, saying, "Thine are the stars, O Spirit; far be it from us to dare to occupy thy mansions." The Spirit let them weep as many days as the voyage had lasted years, but then He took pity on them and spake, saying, "Great is thy fault. You will not reach the stars, neither will you return to the Earth. Prisoners you are and prisoners you shall remain. The name of the Ship is hateful to me, but I shall make a covenant with you and shall give to that place in which you are a name of hope that shall be pleasing unto me. That name shall be Drudania, which signifies the place of my love. And the terms of my covenant shall be that you shall forget the Earth from which you came and the stars to which you tried to go; instead you shall wander in the wilderness. And thus it shall be throughout the course of your days, but once you are dead I promise to give you Outer Space, where the stars sparkle in the immensity that sight cannot pierce. And you, the Technicians, my best beloved among men, shall be the guardians of the Hall of Machines, and, from being a place of guilt, it shall be converted unto a holy sanctuary. The Technicians shall guard the levers that move the Ship that they may never be disturbed again. Neither may you, O Technicians, touch them, excepting one through whom I shall maintain my bond with you. Neither may any other enter the Hall of Machines or touch the levers, for on the day the multitude of men enters, there Chaos will ensue." (*Pause.*) The first chapter of the *Book of Man's Fate*. You have given ear and heard.

The man closes the book and the light goes out on the screen. As the light increases, the scene becomes clearer and a long box with a shiny surface becomes visible. The man continues speaking naturally, though in a slightly declamatory style.

It would seem that almost any part of the Book would be more appropriate than this one to console us for the death of our friend

Josep whom we are bearing company at the moment of beginning the last and only true Voyage. The Book tells us that Josep will find a place that will compensate him for the sorrow and longing that was his lot in this life. The Book was written centuries upon centuries ago and was inspired by the very Spirit Himself. Everything in it is symbolic and true unto itself in its symbolism. The paradise of milk and honey called the Earth is a symbol, the stars are a symbol, and symbolic also is Outer Space whose far reaches the eye cannot pierce. With the Ship, none of these may be reached. But these symbols turn to reality when we think of Drudania, the name through which the Spirit made His covenant with us. Everything is possible, everything is real, after death, in an ineffable dimension that the Book attempts to explicate. Josep is just now beginning to understand the richness of these symbols. His lack of satisfaction, his longing for a state greater than that of the Ship, that longing that is so real and meaningful he is now beginning to overcome. The Spirit has made us a promise — death is the real beginning of life. He has said, "Once you are dead I promise to give you Outer Space, where the stars sparkle in an immensity that the eye cannot pierce." This is a time of rejoicing and not of tears; for Josep the time of the promise has begun. May your voyage be one of peace, Josep.

The speaker has finished and makes a sign. Several persons separate from the group and lift the casket while others open a hatch. They slide the casket into the hatch and close it again. The speaker goes to the hatch and presses a button. A light goes on for a moment, there is a faint whistling sound; then silence. Here and there a sigh, here and there a suppressed sob rises from the group — the first noticeable individual gestures. Some speak to the veiled woman, **Jove** *being the first to do so. On the other hand, some keep away from her and observe an old man with a somewhat absent air who seems to be peering out beyond the hatch through which the casket disappeared. A rather daringly dressed slender and sexy-looking young girl seems undecided what to do; she seems to be attracted to the events more by curiosity than by any direct personal relationship. She gives the impression of having come to show off her legs. Two young men get together and start to talk. The others have by now formed a compact group around the veiled woman and the speaker, and gradually move away. The girl makes up her mind to go in the opposite direction, thus attracting the attention of the two young men who are talking to each other. As she passes them, the girl pulls her hair back and smiles slightly.*

Marso: Not bad.

Dan: Who?

Marso: That broad. You took a good look at her yourself — don't pretend.

Dan: Yeah? Maybe for a moment. It's good to have run into you. I've been meaning to visit you for some time and never got around to it.

Marso: There's no need to apologize.

Dan: You know, it sounds kind of silly to say so, but your brother's death took me by surprise.

Marso: Naturally. You were friends.

Dan: But it doesn't stop me from looking at a girl's legs . . . You going back to work? I'll go with you, if you like.

Marso: I'm not going to work today. I've taken the day off in my brother's memory. His wife's completely broken up, and her parents are taking her away for a few days, so now there's no one in his apartment and I have to go and be there when the inspectors come.

Dan: What inspectors?

Marso: The ones who are conducting the investigation. Josep wrote a lot and they want his papers to see if there's anything in them that might show a motive. I doubt it.

Dan: Motive for what? What's this investigation all about?

Marso: Didn't you know? I thought you knew all about it. It wasn't an accident. My brother committed suicide.

Dan: No, I had no idea.

Marso: They're keeping it a secret — for what that's worth. Well, I'm off. I'd rather you didn't come with me, but come and see me whenever you like.

Dan: Yeah, I'll do that.

Marso: I see that three years of marriage haven't given you a pot. How do you manage it?

Dan: I go to the gym. You have to amuse yourself somehow.

Marso: I'll tell the guys I saw you. So long!

Dan: So long, Marso!

Marso *leaves.* **Dan** *remains still for a moment, looking at the hatch and out into the distance. He notices the elderly man with the absent air who is the only other person still remaining. The older man feels himself being looked at. He turns and looks at* **Dan.**

Arbenet (*bowing slightly*): Good day.

Dan: Good day. (*They exit.*)

II

Dan *enters his apartment. It is comfortable and tastefully furnished.*

Candia (*off*): Dan?
Dan: Hi there. (**Candia** *enters. Her attitude to* **Dan,** *whenever possible, is cautious.*)
Candia: Don't shout — the baby's asleep. How'd it go?
Dan: Josep is floating in infinite space, etcetera.
Candia: Don't start that, please. And Helena?
Dan: You can imagine.
Candia: Did you tell her I was coming to see her today?
Dan: I didn't get a chance. You'll have to go to her parents' place. They've taken her there.
Candia: It'll be nearer for me. (*He acts distracted; she seems unsure of herself.*) Listen . . .
Dan: What?
Candia: Maybe I shouldn't give it to you. You're not in a good mood, but still . . .
Dan: What is it?
Candia: You got a letter.
Dan: I'll look at it later.
Candia: It's a bit morbid, getting it just now. I don't know why he had to write to you. You didn't see each other much. And if he wanted to talk to you he could have come over — he didn't live far. (**Dan** *begins to look alert at these circumlocutions.*) He must have written it before the accident.
Dan: It's a letter from Josep?
Candia: Yes. Here. (*She goes to get it.*)
Dan: It wasn't an accident. He committed suicide.
Candia: What do you mean, suicide? Why?
Dan: Who knows?
Candia: Poor Helena! It's horrible! Suicide! It ought to be possible to punish people after they die.
Dan: You going to give me the letter?
Candia: I shouldn't have told you about it. Wait a few days before you read it.
Dan: What's the difference?
Candia: It can't be anything good. If people want to die, let them and so much the worse for them, but there's no reason why they should make life miserable for others. What did he have to write to you for?

150

Dan: We'll know that as soon as you give me the letter.

Candia: He wasn't right in the head. He always acted peculiar.

Dan: I act peculiar too and I haven't killed myself yet.

Candia: That's not what I meant. All right, but at least read it aloud.

Dan: Just as you like. (*He reads.*) "Dear Dan, I thought this would be a good time to write to you. I'm sorry if it seems a bit strange, but remember I haven't bothered you much with anything lately. Listen, do you remember that project we worked out when we were kids about breaking down the Ship's walls? Well, right now I'm on the point of doing something a good deal better than that and less childish. I've got friendly with an old man and he says that once I do what I'm planning to do, I'll know where I am and my horizons will broaden. That sounded just as enigmatic to me as I'm sure it'll sound to you, but I'm going to follow it up and find out what it's all about. Right now I feel like I'm being sacrilegious and blasphemous, but instead of horrifying me, it amuses me. To be sure, what I'm going to do is dangerous, and that's why I'm not giving you more particulars. By the time you get this note I should know all about it, and if I've aroused your curiosity with it, I hope you'll come and see me. Till then." (*Pause.*)

Candia: I don't get it.

Dan: Neither do I. I imagine he was being secretive on purpose to get me interested, but the trouble is I can't go to him now and ask him what he meant. He must have written this just a few hours before he died. Very peculiar.

Candia: Don't lose any sleep over it.

Dan: He seems hopeful in this; but then he went and killed himself. Looks like things didn't work out the way he hoped they would . . .

Candia: You're just playing guessing games.

Dan: He made up his mind to do away with himself. But why? What was he up to between writing this and killing himself?

Candia: That's enough, Dan, you're making me nervous. Josep was a visionary. You know what I mean — he was always going around in a fog. I don't like to say it, but it doesn't surprise me that he came to a bad end.

Dan: Yeah, he was a visionary, all right.

Candia: And you yourself were getting tired of his peculiarities.

Dan: Yes, that's true, even though we used to be close friends, the kind where what one does, the other does too. And then he got married to Helena and I got married to you.

Candia: I don't know if you're trying to be funny, but it's all the

151

same to me.

Dan: No, I'm not trying to be funny. You know Marso, Josep's brother? I talked with him a moment. He's still working at the Central Power Plant. I seem to recall that I used to work there too. But both Josep and I got out. I'll never be able to thank your father enough for the job he got me and all the privileges that go with it. You needn't look at me like that — what I'm saying doesn't mean I don't care for you.

Candia: It doesn't mean that you do, either. Poor me.

Dan: Poor little you. Come here, I want to explain something to you. There's a part of that letter that I do understand. He speaks about how when we were kids we had this plan of tearing down all the walls of the Ship.

Candia: You were crazy. The walls are the Ship.

Dan: I don't think we could have been more than sixteen years old. We were just finishing our courses for going to work at the Plant. We talked and talked. His brother always laughed at us. When we were small we thought that Outer Space really existed. Everyone's gone through that phase — you too — but I think I might say that we had a real mania about it. We'd crouch down in some corner and play at imagining the Earth, inventing it, detail by detail, and describing it to ourselves. The stars too. We used to wonder how much longer the voyage would last. Later they told us that all that was symbolic and that it wouldn't be converted into reality until after death. Then, when we were about fifteen, Josep and I figured out that once you're dead, you're dead. That's when we were overcome with what they like to call longing and started figuring out projects to break down one wall after another until we reached an enormous and ideal place. You'll never understand why we felt that way. It was a longing for the Earth, for the stars, for Outer Space . . . A longing for imaginary places — how silly we were!

Candia: It would have been much easier to go on believing in the symbols of the Book. You can get it all explained to you today because the Technician Jove is coming to dinner.

Dan: Oh, no! He's the one who conducted Josep's funeral, and I've had about enough of him!

Candia: He's not a phony. On the contrary, he's a great man. I don't understand why you don't like him, what with all the weird things you manage to put up with otherwise.

Dan: Maybe.

Candia: The truth is you don't like him because he's a relative of mine, not because he's a Technician. I don't see what you've got against my family. Did they ever oppose our marriage? No, on the contrary, sometimes I think they think more of you than of me; but you always look down on them.

Dan: You always manage to bring everything down to the domestic level. Forget the whole thing. I'm going out, I've got some things to take care of . . . For one thing, I want to talk to Josep's brother again and tell him about this letter . . .

Candia: Damn letter! What did he have to write it for? Josep never knew how to do anything right. He never gave Helena a child and when he's finally decided to leave her in peace he has to go and foul up other people's lives to boot!

Dan: It just makes you ugly when you let your dislike get the better of you like that.

Candia: Josep's dead, Dan. I'm sorry about it, but there it is. His body is at rest in Infinite Space on its way to the stars. Leave it.

Dan: Sure, if you'll agree to leave a few stars that you've never seen as well. I'm going to find someone who can explain to me why Josep killed himself.

Candia: Please don't get mixed up in something.

Dan (*leaning down to give her a kiss*): 'Bye. (*He leaves.* **Candia** *watches him, uncertain what to do.*)

Candia: Wait, Dan, I'll go with you. (*She grabs her purse and is about to follow him when she hears the baby's crying. She stops, puts the purse down and now, not hurrying anymore, starts to go to the inner room.*) Don't cry, Mama's coming.

III

Dan *arrives at the apartment of his dead friend. It is very much like his own. The door stands open, and two men in uniformlike dress are preparing to leave. They carry a pair of files and a brief-case.* **Dan** *stands at the door without entering and makes way for them. They nod at him absently and leave.*

Marso: What are you doing here? Did you get lost?

Dan (*entering*): Were those the inspectors?

Marso: Yes. They took Josep's papers.

Dan: That means I've come too late. I'd have liked to go through them, but it doesn't matter. I wanted to see you too. I'm not disturbing you, I hope?

Marso: I've got nothing to do for a bit. We can talk. Make yourself at home. I'm surprised you came.

Dan: I told you earlier I wanted to come and see you some time. The fact is, if you don't mind, I've got a few questions to ask you. And I'd rather ask you than your sister-in-law.

Marso: What do you want to ask about?

Dan: Your brother.

Marso: Everyone takes care of his own affairs.

Dan: How did he kill himself?

Marso: Oh, that — he shot himself.

Dan: Here?

Marso: No, in one of the corridors of the Ship — not a place that many people went to. When he didn't show up for dinner, Helena got worried. A little later, someone stumbled on him.

Dan: Does Helena have any idea why he did it?

Marso: I don't think so.

Dan: Doesn't she even have a suspicion?

Marso: You're upset. My sister-in-law doesn't tell me what she knows or what she suspects. I didn't see them much. Same as always, what're you gonna do? Ever since you and Josep drifted away from each other things haven't changed. Helena and I never confided in each other, thank goodness, and I may as well tell you frankly, that my brother's death interests me only in a relative way. He went right on acting peculiarly after he got married, although I'd say he made a hell of a lucky match. I can't figure out whether that affected manner was real or whether he was just pretending. What do you say?

Dan: Defending your brother would be the same as defending myself, as far as I'm concerned. Think what you like.

Marso: I don't give a damn. Spend all of your time jeering at everything and you see how it all ends up. That's the whole point. I take it you've got a bit more sense.

Dan: Josep wrote to me just before he died.

Marso: That right?

Dan: It doesn't seem to make too much sense.

Marso: Give it to the inspectors; they might be able to use it in their investigation.

Dan: The official version is that he died of illness. I'm not under any obligation even to know that they're conducting an investigation. It seems your brother had high hopes for something he was planning to do. And right after, he felt he had to do away with himself. I'd like to know what happened to him.

Marso: I can't help you there.

154

Dan: He said something about an old man, a friend of his. I don't recall that he had any elderly friends. I'm sorry to keep pressing you like this, Marso. You're a hard man, and since you've got a bit of right on your side, I feel sort of embarrassed.

Marso: There's no need to make things more complicated than they are. The old man was probably Arbenet.

Dan: Who?

Marso: Arbenet. A bit touched himself, in my opinion, but about the right age. Josep told me a short while ago that he knew him and got along well with him. I never saw him until someone pointed him out to me at the funeral.

Dan: At the funeral? What did he look like?

Marso: A thin man — bald, I think.

Dan: Oh yes, the one that came alone and never opened his mouth. He stayed until all the others were gone.

Marso: You've got a good memory.

Dan: He attracted my attention somehow. You don't know who he is or where he lives, I suppose?

Marso: No.

Dan: It doesn't matter. I know someone who can tell me. Mind if I use your communicator? I know someone who works at the Identity Office. (*Goes to the apparatus.*) Her shift must be about over but I might still catch her. (*Speaking into the communicator.*) Section III, please. Jana? Dan here. Could you do me a favor? I need to know where a certain Arbenet lives. That's all I know about him. Tall, probably in his sixties. If it's all right with you, I'll come over to your place later. I'll call you again. Thanks, see you later.

Marso: How many hours do they work at the Identity Office?

Dan: Depends. They do alternate shifts of two and four hours. More or less, I'm not sure really. They can't keep them on long shifts because those machines require your total attention.

Marso: Yeah.

Dan: And how about you . . . How're things going for you at the Central Power Plant?

Marso (*laughing*): The shifts are a little longer there. Still, it's getting better; a bit better than when you were there.

Dan: Yeah, I read about it.

Marso: Everything works out in its own good time. Whether you work in groceries or in electricity, you can put up with things these days. Of course, the hours don't go by very fast.

Dan: I remember.

Marso: But you can put up with it these days and, pretty soon, things will be even better. (*Changes his tone.*) That's what they

155

say, anyway. You were smart to get out, but you weren't smart enough. It isn't enough just to get to the point where you can live as comfortably as a Technician, and in any case it's just plain stupid to think you can get to that point anyway. But it wouldn't be enough in any case. Nothing's going to happen until we get rid of the Technicians.

Dan: Get rid of them?

Marso: My brother and you dreamt of pulling the walls of the Ship down. I've got a better dream. I want to occupy the Hall of Machines.

Dan: But that's impossible! It doesn't make sense! What do we care about the Hall of Machines?

Marso: I care.

Dan: According to the Book, the day the people get in there, Chaos will ensue.

Marso: And you believe that?

Dan: No, and I don't believe the rest of it either. And if you don't believe it either, I don't see why you're saying all this.

Marso: The Hall of Machines is the Ship's nerve centre. Out of its shadows come the Technicians' edicts about what's good and what's bad, where my place is and where yours is. I know what I want.

Dan: And how do you think you're going to do it? All by yourself?

Marso: No, I can't do it alone. We'll see. Most of the people I know are kind of shortsighted. But sooner or later . . .

Dan: I wish you luck.

Marso: Very kind of you. Some friends are coming here today. I'm sure I'm right in what I'm trying to do.

Dan: You're going to discuss this project of yours?

Marso: That's what we meet for.

Dan: The Hall of Machines is just an empty symbol.

Marso: If that symbol falls into our hands things can never be the same as before.

Dan: Do you realize what you're saying? It's inconceivable! You really believe in Chaos! (*Lights down.*)

IV

A door opens in the darkness. In the faint light streaming in we can see a girl standing on the threshold. She freezes, then she tosses her hair back with an automatic motion. She is the same girl whom **Marso** *pointed out to* **Dan** *after the funeral.*

Jana: Who's there?

Jove: Don't be frightened, it's only me. (*The light goes on, revealing the man who conducted the funeral seated in an armchair. The room is small and furnished in a very personal manner.*)

Jana: I don't know what I was thinking of. (*She enters and shuts the door.*) What are you doing, sitting in the dark? (*She puts a filing card that she has been carrying in a spot where it remains visible.*)

Jove: I was resting. Or, to be more precise, I was thinking. Does it bother you that I came?

Jana: I gave you my key, didn't I?

Jove: I'm never sure if you're pleased when I use it.

Jana: You've got bloodshot eyes.

Jove: They're tired.

Jana: From sitting in the dark? (*He shrugs.*) The dead man's family bother you a lot?

Jove: Why did you come to the funeral?

Jana: I didn't have to go to work until later today — and I hadn't seen you much in your official capacity.

Jove: Come on, you just wanted to laugh at me behind my back. The Technicians and their silly babble, eh? I tell you, when I think about the death of that young man my head feels like it's bursting! I'm fed up with my job. You're responsible for everything and everyone, and there's no one to tell you whether you're deciding the right thing or not.

Jana: You must really be tired of thinking up new ceremonies to distract the people, you poor thing.

Jove: We haven't invented them; they were handed down to us. But never mind that — I didn't come here to argue with you. Come on, come here. The ceremonies are beautiful — you won't deny that. And they serve to bring people together. You know what it's like to be a Technician? We're always in a state of tension, hanging on the words of the Book.

Jana: Hey, forget the Book; you're not in the pulpit now.

Jove: I'll wind down eventually — don't get impatient. There are days when I get fed up, Jana, with watching over people who are either stupid, or don't believe in the sacrifice we're making for them. You belong to the latter type, but with you it doesn't matter. The worst are the ones who substitute vicious and sterile obsessions for belief in the Book. People like Josep. And, after him,

157

there will be others. There are parts of the Book that even the Technicians can't decipher. One of these days Chaos will conquer all.

Jana: Chaos ... That's an abstract word that doesn't make any sense to me at all.

Jove: If the people ever get into the Hall of Machines and move the first lever, nothing will ever be the same again. The order of the world and its customs will be turned upside down ... I don't know. The laws that govern life in the Ship, built up and refined in the course of many years, will lose all meaning. It's very difficult for me even to imagine what it would be like after such a thing happened. That's what Chaos must be like.

Jana: On top of exaggerating everything, you're talking in abstractions, as usual.

Jove: I swear to you that what we're protecting in the Hall of Machines isn't an abstraction. At least it's something that can be felt by the five senses, just as the things in this room can. Just as your beauty can ... No, you're right, I can't seem to be able to get away from abstractions. And maybe I'm just talking for the sake of talking; and anyway I couldn't allow you to understand me.

Jove grasps **Jana** by the elbows, his face expressing an intense anxiety. Pause. **Jana** looks at him worriedly. A bell rings. He lets her go and passes his hand over his face.

Jana: You'll wind up going crazy. (She goes to the communicator.) Oh yes, that's right. It's just that right now ... Wait a minute. (To **Jove.**) It's Dan. He asked me to look up an address for him and wants to come round to get it. I'll tell him I can't see him now.

Jove: You like Dan, don't you? (She shrugs; he moves away from her.) Don't let me disturb you. I'll be on my way.

Jana: You're getting overexcited. Stay here and tell me what's the matter with you.

Jove: You want more? Haven't I given you a hard enough time already?

Jana: So much the worse for you if you need to. (Into the apparatus.) All right, Dan. I'll expect you.

Jove: I've been here long enough already. Dan can amuse you better than I. He's an interesting young man. How come he calls before coming?

Jana: He's very discreet. He always calls from right near here.

Jove: I'm afraid Josep's death will have depressed him. They were like brothers.

Jana: Yes, I suppose so.

Jove: Try and cheer him up.

Jana: What's his wife like?

Jove: Rather quiet and withdrawn, I'd say. In any case, she's very much in love with him.

Jana: I really don't want you to go. You need me today. You're the one who's depressed by Josep's suicide. Forget about it, there's nothing you can do for him anymore.

Jove: You've got a completely rational mind. How do you do it?

Jana: What do you want me to do? I've got a good enough job, and the only thing I'm afraid of in life is boredom. If I'm going to get upset, it won't be about things I can't do anything about — and I don't like the people around me to pull long faces either.

Jove: You're in love with Dan, aren't you?

Jana: I'm in love with you.

Jove: No.

Jana: I'm in love with both of you, and right now I prefer to have you here.

Jove (*laughs*): I'm afraid Dan doesn't like me very much — I doubt he'd go for that kind of game. (*The bell rings.*)

Jana: There he is. (*She opens the door to reveal* **Dan.** *He gives her a kiss before he notices* **Jove.**)

Jove: I'm just leaving.

Dan: There's no need, I just came to . . .

Jove: You and Jana make a handsome pair. I'll leave you together. Oh, by the way, Dan, your wife invited me over to dinner at your house tonight.

Dan: I know, she told me.

Jove: Well then, we'll see each other later. (*He leaves, kissing* **Jana**'s *hand as he goes by.* **Jana** *closes the door.*)

Dan: Did you tell him we were friends?

Jana: Quite some time ago. He thinks very highly of you. He's a good man — I'm very fond of him.

Dan: Did you look for the address I asked you for?

Jana: Yes, it's over there. (**Dan** *goes and picks up the card that* **Jana** *had brought with her.*)

Dan: Very good. Many thanks, you're very efficient. (*He puts the card down again.*)

Jana: Who is this Mr. Arbenet? Why are you looking for him?

Dan: I don't really know. It's not worth talking about. (*He embraces her.*)

Jana: Well, someone else in a bad mood. It's almost as if you'd gotten together and planned it in advance.

Dan: Be nice now, and don't talk to me about that Technician.

Jana: What d'you want me to talk about?

Dan: I got a letter from Josep.

Jana: But he's dead!

Dan: He wrote to me just before he died.

Jana: Jove said he was the sort of fellow who succumbed to all sorts of vices and I don't know what else. Sterile obsessions! There, now you know. Watch out it doesn't happen to you too!

Dan: If it does, your Technician will come and save me. He thinks very highly of me and, besides, it's his business to do so.

Jana: And if you lead him astray, I'll intercede for you.

Dan: Well then, I can go ahead without worrying. But that's enough now, Jana, please, just don't talk to me about that Technician anymore, just don't talk to me about him . . .

V

Dan's *apartment.* **Candia** *is walking back and forth. The door-bell rings.* **Candia** *opens; it is* **Jove.**

Candia: My husband isn't home yet. You're a bit early. I was just finishing up with the cooking.

Jove: I wanted to sit down and rest a bit. That's why I came early. Have you got something to drink?

Candia: Help yourself.

Jove: Thanks. You're a good girl.

Candia: Good? (*Laughs.*)

Jove: How's the child?

Candia: Fine. I'm glad you got here early. I can't talk with my husband about anything.

Jove: I'm sure you make his life easy.

Candia: Getting married to me has given him an easy life, all right. I don't want to think about it. I'm afraid for him.

Jove: Afraid? Of what?

Candia: Oh, I can't exactly explain it . . .

Jove (*drinking — casually*): Something specific disturbed you? Or are you exaggerating a bit?

Candia: I'm not exaggerating. You should have seen him. But it isn't his fault. Josep sent him a letter before he died.

Jove (*suddenly interested*): A letter?

Candia: Yes, that's what upset him.

Jove: Where is this letter?

Candia: He took it with him.

Jove: Do you know what was in it?

Candia: Certainly, but it was hard to understand. Just a lot of vague remarks.

Jove: Try and remember them.

Candia: I don't know if I can. You can imagine — references to when he and Dan were boys, blasphemies, profanities . . . Well, almost anyway. It was as if he was planning to do something sinful . . . It was all very garbled and I'd just as soon not remember it at all. After all is said and done, he's dead now and one shouldn't speak ill of the dead. But that's what's to blame for Dan's . . . Can I fill you up again? I don't think I should drink anymore myself. (*She takes some more anyway.*) Thanks for having come anyway. It feels so good to talk about these worries . . .

Jove: Candia, you've got to get me that letter. (*She looks at him, surprised.*) I've always helped you, so trust me now.

Candia: I trust you completely.

Jove: I want to help you. Get that letter. I'll look into it and tell you what to do.

Candia: What if he finds out? He won't like it.

Jove: Just trust me.

Candia: All right. Today or tomorrow he'll leave it somewhere and I'll be able to get it.

Jove: It's got to be today.

Candia: Today? What's so urgent? Ah, I was right to be scared. I knew it instinctively, and now you've confirmed it for me. You can see further into things than I can.

Jove: You're upset — Dan mustn't see you like this. You've got to try not to let him see you like this ever, and especially not today. Now, calm down — nothing's going to happen. These are just precautions that don't really mean anything. They're not things you could understand. Get that letter, get it any way you can, and give it to me.

Candia: All right, I'll do it.

Jove: Just remember that I'm right here at your side, that there's a Technician at your side. I know that means something to you.

Candia: I . . . always try to have the Spirit within me. That all my acts . . . I'm weak.

Jove: No, you're a strong woman. Your strength is the most difficult strength, for it is the strength that comes from blind faith. The Spirit resides in women like you. (*He speaks a little sadly and with some difficulty.* **Candia** *listens to him with deep atten-*

161

tion.) Being a Technician is not easy; there are obstacles to be overcome; an invisible circle separates us from other people. At times we feel like breaking the circle, forgetting the Book. You may find it hard to believe, but it is strength like yours that sustains us in such situations. So you'll get the note and slip it to me without him noticing — all right?

Candia: I don't know whether it's because I've drunk too much or whether it's the way you talk, but it suddenly seems quite easy to do what you ask.

Jove: Just take care and don't do anything rash. Have you thought about how you're going to do it?

The door opens and **Dan** *enters.*

Dan: Hello — am I late?

Candia: No, no.

Dan: I've had a busy afternoon. (**Candia** *goes and gives him a kiss.*) Hey, what's that on your breath?

Jove: Your wife and I have been drinking a bit. Does that seem terrible to you? Candia's taken on a very pretty color, and I like to warm myself up now and then too — just to forget my duties for a bit, you know?

Dan: The Technicians' duties? If there are so many of them, you can always share them out among yourselves.

Jove: I keep asking myself if it isn't envy that makes you say things like that.

Dan: Sure it is.

Jove: And what, precisely, is it that you envy?

Dan: Your power.

Jove: The Spirit gave it to us.

Dan: Oh, to be sure — sorry I asked.

Candia: You mustn't talk that way, Dan. Don't start that now.

She is somewhat drunk and embraces her husband in a clumsy attempt to find out where he has put the letter she wants.

Dan: What's the matter with you? You're drunk!

Jove: The Book is not something that someone made up. Do you think that the Technicians are a bunch of swindlers? Look me straight in the eyes if you dare, and try and deny that for me the Book is the one truth.

Dan: I couldn't care less. Calm down, Jove. It isn't just my wife. You're drunk too!

Jove: The words of the Book are the one truth. And the Hall of Machines is the sanctuary in which that truth is guarded.

Dan: Blessed Hall! And blessed the levers you worship in there! What's the good of those levers? They don't produce the light — that's produced at the Central Power Plant by the 500 men that work there, one of whom used to be me. They don't produce food — that's produced in the artificial gardens and in the mechanized granaries and in the provision warehouse. They don't produce clothes or heat either. So what *are* they good for?

Jove: The Spirit uses them to communicate with us!

Dan: That's a marvellous answer, but I'm talking seriously. What have you got stashed away in that Hall of Machines that makes you guard it so carefully? Maybe nothing at all?

Candia: That's enough, Dan. Tell Jove you're sorry. Go on, apologize, you have to.

She has come close to him again in order to say this and suddenly leaps backward, the letter in her hand. She stands in the corner and hugs it with a childish gesture.

Dan: What did you take from me? Ah, Josep's letter. Come on, give it back to me. I don't know what these games are supposed to mean.

Candia: No.

Jove has calmed down and is now scowling at **Candia,** *but she is no longer in command of herself.*

Dan: Come on, give it back to me and I'll go on discussing things with our friend the Technician. Who knows? Maybe he'll manage to convert me. Don't give up hope.

Candia: I'm not going to give it back to you. It's for him.

Jove: Candia!

Candia: Jove's got my complete confidence, I trust him absolutely, and he's going to check out this letter to see if it might be bad for you.

Jove: You're not in your senses, Candia. You'd better go and lie down while Dan and I continue discussing things.

Dan: That's a good idea. Go on, Candia. Actually, I rather like you like this. I've never seen you drunk before. Give me the letter and go on.

Candia: No.

Jove: Let her stay. It'll calm her down. (*A long silence.* **Dan***'s expression has changed.*)

Dan: Now then ... just what is going on here? (*Goes over to* **Candia** *and roughly takes the letter away from her.*) Did he tell you to take it? You have to do what he tells you to, eh? So that's what things have come to with you!

Jove: You're putting the worst possible face on this matter, Dan. You can't begin to imagine how much your wife loves you, and I myself ...

Dan: You think very highly of me too. You are graciously extending your friendship to me. You hear, Candia? You behave yourself and maybe I'll be nice and let you out to play again. What d'you want the letter for, Jove? What are you afraid of? I like to see you worried. Why did Josep kill himself? You clumsy fraud! Compared to you, my friend Marso, a person of absolutely no account, is a thousand times ...

Jove: There's no need for you to compare me with anyone: I know myself perfectly. Listen, Dan, I'd like ...

Dan: You'd like this letter. You figure this letter might have something interesting in it. And what I'd like to know is what, precisely, this interest of yours is directed to. And I'll find out, don't you worry! And it won't be tomorrow or the day after that I'll find out, either. It'll be today! If I had any doubts before, you've managed to get rid of them for me. You two can stay right here and have your dinner without me. I'm sure you have plenty of interesting things to discuss yet. I'm going to go out and look into the things that interest me. Thanks for having opened my eyes for me. Don't worry if I'm late, Candia, you can sleep it off while you're waiting! (*He leaves.*)

Candia *starts sobbing, obviously not clear as to what is going on.* **Jove** *takes a glass of water and splashes her face, startling* **Candia.**

Jove: Try and clear your head. You've fouled things up completely. I don't even want to think about it.

Candia: Oh, Jove ... My husband ...

Jove: You calm down or do you need some more water?

Candia: No, no more. I've got a headache.

Jove: You got any idea where he would have gone?

Candia: How should I know? Let me think. Why don't you follow him?

Jove: Because he wouldn't let me. But we have to know what he's up to.

Candia: Earlier today he said . . . he said he wanted to go and see Marso, Josep's brother. I don't know if he did yet. I don't think so. If he hasn't, maybe he went there.

Jove: You know I've got a high regard for your husband, don't you, Candia?

Candia: Certainly I know it. What could happen to him?

Jove: Now, listen — get someone to look after the child for you. Then, go and see if your husband is with Marso. But don't go to Marso's place. The inspectors have to go over Josep's house and Marso will be there. Go and see.

Candia: And what if he isn't? Is it important that we find him?

Jove: I don't know. I hope not. But we'd better, just in case.

Candia: He could have gone to that girl's place too, Jana's.

Jove: Oh, you know her, do you?

Candia: I've never been bothered by that sort of thing. I don't mind going there if it's necessary.

Jove: It isn't. I've thought of it already and I'll go. I know her.

Candia: Dan's in danger, lots of danger, isn't he?

Jove: Don't start imagining things now.

Candia: You're worried yourself.

Jove: I'm just taking some simple precautions.

Candia: Against what? You think . . . you think that what Dan might do . . . is he might end up the same way as Josep.

Jove: I forbid you to say things like that, Candia!

VI

Jana's apartment. **Jove** *enters;* **Jana** *is surprised.*

Jove: You alone?

Jana: As you see.

Jove: Where's Dan?

Jana: He left hours ago.

Jove: Hasn't he come back?

Jana: No. Weren't you supposed to be going to have dinner at his house?

Jove (*collapsing into a chair*): I'm looking for him. He had a fight with me and Candia and left. I'm worried. I thought I might find

165

him here. He could have gone to Josep's house with Marso too. If he did, it's all right. I sent Candia to look there. He was furious. How did he seem to you? Did he say anything to you?

Jana: About what?

Jove: Anything that seemed peculiar to you.

Jana: He seemed to be in a bad mood. But then so did you. He said something about a letter that Josep sent him before he died. I wasn't interested and changed the subject. What else? I asked him what he wanted that man's address for.

Jove: What address?

Jana: I mentioned it to you earlier, remember? The main reason Dan came here was to get an address he asked me to find for him in the office archives.

Jove: I didn't take any notice. What did he need the address for?

Jana: Search me.

Jove: Whose address was it?

Jana: A certain . . . Wait a minute. An older man. (*She gets the card.*) Some silly sounding name — Arbenet.

Jove: Of course! (*He sighs.*)

Jana: You know him?

Jove: I know who he is. (*He is paler but calmer from now on.*)

Jana: You could sniff up that trail.

Jove: Eh?

Jana: I said you could sniff up that trail. You're hiding something from me, and you're not acting normally either. So Dan got mad and left. He got fed up. Maybe he'll ask Marso to put him up for the night. And tomorrow it'll be all forgotten. Or maybe not, but either way it's no business of yours.

Jove: He doesn't know what he's doing. And it's only a few hours since we kept Josep company as he began his last Voyage.

Jana: You don't think he'll kill himself too, do you? That's ridiculous! I know him — and so do you, for that matter. What would he kill himself for? What do you want me to tell you? If they carried his body in here right now and told me he'd killed himself, I wouldn't believe it. No matter how many times they told me.

Jove: Well, what would you think?

Jana (*quietly*): I'd rather not say. You've got inspectors you can order around. I just hope you're not satisfied with easy answers either.

Jove: I'm a Technician. I'll do my duty no matter what happens.

Jana: That's what I mean. But let's not imagine any tragedies or talk about things that don't make any sense anyway. Come on,

Jove, don't get upset.

Jove: You're right. I've got myself mixed up in this for no reason. Let Dan do what he likes. He's free, after all.

Jana: Well, you've managed to get me worried too now.

Jove: I'm sorry, I've been a beast, really. Come on, I'll go and leave you in peace.

Jana: What are you going to do?

Jove: I'm on duty tonight. It's almost time.

Jana: And what about Dan?

Jove: Never mind him. You've convinced me it's nothing.

Jana: All right, but call Candia or Marso to see if he's there.

Jove: I've got no time and it isn't important anyway.

Jana: What is this? You came here expressly to find out where Dan was and now you wash your hands of the whole business?

Jove: I'm just doing what you said I should.

Jana: Mysterious and enigmatic, like all the Technicians.

Jove: That's why you like them. I'm on duty, there's nothing I can do about that, and I'll be late. I'd like to stay with you, you know that!

Jana: Mysterious and enigmatic. Give me a kiss.

Jove: Sleep well.

He leaves. **Jana** *tries to do something or other, but it is obvious that she is worried. She drops what she is doing, looks in a notebook, and calls a number on the communicator.*

Jana: Excuse me, is Marso there? Oh, he's busy. No, don't disturb him. I really only wanted to know if a friend of his was there. A friend of his named Dan. Is he there? No? My name's Jana. And you're . . . you're Candia. I know, Jove told me. No, he hasn't come here either. I assure you he isn't here. Jove saw that himself. I called up simply to see if I could help. I'm sure he'll come back home. Calm down. No, don't upset yourself. If I see him, I'll let you know right away. Just stop worrying — after all, nothing terrible's happened. That's right. As soon as I know anything, I'll call you.

She cuts the connection, but does not seem to have calmed down. Quite the contrary. She walks nervously back and forth. Suddenly she stops, her eyes fixed on the card with the address on it. She looks at it for a moment from a distance, then makes up her mind and goes over to pick it up.

VII

In the middle of this scene, very faintly, we begin to hear the sound of the Ship's motors again. **Dan** *and* **Arbenet** *are facing each other with a communicator behind them.* **Arbenet** *is an old man, thin and of average height, bald, and with a large nose that dominates his otherwise unremarkable face.*

Arbenet: Yes, my name's Arbenet.

Dan: I'm a friend of Josep's, whom you knew. We saw each other at the funeral, remember? My name's Dan.

Arbenet (*enigmatically*): What can I do for you?

Dan: I realize that it's a rather unusual time for . . . It's just that I happen to know that Josep had a lot to do with you lately. I suspect that you know more than anybody else about what he was thinking. Maybe you had some influence over him. Maybe I'm assuming too much, but if anyone might know what Josep was up to or what he wanted to do in his last hours, you might. (*Pause.* **Arbenet** *says nothing.*) Very well, no doubt I'm mistaken. In any case . . . I got a letter from Josep. It seems to allude to you. I'd like to know what he was really thinking when he wrote that letter. He seemed to be thinking about something — what, I can't figure out, but it wasn't suicide. But then he killed himself. Did you see him recently?

Arbenet: No, not recently. And I'm surprised to hear you say he killed himself. I thought he had had an accident. Or rather, I still think so. Nobody commits suicide on the Ship.

Dan: Everyone knows he committed suicide. I've spoken with the Technician Jove, and not even he denied it.

Arbenet: I wouldn't know what to tell you.

Dan: You can believe, or pretend to believe, whatever you please about it. What I'm interested in is finding out what things you and Josep had been discussing recently.

Arbenet: We just talked about general matters — nothing of any special interest. On the other hand, I'm very sorry that you've been given a false impression, but the fact is that my acquaintance with Josep was only a superficial one.

Dan: That's strange. I was told . . .

Arbenet: It wasn't true.

Dan: I see I'm annoying you but, despite your attitude, I'm as eager as ever to find out more about this matter. In fact, your refusal to answer me strikes me as very peculiar, and simply serves to convince me that there is something extremely mysterious about Josep's death. I'll get the information you're holding back one way or another. Good-bye!

Arbenet: Any information you fail to get from me you won't get anywhere else! Wait a minute! What interests you so much about this matter?

Dan: Josep was a friend of mine.

Arbenet: That needn't necessarily make you curious about his death.

Dan: That's all.

Arbenet: In that case, it might be better for both of us if you did leave.

Dan: What do you want me to say to you? Tell me and I'll say it! I want to know why Josep killed himself. We shared lots of dreams together. Just to pass the time and not be bored, we thought up the most enormous projects. We created — I suppose you'd call them unhealthy — visions of a real Outer Space and dreamt that one day the Voyage would end and we'd step out of the Ship into a land of milk and honey . . . We really longed for the Exterior. It's embarrassing to tell about it, but it's the truth. It all happened. Youth is a hard time to live through, but it passes. Now, Josep went right on being a bit of a child maybe, but I can't believe he killed himself to be consistent with his visions! The letter was written very vaguely, as always — but why is Jove so scared of it? He doesn't get scared about things that are vague!

Arbenet: All right. You're all worked up and even if I don't say anything . . . I don't know everything I'd like to know, but I do know a good deal more than I need to know to live peacefully. Listen, I saw Josep the day of his accident. And I knew what he intended to do because I was in a way partially responsible. Josep went into the Hall of Machines.

Dan: The Hall of Machines! . . .

Arbenet: Come here, It must have happened when he came out . . . the accident, I mean. I had told him that all questions could be answered in the Hall of Machines. Understand me, I meant answered in a meaningful, that is to say, rational way. What I told him fitted in so well with his old dreams of tearing down the walls of the Ship and with the remembrance of that longing you've mentioned to me, that he didn't think about it twice. (*Animatedly.*) Listen, let me tell you. We don't know where we come from or where we go, but in there is the answer that we need to know where we are.

Dan: We're in the Ship. But he did write something very close to

169

what you've just said in his letter to me. I didn't understand what he meant and I still don't.

Arbenet: I can try and explain it to you more or less.

Dan: Who are you? Arbenet is an official sounding name.

Arbenet: Let's just say I'm a student — or a visionary, if you prefer. In any case, I'm not a Technician, and consequently I haven't had access to their knowledge or their secrets. But I enjoy thinking about things. When I was young, I used to get carried away with the same sort of ideas as yours or those of your friend. I didn't stop being interested in the myths of the Book the day I stopped believing in them. I've dug through as many ancient documents as I could in order to learn more about the Book. And the older the documents, the less rigid and formalized was their version of the myths . . . the myths seemed fresher, more . . . It was strange. Listen, what's the point of the Technicians creating a forbidden place? What's the Hall of Machines supposed to do? It's dangerous to forbid something because, no sooner do you do so, than you give birth to the wish to have it. Why do those abstractions that the Technicians claim explain the Book have to be forbidden in such an aggressively concrete way?

Dan: If you're not a Technician you can't get into the Hall of Machines. There was no way for Josep to satisfy the curiosity that you no doubt started up in him.

Arbenet: There was a way — with this.

Dan: What's that?

Arbenet: One of the keys to the Hall of Machines.

Dan: How come you've got it?

Arbenet: I don't answer that kind of question.

Dan: It's just that I'm surprised that it's so easy to get into the most inaccessible part of the Ship.

Arbenet: It can be.

Dan: Let's suppose it is. There's still the fact that Josep killed himself after going in there. (*Long pause.* **Dan** *stretches out his hand.*)

Arbenet: As you've just pointed out, the only thing Josep accomplished was his own death. You sure you want the key?

Dan: Sure that you hope I do.

Arbenet: Very well. (*He hands it over.*)

Dan: You've never used it yourself?

Arbenet: I've answered everything you've asked me about Josep, but I will not say one single thing about myself. Oh, one more thing. The key is only good tonight.

Dan: Am I supposed to believe that?

170

Arbenet: You have no choice. I'm your only contact. Good luck.

Dan: Thanks.

Arbenet: What do you think of me?

Dan: That you're either crazy and are pulling my leg or that you're a coward who hopes other people will do what he's afraid to do.

Arbenet: You're not very imaginative.

Dan: And I don't have any time to argue with you either. (*Pause.*)

Arbenet: Get going then. (**Dan** *turns and goes.* **Arbenet** *watches him disappear with a sudden expression of panic, which, however, is instantly replaced by his customary neutral expression. He turns to the communicator.*) Technician Jove, please. Yes, I know he's on duty. Tell him Arbenet wants to speak to him. (*Pause.*) Jove? Arbenet here. A young man, named Dan, I think, was just here to see me. I gave him the key.

VIII

During this scene the sound of the motors will increase gradually. **Josep**'s apartment. **Candia** *is seated and waiting. The bell on the communicator rings. Since there does not seem to be anyone else to answer it,* **Candia,** *after a moment of doubt, lifts the receiver.*

Candia: Hello. Yes, Marso is here, but I don't know if he can come. He's talking to some friends, and I'm waiting myself for him to be finished so I can speak with him. You want me to give him a message anyway? Oh, you're really calling his friend, Dan. Who are you? No, Dan hasn't come here. You're Jana, aren't you? This is Candia. I'm looking ... well, I'm looking for my husband. Of course. Excuse the question, but haven't you seen him either? Yes, he'll probably go back home. At least I hope so, although I don't know what to think. Look, if you find anything out, no matter how late, I'd be very grateful if you'd ... Thanks. Sure. Probably it's nothing. Thanks again. (*While she is still talking, a door opens and* **Marso** *enters.*)

Marso: Was that for me?

Candia: No — just a friend of mine.

Marso: They knew you were here?

Candia: She was calling to find out if I had found my husband.

Marso: Dan won't show up here. There's no reason for him to. I'm sorry — I'm busy.

Candia: Dan spoke of coming to see you today.

Marso: And so he did — hours ago.

Candia: Oh, he didn't tell me that. Did he come before dinner?

Marso: Quite some time before. Look, I can give you a few minutes while the men in there are making up their minds about something, but that's all. I've got my own problems.

Candia: I'm sorry, I'll go. I'm bothering you for no reason. I'm worrying like a fool, and I really don't know why. Sometimes I get furious at myself for putting up with the things I put up with and still being happy.

Marso: Excuse me . . .

Candia: Dan's never responded to my affection. I've got a right to . . . the same as anyone else. You work at the Central Power Plant, and you know what that's worth. Dan's taken everything I've given him without the slightest surprise or gratitude. I've never said anything, I've never even thought about these sordid things until today, I swear. I've always been satisfied to get along evenly, trying to guess what Dan wanted or didn't want . . . Often enough I've felt that it might be a relief if Dan disappeared!

Marso: You tell him all that tomorrow and, afterwards, you'll feel like a new woman.

Candia: You're making fun of me. Well, good for you. I hardly know what I'm talking about. I must be crazy. I'm sorry, it's just nerves. I'll be on my way — forgive me. Oh, one more thing . . . if you see him . . .

Marso: I'll let you know, don't worry.

Candia: Thank you and forgive me again. (**Marso** *shuts the door after she leaves.*)

Marso: Pleasant dreams. (*He goes rapidly into the room he came from, leaving the stage empty. Immediately, the door of the other room opens again. Two men and a woman cross the stage and leave. Pause.* **Marso** *comes back, looking disappointed. He stands still for a moment without looking around. Then he takes a drink and sits down. He gets up eagerly when he hears the doorbell but is disappointed when he sees it is* **Dan.**) Well, so you came after all. I've just had the pleasure of talking to your wife.

Dan: My wife?

Marso: She was looking for you. You're in demand.

Dan: I'm in a hurry. I'd like to talk to you if you can spare me a moment.

Marso: Sure I can. You'll keep me company.

Dan: I've got to go again right away. I want to make you a proposition.

172

Marso: That's good, I like propositions. The people that were here just now turned my proposition down, so yours'll get a friendly hearing as a contrast.

Dan: You told me this afternoon that you dreamt of taking over the Hall of Machines.

Marso: A dream. I daydream, yes. But my friends say I'm crazy, that I'm a brainless radical, and that there are a thousand more important things. They say it's possible to reform the system from the inside without going to extremes. They represent the view of practically all the workers so that it's pointless for me to beat my head against the wall.

Dan: Yeah.

Marso: At bottom, I suspect they're right. I'm a visionary — my brother's brother, apparently.

Dan: In that case, I've come at the right moment. Look.

Marso: A key.

Dan: The key to the Hall of Machines.

Marso: You're crazy!

Dan: No, I'm not. I managed to get it.

Marso: You weren't interested in the Hall of Machines.

Dan: I am now. Josep went in there. Don't you believe me?

Marso: No. I know you.

Dan: The proposition is that you come with me and that we go in there together. What have you got to lose? If I'm lying, you'll just have to turn round and come back again and that'll be all. But if the key is good . . . What do you say?

Marso: If that's a good key, it's a dangerous one. Where'd you get it?

Dan: Arbenet gave it to me.

Marso: If it's good, it's dangerous. I haven't lost my head yet.

Dan: But you wanted to take over the Hall of Machines!

Marso: And you think that I can take it over alone, or even with you? We'd have to get others. Then we could give it a try.

Dan: The others turned you down.

Marso: So I'll just have to say, the hell with it!

Dan: I've got the key, Marso!

Marso: That key plus yourself equals nothing.

Dan: I'm sorry if I've bothered you.

Marso: Wait a minute. I don't want to run any risk — I've got no stomach for that sort of thing; but if you're set on doing it, I'd like to get something out of it.

Dan: That's what I call sincerity!

Marso: If you manage to get in, leave the door open. I'll follow you at a distance. If the coast is clear, and I find the door open, maybe I'll make up my mind to follow you in.

Dan: If there's any danger you'd rather save your own skin, eh?

Marso: Precisely.

Dan: And that's what I call cynicism!

Marso: What do you mean, cynicism? You talk like someone who's never been hungry. I'm still undertaking to do too much. The whole affair isn't at all clear to me.

Dan: Well?

Marso: If it's okay with you, we'll do it the way I said.

Dan: Okay with me.

Marso: Fine. Good luck.

Dan: You'll be the first to know if I've had any.

IX

The sound of motors. A door opens and **Dan** *enters. He stops, trying to orient himself in the shadows that surround him. The first thing he is able to distinguish is the flickering yellow light of some oil lamps. Silent, gray forms can be seen spread out in the light.* **Dan** *takes a step forward. The door closes behind him.* **Dan,** *noticing it, hesitates.*

Voice: You are in the Hall of Machines, Dan.

Dan: Who's that?

Several strategically placed lamps light up, causing the shadows to fall back into the corners. The oil lamps, surrounded by censers and other holy objects, are lined up along the Ship's control panels. Everything is silent and stained with rust. The levers dominate the whole assembly. Only one of them glistens as if it were constantly in use. **Dan** *glances at these things only in passing since his attention is taken up by more disturbing matters: to wit, the presence before him of* **Jove** *who looks at him with a mixture of irony and discouragement. Behind him* **Arbenet** *tries to efface himself, while, further on, a Technician may be seen watching alertly.*

Jove: It's me, Dan.

Dan: I see that you're expecting me. Arbenet too?

Jove: Arbenet is a modest but indispensable servant of the cause —

a faithful one, I must say. Yes, we're expecting you. You like this place?

Dan: Not with you in it.

Jove: I'm afraid you can't leave. That door is only for entering.

Dan: I've got the key and I didn't lock it.

Jove: You didn't? In that case someone else could come in, but not go out. Once you're in here, you've got to use other methods to get out of here. You may not care for my company, but you'll have to put up with it. What was it you came to see? The levers? Take a good look at them. They're real, all right. We Technicians have fulfilled our task. None of us has touched them, except the first one there, of course. Just as the Book says.

Dan: Arbenet isn't a Technician.

Jove: All that Arbenet knows about this Hall is about the same as you know now — not much. Right, Arbenet?

Arbenet: Right.

Jove: We Technicians never lie, Dan.

Dan: Sometimes. Josep didn't kill himself.

Jove: Since entry into this Hall is forbidden, coming in here is exactly the same as committing suicide.

Dan: You killed him.

Jove: I did my duty, and will do it again, if necessary. It's my watch, and it's just too bad if problems arise during one's watch. But I know what I have to do, and I can't pick and choose. You think I'll enjoy talking to your wife afterwards? Now listen, you've got just one chance — yes, there is one. It's either that or nothing. Like you, or your friend, Arbenet was one of those people who wanted to know too much. And, as you can see, he's still alive. But he's old now and when he goes he'll have to be replaced. By you, for instance.

Dan: Replaced at what?

Jove: Every so often people who want to know too much show up. Such people could make problems if they're not controlled. Arbenet finds them or lets himself be found by them — and brings them to us.

Dan: And you kill them. But what for? Why do you have to kill them? Do you suppose I'm deeply impressed by this place? Do you really think anything would be changed if you let me go? You'd get me to the point of thinking that maybe there was something extraordinary about this place, after all. And now? Total disappointment! All you want is to be alone here so you can play at your visions undisturbed. Let anyone who wants to come in. In four days, everyone will lose interest and you can be in peace again.

Jove: You don't know anything, Dan. The people must never have access to the levers! I don't want to argue about it. Your situation is desperate, but there is a way out. One day you'll take over Arbenet's job. You've got no choice except to agree.

Dan: I'm afraid I wouldn't make a good decoy. You've got a very good one there, and I'd never be able to come up to his standard.

Arbenet: Listen to Jove, Dan. There have been plenty before you who would have wished for this opportunity.

Dan: What's it to you?

Arbenet: I don't like killing.

Jove: Nobody here does. I want to save you, Dan.

Arbenet: If you accept, you won't be taking the easiest way. No, don't imagine there'll be anything easy about it! If you accept, you'll be able to enter the Hall of Machines, but you'll never know its secrets, as the Technicians do. You'll never be allowed to know what happens when that first lever is moved. You'll know the disappointment of realizing you're at the gates of a mystery which it will never be given to you to know, although each time you see it, it will seem more important to you. It won't be easy, believe me.

Dan: And on top of that is how I'll feel every time I give someone the key and lead him into the trap! That's a little detail you forgot to mention as part of the complete picture!

Arbenet: I don't deny that I give the key to people and do what you say! But there's two sides to what I do. I stimulate the adventurous types and give them the key. And they die. But one day, I hope, those ideas and that key will be used by someone as weapons with which to overthrow the Technicians. If I didn't do this job, they wouldn't die, but, on the other hand, there wouldn't be even this remote chance of defeating the Technicians and learning the true meaning of the Book. If that day ever comes I won't expect any mercy, but meanwhile somebody *has* to do this job!

Dan: Your indispensable servant speaks rather insolently, Jove. Is that allowed?

Jove: If it helps you to make up your mind, why not? Besides, anyone is free to say what he likes.

Dan: To say, but not to do. All the same, I can't accept. Your pathetic words are just so much hot air, Arbenet. I refuse.

Jove: Your stubbornness will simply cost you your life. Once a man reaches a certain age there isn't all that much he can do to amuse himself anyway — making love, talking. There isn't much, and to destroy it all is too painful. (*He points to the levers.*) Look, that's the first lever, the one that unites us with the Spirit and with His covenant. That bond and that covenant I will defend with my life.

The Ship will continue to keep its sacred name, Drudania, and the Spirit will continue to reign in it! You will not stop me, Dan! (*Pause.*) Accept!

Dan: No.

Jove: Very well. (*Tonelessly.*) Since we are on sacred ground, we cannot finish this matter here. Do you want to come voluntarily or will you have to be brought? We will give you a short time to decide.

Dan: You're going to leave me alone here? (*He glances at the levers.*)

Jove (*following his look*): Yes. There's no way out and what you do here makes no difference.

Dan: I'm not going to make things easy for you. You'll have to come and get me.

Jove: That's up to you. There's nothing we have to talk about anymore.

Dan: Thank goodness!

Jove: You've always insisted on the last word.

Dan: Right!

Jove *smiles resignedly. Then he,* **Arbenet,** *and the other Technician turn round and leave.* **Dan** *remains alone. He is terrified but succeeds in controlling himself. He looks around mistrustfully, listening to the motors. After a moment, he approaches the levers and stops in front of them. He looks at them suspiciously. He is just stretching out his hand to the first one when the door opens silently and* **Marso** *and* **Jana** *come in.*

Jana: Dan! (*Startled,* **Dan** *takes in the situation.*)

Dan: The door! Don't let that door close! (*But it has already closed.*) Damnation! Now we're in a fix — that door lets you in but not out.

Marso: Are you sure? (*He tries it.*)

Dan: Certainly I'm sure. You should have stayed suspicious, Marso. You shouldn't have come. It's my fault. In a moment, they're coming to get me and kill me, and when they find you here, they'll do the same with you.

Jana: Don't talk nonsense — I don't like being frightened.

Dan: I didn't figure on you coming here. That just makes it worse. Where'd you come from?

Marso: She found me wandering around here and persuaded me to come in.

Jana: I was looking for you. Oh, don't look at me like that — I've

177

already told you I don't like people who pull long faces! I'm a good detective, know that? I went to that old guy's house and followed him here. I haven't enjoyed myself so much for a long time, except I was worried about you. Stop looking so miserable. Jove's on duty and he'll be a little mad, but he won't dare to bother us too much.

Dan: I just got through talking to Jove. Nobody's allowed to enter here. Jove himself decreed my death, and he'll do the same to you. I'm sorry.

Jana: You're joking.

Marso: I don't think he is.

Jana: It would be stupid to die like this. Jove's in love with me and won't kill me.

Dan: He won't want to, but he has no choice. And, if he doesn't do it, the other Technicians will.

Jana: You're crazy! It's those crazy ideas of your again! I'll never forgive you for talking to me like this, no matter how much you apologize!

Dan: I can't apologize.

Jana: I'm not trying to take over here. I just wanted to help you! Jove will understand. Nothing can happen to me, even if you have gone crazy and want it to happen!

Jove's *voice, metallic and inexpressive, is heard through a loud-speaker.*

Jove: Your time is up, Dan.

Jana *shrinks when she hears the voice, but then reacts hysteri-cally.*

Jana: Jove! It's me — Jana! Help me, help me, Jove!

She runs into the shadows. **Marso** *tries to stop her, but* **Dan** *holds him, and the girl disappears.*

Dan: Let her go. We can't save her, and it'll be better for her to die sooner.

Marso: Save her? You and your noble sentiments! There's one chance in a thousand that the Technicians don't know yet that the girl and I have got in here — or that they don't know that two got in. And now she'll tell them. (*Pause.*) If they give her time.

178

Dan: I'm sorry, you're right.

Marso: What good does it do me? It's not very nice waiting here for them to come and liquidate you.

Dan: We don't have much time, but we have to do something. I'm going to try to move the levers. I'm still curious — I want to know why they want to kill me.

Marso: Right — but we have to think of afterwards; I don't like to give up. Listen, when they come to get you, I'm going to hide. I know it's almost impossible, but let's suppose that they don't know I'm here. We'll try and surprise them. Okay?

Dan: Sure, but it's useless.

Marso: All the same.

Dan: All right. And now, the levers. (*They pass between the oil lamps and stop in front of the levers.* **Marso** *examines them.*)

Marso: They're rusted. There's no way they can be moved without being oiled.

Dan: What about this one?

Marso: This one looks in good shape.

Dan: According to the Book, it's the only one the Technicians are allowed to move. And now I'll move it! (*But first he looks questioningly at* **Marso.**)

Marso: Go ahead.

Dan *moves the lever. The lights go out; the motors become louder. The oil lamps keep burning near the men. Slowly a part of the wall at the back lifts up and a cold, blue light streams through a thick, almost opaque, window. Beyond the window can be seen the nighttime sky. The fascinated eyes of* **Dan** *and* **Marso** *stare out at the circling of the spheres, the glittering stars, and the gentle brightness of the galaxies.*

Dan (*softly*): It can't be anything else! It's Outer Space!

Marso: It really is! Doesn't look a bit like the metaphors.

Dan: We didn't know where we were! We didn't know where we were! They deceived us!

Marso: We've got to tell people, get the other levers operating, get rid of the Technicians, and learn to run the Ship!

Dan: That's what we always longed for!

Marso: That's what we've got to do!

Jove (*inexpressively, from a loudspeaker*): Your time is up, Dan.

Total darkness descends on the scene and the two men disappear from view. The panorama of the skies, illumined by the flickering oil lamps, remains visible. The Ship's motors become louder and louder, but their timbre changes. Little by little they become the sound of factory machines, as at the beginning of the play. The sound serves as a frame for the spheres, the stars, and the galaxies.

The Legend of the Piper

(El retaule del flautista)

Jordi Teixidor

English version by George E. Wellwarth

CHARACTERS

Frida
Hans
Schmid (the Mayor)
Batts
Webs and Kost (Aldermen)
Rush
Blacksmith
Weis and Baun (Guild Officials)
Reverend Grundig
Shoemaker
Walter Romberg
Bailiff

Lisbeth
Grete

Citizens, Militiamen, Jailers

PROLOGUE

The Ballad of the Pied Piper of Hamelin

Lisbeth's Voice:

> On the banks of the Weser
> There once was a town
> Where rats ran all over,
> Rats black, gray, and brown.
>
> They were so many and so big
> That the cats ran away,
> And the poor people in town
> Couldn't keep hunger at bay.

Hans (*in front of the closed curtain*): Once upon a time there was a very beautiful city in Germany called Pimburg which lay on the north bank of the river Weser. At the time this story begins, more than six hundred years ago, the Pimburgers and their town were the victims of a terrible plague: rats! There were so many of them and they were so big that they attacked the dogs and ate the cats. And as far as the town's food supplies were concerned, well, they ate everything: piles of cheese, barrels of herrings — everything. They even tasted the soup in the kettles and made their nests in the people's hats. And on top of all that, the noise they made was so great that people couldn't hear each other gossip about their neighbors' affairs. One day the Pimburgers decided to gather in front of the Town Hall.   (*The curtain rises.*)

Scene 1

Frida: Scene One, in which the citizens are shown pleading for the Town Council's help — and how much help they got.

*The **Bailiff** enters running, heading for the Town Hall.*

Bailiff: Mr. Mayor, Mr. Mayor! (*Enter **Alderman Batts.***)
Batts: What's up? What's all the noise about?
Bailiff: Where's the mayor?
Batts: He's taking his after-dinner nap, why?
Bailiff: Wake him up, wake him up!
Batts: Are you or are you not going to tell me what's up?
Bailiff: There's a huge crowd on the way! The shoemaker's leading the whole waterfront district over here.

*Batts leaves. The **Bailiff** sits down and wipes the perspiration from his brow. Enter **Batts** with **Schmid,** the mayor.*

Schmid: What's this? An uprising?
Batts: Could be.
Schmid: What's it all about?
Batts: The shoemaker's leading it.
Schmid: The shoemaker? Why him?
Bailiff: The rats — it's all because of the rats!
Schmid: Mother of God! Bailiff!
Bailiff: Sir!
Schmid: Listen! Go and see if you can find the Reverend Grundig — and make it snappy. Tell him it's urgent. And while you're about it, give the word to the blacksmith.
Bailiff: You want me to sound the alarm?
Schmid: No, no! Go on, run!

*The **Bailiff** leaves. **Batts** and **Schmid** peek out the window while the square below fills with people.*

The Song of Going Through Regular Channels

Various Citizens:

> I wrote the mayor a letter
> To tell him we can't live in peace,
> Than this the plague would be better;
> It's over a week since he got it,
> And no answer yet has come back;
> Perhaps it got lost in the shuffle,
> Or thrown in the wastepaper sack.

One Citizen:

> I can't do a thing by myself,
> Nobody listens to me;
> I can't do a thing by myself,
> Alone I can't do more than a flea.

> I went to see him and told him,
> "We've got to get rid of the rats,
> Because those filthy creatures
> Are ready to eat up the cats.

> We'll all of us, everyone, suffer
> If we don't get rid of them soon."
> He listened to me with patience,
> Then told me, "Don't ask for the moon."

Two Citizens:

> You can't do a thing by yourself,
> Because nobody gives a hoot;
> You can't do a thing by yourself,
> But two can spring from one root.
> It's almost a week since I met him,
> Strolling across the square:
> He hardly bothered to listen,
> And really did not seem to care.
> Two days ago he was rushing along,
> But he stopped for a moment to chat,
> And he told me the Council was busy,
> And had other problems than that.

Three Citizens:

> We can't do a thing together,
> Because nobody gives a hoot; .
> We can't do a thing together,
> But three can grow from one root.

I went to his shop to see him,
And to buy a piece of his goods,
And also to tell him quite frankly
That the rats would put us out in the woods.
"If you want to complain about conditions,
The Town Hall is the place to go;
When I'm here behind the counter,
I can't deal with everyone's woe."

All:

Together we *can* do something,
If only we keep in mind how;
Together we *can* do something,
Since there's a thousand of us by now.

Shoemaker: Silence, silence! Fellow citizens, are we or are we not resolved not to stir from this place until the Council agrees to start the anti-rat campaign this very day?

All: Yes, yes!

Shoemaker: And just to make sure that they don't send us away with vague promises, we've got to insist that the Council receive a representative from us who will tell us what action they've decided to take. Agreed?

All: Yes, yes!

Schmid: Now I get it: the shoemaker wants to be an alderman, and since he didn't get elected . . .

Shoemaker: Let's choose our representative right now. Who do you nominate?

All: You!

Shoemaker: I accept willingly, and I promise you I'll defend your interests. And now let's call out the people we've put in power. Come on out, Mr. Mayor!

All: Come on out!

Shoemaker: The aldermen too!

All: Everyone out!

Shoemaker: Out on the balcony!

All: Get out here! We want to speak with the Council! The mayor — we want the mayor! No hiding! Schmid! Schmid! Schmid!

Schmid: We're gonna have to go out there, Batts.

Batts: It looks that way . . . yeah, you'll have to go out there — they're yelling for you.

Schmid: Yeah, but you're coming with me. Let's go. (*They go out.*)

186

All: That's it! They must have been eating . . . or sleeping! Quiet now! Silence!

Shoemaker: Silence! Everyone quiet now!

All: Shhh! Shhh!

Schmid: All right, good people, what's the matter!

Everyone talks at once so that only the last word can be understood.

All: . . . . rats!

Schmid: What?

All: . . . . rats!

Schmid: One at a time, or we'll never find out what's the matter.

Shoemaker: We've had it up to here with the rats!

Schmid: That's a problem that everyone has to solve for himself, my friend.

Shoemaker: We demand that the Town Council do something about it. Every corner of the town is infested with rats. The shops and warehouses are full of them and they just come and go as they like.

Various Citizens: Especially in our neighborhood . . . They've eaten all my flour — three whole sacks! . . . All my corn's been eaten up . . . And the mess they make! . . . They won't even let us sleep . . . And how about our children? . . . At this rate they'll chase us out of our own houses.

Shoemaker: And what's the Council doing about it?

All: Nothing! Not a thing!

Shoemaker: We elected you to solve the town's problems, and all you do is sit there doing nothing.

Various Citizens: Isn't that what we pay you for? . . . The only people in the Town Hall who do any work are the tax collectors . . . The aldermen are a bunch of crooks! . . . And the mayor's an ass!

Schmid: You speak first, Batts.

Batts: And just what do you expect me to say?

Schmid: You know how to speak. If you're a good speaker, it doesn't matter what you say.

Batts: Citizens of Pimburg!

All: Shhh!

Batts: Citizens of Pimburg, it's been ten years now since our beloved mayor . . .

Various Citizens: Aaaaaaaaah! . . . Shut up! . . . Never mind the speeches! . . . Tell it to the rats! . . . Now it's our turn to talk!

Schmid: Quiet, please, quiet! My good friends, the Town Council has put the rat problem at the top of its agenda . . .

Various Citizens: But you haven't even started doing anything!
. . . The only thing they know how to do is make speeches . . .
They've got speeches on the brain.

Shoemaker: Mr. Mayor, we demand that the Council start the
anti-rat campaign this very day and that a delegate from the people most affected by the plague sit in on the proceedings. We're
not budging from this place until you agree.

Schmid: We can't form an Anti-Rat Committee because there isn't
any money in the treasury . . .

Various Citizens: Yeah, what happened to it? . . . Maybe you'd
like to levy another tax, eh?

Enter the **Blacksmith** *with two soldiers, who guard the entrance
of the Town Hall with their pikes. The* **Blacksmith** *goes up to
the balcony.*

Blacksmith: At your orders, Mr. Mayor. Do you want me to call
out the militia?

Schmid: I don't think that'll be necessary.

Blacksmith: I can clear the square in two minutes.

Schmid: Just take it easy . . . Citizens of Pimburg, listen to me!
You've been brought here under false pretences. He resents the
fact that you didn't elect him alderman. Don't take any notice of
him; don't follow his lead. Go back to your homes, and the Council will do its duty.

Shoemaker: We're staying right here!

Schmid: Tell them to go back to their homes, Shoemaker!

All: We're staying! We're staying! (*Silence falls as the* **Reverend
Grundig** *enters the square.*) Reverend Grundig! He'll help us!
Put yourself on the side of the poor, Reverend!

Grundig: Be calm, my children, everything will work out for the
best with the help of God. (**Grundig** *goes up on the balcony.*
Schmid *whispers in his ear with expressive gestures.*)

Schmid: Speak to them I beg you, Reverend.

Grundig: My dear children, I am aware of the misfortune that has
befallen you. I know that you are undergoing a terrible trial. But
tell me, who has brought you here? Why have you let yourselves
be led astray? What do you hope to accomplish with this attitude
of provocation? If the Lord, my dear children, has allowed rats to
take over your neighborhoods, have you not asked yourselves
why he has done this thing? You accuse the Town Council of not
doing its duty, but I ask you what sins you have committed. Of

what do you accuse yourselves? Think a moment: these things never come about for no reason at all. Repent, my children, repent and let us all go right now to prostrate ourselves before the sacred relics of St. Rogatia and pray that she will intercede for us. (*Several citizens kneel.*)

The Sermon of Divine Punishment

> Resignation and conformity,
> Patience and humility.
> Think of Egypt and its wrongs,
> Caught within the Devil's tongs.
>
> And how Our Lord, infuriated,
> The land almost depopulated
> By launching, as told you many times,
> Plagues as punishment for crimes.
>
> Resignation and conformity,
> Patience and humility.
>
> And from the sky, from time to time,
> Came fire and other calamities,
> Destroying cities in their prime
> To punish their carnalities.
> We must supplicate and pray,
> To earn God's pardon as we may.
> Repent ye now in God's own sight,
> For who has faith will be all right.
>
> Resignation and conformity,
> Patience and humility.

The crowd is silent. **Schmid** *coughs.*

Various Citizens: You know Latin, Reverend, can't you give us a more practical solution? . . . Can't you put a spell on the rats?
Grundig: Infidels! At least have faith in the authorities.
Various Citizens: There aren't any rats where the authorities live!
Grundig: Drive envy and hatred out of your hearts. Do not doubt that the authorities know what they have to do and that they will do it. Respect for your superiors is welcome in the eyes of the Lord. He has set people above us whom we must obey, for disobedience brings about disorder, and disorder leads to sin.

189

Various Citizens: The Lord didn't set them above us — we elected them!

Grundig: Then why do you complain?

Various Citizens: We have the right to kick them out again!

Grundig: In the Name of the Lord I appeal to you to return to your work. Do not provoke violence. Blessed are the meek, for they shall inherit the earth.

Shoemaker: We're staying right here!

Some people leave; the rest sit down.

Schmid: If you don't leave, I shall be obliged to have the square cleared by force of arms!

Shoemaker: The militia won't obey you — they've got rats in their houses as well!

Blacksmith: I'll answer for the discipline of the militia, Mr. Mayor.

Schmid: Thank you, Captain, I don't doubt it . . . All right, if they want to stay, let them stay. They'll soon get tired of it.

Blacksmith: A little prudence, if you please, Mr. Mayor. What about the principle of authority? What will the honorable citizens think of us if we allow this riotous behavior?

Schmid: I'm trying to do everything I can not to aggravate the situation.

Grundig: You are showing a forbearance worthy of the confidence reposed in you by the town.

Schmid: I'm just doing my duty. I thank you for your support, Reverend Grundig. Batts, call the Council together.

Batts: Very good, Mr. Mayor. (*They exit.*)

The **Citizens** *sing The Gospel Song of Passive Resistance*

Refrain:

> We will not budge from this place,
> From this place we will not budge,
> Till they drive us out by force,
> Till they drive us out!

> Keep your hind-end on the stones,
> Keep them warmed-up with your bones,
> If they throw us out of here,
> Others will come, never fear.

Refrain   (Repeat of first verse.)

No matter what they say,
We know we're right, all right,
And high time 'tis they found a way
To get those rats out of our sight.

Refrain   (The lights go down.)

Frida (*coming downstage*): We don't know if passive resistance will get us anywhere, but it's a good way to start.

The **Citizens** *repeat the refrain:*

We will not budge from this place,
From this place we will not budge,
Till they drive us out by force,
But we must resist, resist.
Come and sit at our side,
Come and sit at our side . . .

Scene 2

Hans (*in barber's dress*): Scene Two, in which is presented the solution of the Most Ingenious Guild of Locksmiths and the most Learned Corporation of Apothecaries.

The lights go up. **Hans** *is soaping the mayor's face.*

Schmid: See that you soften that beard up properly — you nicked me three times the other day.
Hans: I've got three nicks in my razor too: I've never seen such a tough beard. (*Enter the* **Bailiff.**)
Bailiff: Mr. Mayor, the syndics Weis and Baun would like to see you.
Schmid: Together?
Bailiff: Yes.
Schmid: Very strange! Tell them to come back this afternoon; I've got a Council meeting at eleven.
Bailiff: They claim that's what they want to see you about and that it's urgent.
Schmid: All right, show them in.

The **Bailiff** *exits and the two syndics enter.*

Both: Mr. Mayor . . . !

Schmid: Good morning, gentlemen. I'm surprised to see you together. I was under the impression that you were enemies.

Weis: Quite right, Mr. Mayor.

Baun: The competition between our two guilds was terrible.

Weiss: But finally we've been able to patch things up and reach a truce.

Baun: Togetherness makes for strength.

Schmid: Prices have gone up lately.

Baun: Demand outrunning supply.

Weis: Raw materials are expensive and have to be brought here from far away.

Schmid: In other words, the plague of rats is stuffing your coffers with gold, right?

Weis: I wouldn't put it that way, Mr. Mayor.

Baun: We've got a lot of expenses . . .

Schmid: All right, all right, don't start telling me stories. I'm a businessman myself, I know how things work! Ouch!

Hans: Sorry, Mr. Mayor.

Schmid: Watch what you're doing, man!

Weis: To come to the point: we've heard that the Council is planning to launch a big anti-rat campaign.

Schmid: Right! It's a problem the Council can hardly afford to ignore. We're going to do everything we can, and more, to get rid of the rats.

Weis: Mr. Mayor, the Corporation of Apothecaries wishes to place its scientific knowledge at the Council's disposition.

Baun: And the same goes for the ingenuity of the Locksmiths' Guild.

Schmid: I thank you for your generous offers in the name of the Council. I assume you are entirely disinterested . . .

Baun: To the extent permitted by our resources.

Schmid: And as long as it doesn't cost you anything!

Weis: We are not moved solely by material interests, Mr. Mayor . . .

Baun: Our first thoughts are for the families afflicted most severely by this plague.

Weis: And so we have researched better ways of making rat poison.

Baun: And of making more perfect rat-traps.

The Song of Medieval Research

Weis: We have tested.
Baun: We have planned.
Weis: Mixed and matched.
Baun: Fixed and patched.
Weis: Found new ways,
Baun: Worked for days.
Weis: Seethed and boiled,
Baun: Nights on end have we toiled.
Weis: Potions mixed up by the pot,
Baun: Rocks to dust ground by the lot.
Weis: We have dissolved,
Baun: And have resolved,
Weis: And have decided,
Baun: And have concluded.
Schmid: Well?
Both: We have succeeded!
Weis: Mr. Mayor, I have the honor to inform you that the Corporation of Apothecaries has invented a new double-strength rat poison. This new rat poison produces the same effect as the old one, but with only half the amount: ergo, we can kill twice as many rats with the same amount of poison.
Schmid: Aha!
Baun: On our part, the Locksmiths' Guild has invented a new double-strength rat-trap: here it is. This rat-trap has two springs: ergo, it can kill two rats at once.
Schmid: Allow me to congratulate you.
Weis: And there is still one more surprise to come, Mr. Mayor. As you know, it is not unusual to find a rat-trap empty and the bait gone.
Schmid: Yes.
Baun: As the result of the collaboration between our respective Guilds we have brought about another improvement.
Schmid: You don't tell me!
Weis: We will use the new rat poison as bait in the new rat-traps.
Baun: In this way any rat that escapes out of the trap will die as a result of having eaten the poisoned cheese!
Schmid: Obviously, obviously!
Weis: And so, if we have a double-strength poison and a doubly efficient rat-trap, put them together, and what do you have? Quadruple the effect you had before!
Schmid: That's clear enough! And tell me, how much will this quadruple effect cost?
Weis: The new rat poison will cost double the old one.

Baun: And the same goes for the new rat-trap.

Schmid: Hell and damnation! (**Hans** *has nicked him again.*)

Hans: Excuse me, Mr. Mayor.

Schmid: What's the matter with you?

Hans: Well, it's just that my house is full of rats, you know?

Schmid: And how do you figure that's my fault?

Hans: Well, it looks like everything will get fixed up now, right?

Schmid: Of course it will . . . Now, how much do you reckon it will cost to kill the whole lot?

Baun: It'll cost a shilling per rat.

Weis: So many rats, so many shillings.

Schmid: That'll be one hell of a lot of shillings!

Weis: The rats are reproducing themselves at a geometric rate.

Baun: Yes, they're very prolific . . . If today we have, let's say a hundred thousand . . .

Weis: Next week there'll be six hundred thousand.

Baun: And by the end of the month, 3,600,000.

Weis: 3,600,000 shillings.

Baun: And what if we wait till the end of the month?

Weis: And what if we wait till the end of the month after that?

Baun: And another month after that too?

Schmid: Mother of God! The Council meets at eleven. I'll speak to them.

Weis: To be sure, if it's for the town . . .

Baun: And if it's all that important to the town . . .

Weis: We could see our way free to making a good discount in the price . . .

Baun: And even consider giving you a small commission . . .

Schmid: Ouch! (**Hans** *has nicked him again.*)

Hans: Sorry, Mr. Mayor.

Schmid: That'll do, man. You can quit now.

Hans: But you're only half shaved.

Schmid: You're skinning me, not shaving me, today . . . Get out of here.

Hans: Till tomorrow, Mr. Mayor.

Schmid: All right, all right, till tomorrow. (**Hans** *exits.*) What was that you were saying?

Baun: I was talking about a small commission for you.

Schmid: Great natural misfortunes tend to be good for business. Unfortunately for the Guilds, that rule doesn't seem to be in operation this time. The municipal treasury is virtually empty.

Weis: Pimburg is not a poor town.

Baun: In fact, it's a positively prosperous one.

Schmid: All right, all right, we'll find the money somehow.
Weis: Let's hope so, Mr. Mayor.   (*The lights go down.*)

Scene 3

Hans *and* **Frida** *enter with three full sacks and several empty ones.*

Frida: Scene three, in which Hans and Frida undertake a plot whose point is not quite clear and in which the illustrious aldermen of Pimburg are presented to the audience.
Hans: Let's sit down for a bit, Frida, I'm tired.
Frida: I'm not surprised. You've been sweating so much you look like a ball of grease . . . All right, let's rest, but just for a moment. We've still got three sacks to distribute.
Hans: That's right — we've still got to do Schmid's cloth warehouse, Kost's inn, and the Town Hall.
Frida: We've done Batts's cheese store, Rush's granary, the smithy, and Webs's fruit and vegetable market. And that's the lot! Oh, we're generous, all right! It sure makes one feel good to do good deeds!
Hans: Once in a while they're generous too and give to charity.
Frida: Only in moments of weakness, when they let their sentimental side get the better of them. The thing is, from time to time you've got to *make* them get sentimental. Like now.
Hans: It sure was a good idea.
Frida: I usually get good ideas.
Hans: Yeah, well, if we hadn't thought up something good pretty soon, the rats would have eaten us alive.
Frida: Can you imagine Batts's face when he finds his store full of rats?
Hans: And Rush's?
Frida: We've got some pretty influential allies here . . . Come on, let's go, the Council meeting is due to start any moment.
Hans: Have I got to carry the sacks again?
Frida: Naturally! That's so when they ask you what you did for the cause, you can say, "I carried the sacks."
Hans: And what are you going to say?
Frida: I do the thinking, I'm the brains behind the cause. The brain's business is to think up ideas.

Hans: Yeah, but you've got shoulders too and they could do their
    bit for the cause as well. I've had enough of this.
Frida: All right, give me a sack and let's go.

They exit. Enter the **Aldermen,** *singing.*

The Dance of the Aldermen

> We are, we are, we are,
> We are the aldermen
> Of this community,
> Which means we are the best:
> It's the principle of the thing!
>
> We manage, order, decree
> The municipality,
> We manage, order, decree,
> And divide up the pot — for a fee!
>
> We are, we are, we are,
> The incorruptible authority;
> We're the honorable men of the town,
> And we rule the community.
>
> We run the affairs of the town,
> Though when we're tired we stop;
> We run the affairs of the town,
> And we skim the cream off the top.
>
> We are, we are, we are,
> The representatives,
> Elected by the rich
> — And by the poor alike.
>
> We decree and we decide
> The business of the town;
> We decree and we decide
> Who pays taxes to our side.
>
> We are, we are, we are,
> The councillors of the town;
> We're virtuous and sincere,
> The defenders of order around here.
>
> With reason and with sense
> The town's affairs run their course;

With reason and with sense,
And if not, we do it by force.

We are, we are, we are,
The most liberal people around;
Criticism we allow,
In little things, anyhow,
But we'll stay in office, we vow,
By winning elections somehow.

We make what laws we please,
In every political weather,
All us aldermen together,
With the Chief of Police.   (*The lights go down.*)

Scene 4

Hans: Scene Four: the Municipal Council agrees to raise ten thousand shillings to finance the anti-rat campaign.

The lights go up. The Council is in session.

Schmid: The meeting is hereby declared in session. I presume, gentlemen, that you are acquainted with the reason for this extraordinary session. You have all seen the square outside full of citizens demanding a rapid solution to the rat problem. I've been told that the waterfront district is absolutely infested.
Kost: If you will allow me to say so, Mr. Mayor, I don't think this problem is the Council's business. The waterfront district is inhabited by the lowest classes of the town. They have always, naturally, been infested with fleas, rats, lice and all sorts of parasites. In my opinion we're just wasting time here because even if we got rid of the rats, they'd be right back there within a week.
Rush: Or else they'll be demanding that we get rid of their lice next. (*The **Aldermen** laugh.*)
Schmid: Allow me to assure you that the matter is serious. At least, that's what I've been told.
Blacksmith: But haven't you looked into the matter yourself, Mr. Mayor?
Schmid: No.
Webs: Those people are always exaggerating.

197

Schmid: Nevertheless, we have to consider their demands. They may not be very significant, but they are fellow citizens and have a right to be heard; and although I don't want to sound like a bearer of ill-tidings, there is a clear danger that the plague might spread to other districts.

Batts: You think so?

Kost: Nonsense, my dear fellow, rats always look for misery: they'll stay down by the riverbank.

Schmid: Nonetheless, the possibility I've mentioned exists. The annual fair of St. Rogatia begins next week and you may be sure that no one's going to come if the news gets around that the town is infested with rats.

Kost: That would be terrible.

Rush: A whole bunch of businesses would go under.

Webs: Say what you like, I don't think there's anything to worry about.

Blacksmith: Despite everything, Mr. Mayor, I still don't think there's any need for us to intervene. Only a few houses are affected, really.

Schmid: At least a hundred.

Kost: But that doesn't affect the town as a whole. For my part, I'd like to insist that whoever has rats should kill them himself. (*The other* **Aldermen** *nod agreement.*)

Webs: Besides, as treasurer, I am obliged to inform you that the sanitation funds have been used up. I don't quite know how, but . . .

Bailiff (*enters*): One of your employees would like to speak with you, Alderman Rush. (*Exits.* **Rush** *goes to the door.*)

Rush: What's up?

Voice: It's terrible — the store's full of rats!

Rush: My God! . . . Get hold of all the sticks, cudgels, anything you can grab, and kill them! And go and buy a dozen rat-traps. I'll be there as soon as I can.

Webs: As I was saying, I don't see where we're going to get hold of the money.

Rush: Mr. Mayor, Gentlemen, I have just received some news that affects all of us. What we feared—the invasion of the city—has begun.

All: What? What's that?

Rush: The Town Council must act at once.

Blacksmith: One moment. What has happened exactly?

Rush: The plague is spreading!

Webs: Let's get to the point! What did your employee tell you?

Rush: That my store is full of rats!

Blacksmith: Your store isn't the whole city, my friend.

Kost: It's only natural that you've got rats; you've always had them. What do you expect in a granary?

Rush: Those were little white rats and they didn't do any damage. But these are *rats* . . . We're lost! (*General consternation.*)

Batts: Hmmm, we'll have to reconsider the problem.

Blacksmith: Alderman Rush changes his mind now he has rats in his store and Alderman Batts, whose store is next door, is about to change his. Gentlemen, gentlemen, let's try to preserve a little sense of decency! The rats haven't invaded the town yet. They've only invaded Alderman Rush's granary. Whoever has rats should kill them himself! Besides, you've all heard the treasurer: there isn't any money left!

Batts: One moment! Alderman Rush's granary is the storehouse for the whole town's grain supplies, just as practically all of Pimburg's cheese supplies are in my store. Are we to permit our fellow citizens to be deprived of bread and cheese?

Bailiff (*enters*): One of your employees has just been here to say that rats have been seen in your cloth warehouse, Mr. Mayor.

Schmid: Alderman Batts is right. The situation is getting more desperate by the moment: the citizens are on the point of being deprived of their clothes.

Bailiff: The cheeses, Alderman Batts! (*Exits.*)

Batts: The cheeses! (*Goes to the door.*)

Schmid: It's not just a cheese matter, Batts. You're an alderman and you can't leave a Council meeting just like that — especially one as important as this.

Batts: Just for a moment.

Blacksmith: Sit down!

Batts: You've got no right to give me orders just because you head the militia!

Schmid: Gentlemen, there is danger of panic in the town. What kind of an example are we setting here? Let's not get excited! We have to take a careful look at what is to be done.

Blacksmith: Exactly.

Bailiff (*enters*): Alderman Kost! (*Exits.*)

Kost (*running to the door*): Rats?

Voice of His Wife: Like rabbits! All the customers ran out!

Kost: I'll be there as soon as I can.

Schmid: Bailiff!

Bailiff (*enters*): Sir?

Schmid: Nobody is to interrupt the meeting again.

Bailiff: Very good, Mr. Mayor. (*Exits.*)

Webs: What about me? I've got to go see if maybe . . .

Schmid: Pointless, Webs. If you don't have them today, you'll have them tomorrow.

Kost: Rats at the inn! All the guests have gone, and if we don't do something about it fast, no one will come at all.

Rush: Business is paralyzed!

Batts: It's a disaster!

Webs: Ghastly!

Schmid: Quiet!

Blacksmith: I propose that martial law be declared!

All: Hear, hear!

Blacksmith: We'll clear the square with the militia!

Schmid: One thing at a time, please. The first thing that needs to be cleared out is the rats. The square will empty out bit by bit in its own good time. The men have to go to work and the women have to go cook dinner. In a couple of hours the place will be empty. What we have to do is regain the confidence of the townspeople, and calling out the militia isn't exactly the best way to do it. We'll declare a state of emergency, and that'll be it. And now, if you please, we'll get to the point. I have received an offer of rat-traps and rat poison from the Locksmiths' and Apothecaries' Guilds. A well discounted offer.

Blacksmith: That's immoral!

Schmid: What is?

Blacksmith: Doing business with a bunch like that.

Schmid: Let's face facts, Blacksmith. This is hardly the time for going into philosophical discussion about the morality of business. After all, just between us, we're all businessmen here.

Blacksmith: I propose we pass a law applying the death penalty to anyone who speculates in the plague and that forces the guilds to sell traps and poison at cost, at least to the authorities.

Schmid: We have to maintain a free market in business, my dear blacksmith. If we passed such a law, the guilds would simply stop manufacturing traps and poison.

Blacksmith: Then I propose we pass another law forcing them to keep manufacturing!

Schmid: Forcing them? How?

Blacksmith: With the militia, if necessary.

Schmid: We can't force them to support the whole weight of the plague all by themselves. That would be an injustice!

Blacksmith: No more so than their getting rich on the plague!

Schmid: Well, if both solutions are unjust, let's take the one that gets the best results. In other words, let's buy the traps and poison at a reasonable price.

Webs: And where are we going to get the money, gentlemen, where are we going to get the money?

Schmid: Let's take a look at the budget. Mr. Webs, if you please . . .

Webs: Tribute to be paid to the Baron.

Schmid: We can't touch that.

Rush: Maybe the Baron could wait a few months.

Schmid: His Honor the Baron has to eat too, my friend, besides maintaining a standing army, not to speak of all the people that he keeps around him.

Batts: All the same . . .

Schmid: I know him, and I tell you he won't even listen to us.

Webs: Salaries for the Mayor, the Aldermen, the Bailiffs, the Secretaries, etcetera . . .

Schmid: Proceed. What else?

Webs: Donation to the Patron Saint of the City of Pimburg, Saint Rogatia . . .

Kost: Reverend Grundig has a right to expect that.

Rush: It's not really necessary to finish the cathedral this year.

Batts: Particularly since it's so out of proportion to a city of this size anyway.

Schmid: Reverend Grundig would just tell us that right now our best hope for help is in the relics of St. Rogatia and that it would be just as well to stay on the right side of them. Webs . . .

Webs: Money set aside for repairs of the city walls in the northern sector.

Kost: That's it! We can take that. After all, the walls are supposed to protect us from the enemy and the enemy is inside the walls.

Blacksmith: I object! My walls are just as sacred as St. Rogatia's relics! Allow me to remind you that the country is at war.

Rush: The war is being fought on enemy land, my friend.

Blacksmith: The Baron has guaranteed the safety of this city as long as it is fortified, and a city with its walls half down is not fortified. The war is being fought on enemy land, but God knows where it'll be fought next year. I don't mind contributing the militia's services to the anti-rat campaign, but don't anyone dare touch my walls!

Schmid: All right, all right, we're not going to quarrel with the militia. What else, Webs?

Webs: That's all.

Schmid: We've got to find a solution somehow or other. Any ideas?

Webs: We could increase the taxes on the market.

201

Kost: You're forgetting that very probably there won't be any market this year, my friend.

Schmid: I don't see any way out of this unless we float a loan.

Webs: And how are we going to repay it? And what about the interest? Nobody's going to lend us money at less than 30%.

Blacksmith: That's usury!

Batts: Money is dear these days, all right.

Schmid: Perhaps you would be so good as to loan us ten thousand shillings without interest . . .

Blacksmith: If you're leaving it up to me . . . !

Schmid: Once we've got rid of the rats, the people won't mind so much having their taxes raised a bit.

Webs: That sounds good to me. We could repay the loan in two years and by that time everyone will have got used to paying higher taxes and so there won't be any need to lower them again. That way we could have a fund to take care of future calamities.

Blacksmith: All right, if there's no other way to go about it, I say float the loan — just as long as it isn't from a Jew.

Schmid: We're going to have to pay 30% whether we go to a Jew or a Christian, my dear blacksmith. Anyway, the town will do the paying.

Webs: It's better than having everyone pay for getting rid of the rats in his own store, anyway.

Kost: The anti-rat campaign has become a matter of public concern. Mr. Mayor, I would like to request on behalf of the Council that you begin the campaign immediately. The outcome is in your hands from this moment on.

Batts: Move to adjourn! My God, I've got to see about my cheeses!

Rush: My flour! (*Everyone exits, running. The lights go down.*)

Scene 5

Hans: Scene Five, in which an unexpected guest arrives at dinnertime. (*The lights go up.*)

Lisbeth, *the Mayor's daughter, sings while embroidering.* **Grete,** *the servant, is laying the table.*

Ballad of the Pied Piper of Hamelin

Lisbeth:

> The townsfolk went out to protest
> They were afflicted by a pest,
> The city fathers viewed them with alarm,
> And hired a piper to pipe away the harm.
>
> "I'll take the rats away,
> I'll lead them all around,
> If now you promise to pay
> In gold four thousand pound."
>
> "We'll pay you that and more,
> We'll pay you on the spot,
> If on the rats you make war,
> Or else the town will rot."

Grete: That's a very sad song.

Lisbeth: Yes, isn't it? It makes you feel sad for them, doesn't it? (*Suddenly they scream and jump on their chairs: a rat has entered the room. This scene should be "sung" from here to the* **Bailiff**'s *entrance.*)

The Two Women: Eek! (**Schmid** *runs in.*)

Schmid: What's the matter?

Lisbeth: A rat, a rat! (**Grete** *screams.*)

Schmid (*goes out and returns with a broom*): Where is it?

Lisbeth: There!

Grete: Mother of God! (**Schmid** *chases the rat.*)

Lisbeth: There, in the corner!

Schmid: Over here?

Grete: Ayyy, ayyy!

Schmid: Damnation, stop screaming!

Lisbeth: More over to the right!

Schmid: Got it! (*He whacks away with the broom.*) Take that!

Lisbeth: It escaped!

Schmid: Hell and damnation! (*He chases it.*)

Grete: Ayyy!

Lisbeth: There, there, get it!

Schmid: Where?

Lisbeth: To your left!

Schmid: Ouch! (*The rat has bitten him in the leg.*) Filthy beast! (*Trips and falls. The two women scream. At this moment the* **Bailiff** *and* **Webs** *enter and help* **Schmid** *get up.*)

Bailiff: Mr. Mayor!

Webs: What happened?

Schmid: A rat, dammit!

Bailiff: Sit down.

Schmid: It attacked me. It jumped on me like a wild beast, like a bear, and bit me!

Walter Romberg *enters, noticed only by* **Lisbeth** *and* **Grete.**

Grete: Ah!

Lisbeth: Ah!

Webs: Stop screeching, the rat's gone.

Schmid: What?

Webs: Who are you?

Walter: Excuse me, but the door was open. I wanted to speak with the Mayor.

Bailiff: Come back this afternoon. (**Lisbeth** *and* **Grete** *get off the chairs.*)

Walter: The Mayor will see me at once. Tell him that I can get rid of all the rats in Pimburg.

Webs: Let me see your leg . . . Boy, it really bit you!

Schmid: Ouch!

Lisbeth: Are you bleeding, Father?

Grete: Oh, my God!

Bailiff: We can't receive you now. The Mayor's had an accident.

Webs: We've got to do something about that wound.

Lisbeth: Get some bandages, Grete. (**Grete** *exits. Meanwhile, the* **Bailiff** *has pushed* **Walter** *out.*)

Schmid: Who was that?

Bailiff: Some crazy fellow. Said he'd get rid of all the rats in town in a couple of hours.

Schmid: And you threw him out? Call him back and tell him to wait a moment.

Bailiff: Tell him to wait? But he's mad as a hatter!

Schmid: Will you run and tell him to wait! (*The* **Bailiff** *exits.*)

Lisbeth: Does it hurt, Father?

Schmid: Not much, my dear.

Webs: What a bite!

Lisbeth: The bandages, Grete! (*The servant brings them and starts to bandage the Mayor's leg.*) Careful . . .

Grete: Yes, yes.

Webs: Take it easy.

Lisbeth: Not so tight. (*While the servant finishes bandaging the leg, the* **Bailiff** *enters.*)

Schmid: Find him?

Bailiff: Yes, he's waiting.

Schmid: Fine. (*The* **Bailiff** *exits.*)

Lisbeth: Now tie a knot.

Webs: A shot of brandy would do you good. Grete . . .

Grete: Right away. (*Exits.*)

Lisbeth: Are you feeling better, Father?

Schmid: Yes, my dear, don't worry yourself. It's all over now.

Lisbeth: My God, what a fright you gave me! (*Sits down and starts embroidering again.*)

Schmid: Well now, what did you come here for, Webs?

Webs: I brought the loan papers for you to sign.

Schmid: Very good, Webs, let's see them.

Webs: Maybe this isn't the best time for . . .

Schmid: It was nothing; I'm all right, thanks be to God.

Webs: Here's the paper.

Schmid: Hmmm . . . Ten thousand shillings . . .

Webs: At 30% interest. They wanted thirty-five!

Schmid: The town will be in debt for several years . . . but what can we do, Webs, what can we do . . . !

Webs: If we don't want to be thrown out of town by the rats . . .

Schmid: Right — we'll just have to sign . . . (*Gets up.*)

Webs (*helping him*): May I?

Schmid (*sitting down at the table*): Thank you. (**Grete** *brings the brandy.*) Get me pen and ink, Grete.

Grete: Yes, sir. (*Exits.*)

Schmid: Care for some, Webs?

Webs (*pouring*): Allow me. To your health.

Schmid: And may peace come back to Pimburg. (*They drink.* **Grete** *brings pen and ink and leaves.*) And now, let's sign.

Webs: Here and here.

Schmid: Hmmm . . . I'll sign this later on, Webs.

Webs: We've got to have the money by this afternoon, Mr. Mayor.

Schmid: Who knows, maybe we won't need it.

Webs: It hasn't been easy for me to get this loan, Mr. Mayor.

Schmid: I know, I know.

Webs: It's just the way the Council voted it.

Schmid: What's your interest in this, Webs?

Webs: Why, none, of course.

Schmid: Ten thousand shillings would be a nice sum to save. If you'll allow me to say so I find your insistence a little peculiar.

Webs: That's an insult, Mr. Mayor!

Schmid: If we don't get rid of all the rats in Pimburg, neither of us will ever get elected again. Poison and rat-traps are not an absolutely sure way to do it. If we can find some other way, it's our duty to take it. Think of the good of the community as a whole! We've got to take a broad view of the matter. If by any chance you have some special interest in floating this loan — I don't want to know about it! — forget it. Look on it as the price of your re-election. Don't you want to be treasurer for another five years, Webs?

Webs: You're right. I'll leave it to your judgment, Schmid. See you later. (*Exits.* **Grete** *lays the table.*)

Lisbeth: Are we going to eat now, Father?

Schmid: Just a minute, Lisbeth. Bailiff!

Bailiff (*enters*): Sir?

Schmid: Send that fellow in. (*The* **Bailiff** *exits and* **Walter** *enters.*)

Walter: Mr. Mayor . . .

Schmid: Come in, my friend, come in.

Walter: Mr. Mayor, I've come because I've heard that there's a terrible plague of rats in Pimburg.

Schmid: Very nice of you, but who are you?

Lisbeth: He's the Pied Piper of Hamelin!

Walter: Excuse me, but my name is Walter Romberg. I am prepared to see to it that not a single rat is left alive in Pimburg.

Schmid: It's a little hard for me to believe that you can do that, Mr. Romberg.

Walter: It doesn't cost anything to try me.

Lisbeth: Are you really the Pied Piper of Hamelin?

Schmid: Have you been in Hamelin? (**Grete** *enters.*)

Walter: Yes, indeed.

Lisbeth: Look Grete, it's the Pied Piper of Hamelin!

Grete: Mother of God!

Schmid: Do you have any references?

Lisbeth: Teach us how to play!

Walter: I'm sorry I can't oblige you.

Grete: It's the Devil! The Pied Piper of Hamelin was the Devil!

Lisbeth: That's right! He took all the children away with him!

Grete: Heaven protect us!

Schmid: Well now, are you or are you not the legendary piper?

Walter: The legend is just a legend, Mr. Mayor.

Schmid: I don't know what to believe.

Walter: There's no need to believe anything. All I'm doing is offering you my services — for a thousand shillings.

Schmid: Oh? Just a thousand shillings, eh?

Walter: That's all.

Schmid: Nothing more?

Walter: That's all.

Schmid: Not a single soul?

Walter: I wouldn't know what to do with it.

Schmid: Well, in that case I think we can come to an understanding.

Walter: I hope so.

Schmid: Well, go ahead then.

Walter: Just as soon as you pay me.

Schmid: Oh, you want to get paid in advance, do you?

Walter: I'm sure you will understand that after what happened in Hamelin I always insist on payment in advance.

Schmid: You could be a swindler, Mr. Romberg, and just abscond with the thousand shillings. I'm the kind of man who has to be sure he's going to get his money's worth before he pays out any.

Walter: I have to be sure too. If you start shilly-shallying about payment after I've finished the job . . .

Schmid: But I don't know you!

Walter: I don't know you either!

Schmid: I'm the Mayor!

Walter: Hamelin had a Mayor too.

Schmid: I have to know who I do business with — that's certain!

Walter: All right, in that case I'll tell you who I am. (*Sings.*)

The Piper's Publicity Song

> If a plague is ruining you
> And you want to get rid of it,
> The first thing for you to do
> Is call the Pied Piper of Hamelin.

Lisbeth: What a pretty song!

Walter:

> Now listen carefully to me:
> To Verona town I once was called,
> By a plague of locusts they were galled.
> The trees were stripped of every leaf,
> The people overcome with grief.
> I played a few scales upon my flute,
> And into the stream went every brute.

Lisbeth: Oh, father, how beautiful!

Schmid: It's hard to believe!

Walter:

> A cloud of flies to Persia came,
> Its darkness smothered every flame;
> I played a few scales upon my flute,
> And to the desert flew each brute.

Lisbeth: Oh, Father, he's marvellous!
Schmid: I don't know what to think!
Walter:

> The Kingdom of Turkey was in a state,
> The Grand Vizier would meet his fate,
> Because mosquitoes plagued the land
> In numbers great as grains of sand.
> I played a few scales upon my flute,
> The Black Sea made their buzzing mute.

Lisbeth: God must have sent him to us!
Schmid: I don't know what to say!
Walter:

> The Emperor of China
> Gave me this stone,
> For ridding his land of slimy toads.
> In just three days I cleared the roads;
> I played a few scales upon my flute,
> And into the river led every brute.
> For every plague that you can find,
> The Piper's the man to call to mind.

The last two lines are repeated by all three.

Schmid: Amazing!
Lisbeth: It's him, Father, it's him!
Grete: It's the Devil, sir! The Virgin and all the saints protect us!
Schmid: Go to the kitchen, Grete.
Grete: In the name of the Father, the Son . . . (*Exits.*)
Lisbeth: Is it true that you made off with all the children of Hamelin?
Walter: What do you believe?
Lisbeth: If they wouldn't pay . . .
Walter: I know I have a bad reputation, Mr. Mayor. But the citizens of Hamelin didn't keep their word, and now I just don't trust anyone.

208

Schmid: Walter Romberg, I think it might be worth our while to hire you. Now, to be sure, I'm not in the habit of paying for the cloth I sell before I receive it. Here in Pimburg we have a saying that goes, "Prepayment makes for bad faith."

Walter: In Hamelin nowadays they've got a saying that goes, "Prepayment averts disaster."

Schmid: Pimburgers honor their contracts.

Walter: So do I.

Schmid: You'll have to trust my word.

Walter: Very well. I've had a long trip and . . .

Schmid: Not in vain, my friend, not in vain. If you'll allow me to invite you to dinner . . .

Walter: With great pleasure.

Schmid: Grete, Grete! Lay another place. (**Grete** *brings another plate and they sit down at table.*)

Grete: Saints preserve us . . .

Schmid: What are you muttering about?

Grete: May God pardon me, sir, but I don't feel easy.

Schmid: Don't worry, woman, the Devil doesn't work for money. Serve the soup. (**Grete** *exits.*) Did you come from far?

Walter: Oh, yes, from Kunstig — about forty leagues.

Schmid: On foot?

Walter: Yes. (**Grete** *brings the soup and puts it on the table. She remains standing while* **Schmid** *says Grace.*)

Schmid (*observing* **Walter** *stealthily*): In the name of the Father, the Son, and the Holy Ghost. Bless, O Lord, this food for which we thank your bounty. Amen. Serve the soup, Grete.

Grete *takes the lid off the soup tureen and screams: there is a rat inside. Everyone climbs up on their chairs. Curtain.*

Scene 6

Frida: Scene Six, in which the rat extermination monopoly evolves a plan to frustrate its competitor.

The scene is the town square. A few people are still sitting around; after a moment a few others enter.

Proclamation

Town Crier (*sings*):

> By order of the Mayor,
> Let all men be aware,
> Although our problem is serious,
> He has examined it with care.
> He has called upon to save us
> The Pied Piper of Hamelin,
> Who will lead out of our city
> The rats and all other vermin.
> After solving many problems
> He has got him to come without fuss,
> And he's accepted the task we've set him,
> And is already here among us.
> Just as you have been promised
> By the Mayor and Council both,
> Your troubles are taken care of,
> To you they have kept their oath.
> Now go back to your houses
> And make them clean and ready,
> For the Piper will start playing
> His notes both clear and steady.
> Go open all your windows,
> Your doors and cupboards too,
> Your pantries and your larders,
> Run quickly without ado.
> This notice issued and signed
> And displayed by all to be seen,
> At Pimburg the tenth of October
> In the year thirteen hundred eighteen.

Citizens: Great! Terrific! Very good! ... For once they've shown some sense ... Long live the Mayor! ... I'm off ... Me too! (*They exit.* **Weis** *and* **Baun** *are left alone in the square.*)

Baun: This looks like a serious setback for us, my friend.

Weis: Yes, it looks bad for our guilds.

Baun: For their interests, my friend.

Weis: A competitor has shown up ...

Baun: ... who's going to ruin our business deal.

Weis: We've got to figure out a way to discredit him. That contract belongs to us.

Baun: Yes, but how?

Weis: He must have made a lower offer.

Baun: Yes, and it was probably so low that we couldn't afford to meet it.

Weis: And as far as his abilities are concerned, he's just as likely as not not to leave a single rat alive!

Baun: Well, that puts the tin lid on that!

Weis: Could we do the same?

Baun: No, Godammit! Not that we'd want to!

Weis: We've had it, my friend!

Baun: Let's not give up the ship, my friend, our guilds rely on us . . . Devil take that piper!

Weis: That's it! Say that again.

Baun: What?

Weis: Devil . . .

Baun: Devil take that piper! What about it?

Weis: My dear Baun, I have the solution to our problems.

Baun: Pray God you know what you're talking about. What is it?

Weis: You said, "Devil take that piper."

Baun: So what?

Weis: Great Heavens, man, don't you get it?

Baun: No, I don't.

Weis: The pipe . . . he got it from the Devil!

Baun: Eh?

Weis: The Devil helps him . . . that's how he's able to perform all these prodigies.

Baun: Oh!

Weis: Since he's an ally of the Devil, all we have to do is find a more powerful ally.

Baun: Like who?

Weis: God!

Baun: Not bad . . . and how do you figure God is going to help us?

Weis: Well, not God exactly, but his local stand-in. In other words . . .

Baun: Reverend Grundig!

Weis: Exactly!

Baun: God be praised! Of course!

Weis: Reverend Grundig will be a very powerful ally for our cause.

Baun: The just cause!

Weis: The good cause!

Baun: Our cause!

Weis: Amen!

Baun: Off we go!   (*The lights go down.*)

Scene 7

Hans: Scene Seven, in which we see the Pastor saving his flock from the claws of Satan.

The lights go up. The dining room. **Walter** *is finishing his dinner.* **Schmid** *and* **Lisbeth** *are observing him.*

Lisbeth: Are you going to start right away, Walter?
Walter: First, if you'll permit me, I'll have some of those grapes.
Schmid: You certainly eat a lot.
Walter: I was very hungry.
Franz (*enters*): With your permission, Mr. Mayor.
Schmid: Come in, Franz, come in.
Franz: Your servant . . .
Schmid: I'm not very happy with your work, Franz.
Franz: How can you say that, Mr. Mayor? I did everything you told me to.
Schmid: You didn't do much shouting, Franz. I could hardly hear you.
Franz: No, no, Mr. Mayor, I shouted as loud as I could.
Schmid: You're getting old, Franz. Here, here's your two shillings. But next time see you shout louder and don't forget the "Long live the Town Council."
Franz: I won't forget. Many thanks. See you soon, Mr. Mayor. (*Exits.*)
Schmid: Now, my friend, if you're ready, we can begin.
Walter: In a minute, Mr. Mayor. A little more wine, if you please.
Schmid (*serving him*): As much as you like, just as long as it doesn't make you play out of tune.
Walter: Wine always inspires me. (*Drinks.*) Excellent! Is it from around here?
Schmid: From my own grapes.
Walter: Do you pick the grapes yourself?
Schmid: I meant it's made in my own vineyards.
Walter: What beautiful pears! May I?
Schmid: Help yourself!
Lisbeth: When are you going to start, Walter? I'm dying of impatience.
Walter: Just as soon as I've finished this pear.
Lisbeth: There must be people waiting in the square already. I'm going down so I'll be in front.

Schmid: You'll be able to see better from the balcony, my child. You know I don't like you to go down into the street.

Walter: If you go up to the top of the tower, you'll see even better.

Lisbeth: That's true. I'm off. (*Exits.*)

Schmid: Don't lean out too far, my child.

Walter: You have an absolutely enchanting daughter.

Schmid: Thank you. But I'd really like you to get started.

Walter: Don't give it a thought — it'll all be done before the day is out.

Schmid: Care for one last drop of wine?

Walter: If you insist, since it's the last . . .

Enter **Reverend Grundig** *followed by the* **Blacksmith** *and two halbediers.*

Schmid: Reverend Grundig!

Grundig: Good afternoon — and may it turn out well for you.

Blacksmith: Arrest that man! (*The soldiers seize* **Walter.**) Good afternoon, Mr. Mayor. Luckily we've arrived in time.

Walter: Hey, leave me alone! What's going on?

Schmid: Do you mind explaining the meaning of all this, Blacksmith?

Grundig: I'll do the explaining. Do you know who this man is, Mr. Mayor?

Schmid: Sure. He's the Pied Piper of Hamelin.

Grundig: It pains me to have to disabuse you, Schmid. At best he's an imposter or a thief.

Schmid: I haven't the slightest intention of paying him till he's done his work, Reverend. I'm surprised you thought I could be taken in so easily.

Blacksmith: Right now he's just finished dining at the Council's expense — and he's dined pretty well by the look of it.

Grundig: Let's keep to the point. In the event that he's not just a swindler, the matter becomes more serious.

Schmid: I'm afraid I don't understand you.

Grundig: It's perfectly obvious: any man who really has the extraordinary powers this man claims to have must be a witch.

Schmid: Reverend . . .

Walter: That's not true!

Blacksmith: Shut up, you!

Schmid: He never said he was the Pied Piper of Hamelin — he just let us believe it.

Grundig: Have you noticed anything peculiar about him?

213

Schmid: Not a thing.

Grundig: A whiff of sulphur now and then, for example?

Schmid: No.

Grundig: Well, that doesn't mean anything anyway. You're a good businessman, Mr. Mayor, and should be able to smell out a swindler easily enough. If your business sense tells you that this fellow isn't one . . .

Schmid: All I said was that he wasn't about to take me in.

Grundig: . . . my clergyman's sense tells me that he is a witch. And when I smell out a witch . . .

Schmid: Permit me to tell you that you're mistaken.

Grundig: I've been smelling out people like this for years, my friend. It's all part of my work.

Schmid: You mean you've got a second sense for this sort of thing.

Grundig: Nothing less.

Schmid: You've got no reason to suppose any such thing in this case, Reverend. This fellow hasn't done anything wrong.

Blacksmith: And we're not about to give him the opportunity!

Grundig: Blacksmith, do your duty.

Blacksmith: Take him off to jail!

Walter: I'm not a witch! I don't want to be burnt at the stake!

Schmid: Hold it! Blacksmith, allow me to remind you that you take your orders from me!

Blacksmith: Sorry, but in matters of faith, Reverend Grundig is the only legitimate authority. (*The soldiers drag* **Walter** *out.*)

Schmid: This fellow will get rid of the rats for us at a good price, Reverend.

Grundig: If he's a witch, he's got to be burnt. Witches are worse than rats, Mr. Mayor.

Schmid: I'll take the responsibility for his actions.

Grundig: The responsibility is mine.

Schmid: He hasn't done anything that even faintly resembles witchcraft.

Grundig: That's precisely what we're trying to prevent.

Schmid: Let's assume he's a swindler. At least let him try to get rid of the rats. If he fails, we've lost nothing. If he does get rid of them, we've solved our problem *and* we have a good reason to send him to the stake.

Grundig: No, Mr. Mayor, we can't risk it. If he really is a witch, he could put a spell on us and leave us looking like fools. We'll have him tried in the morning. And let me give you a piece of advice, Schmid: forget about putting your trust in easy solutions, because they're full of devilish traps. Good day to you, Mr. Mayor. (*Exits.*)

214

Schmid: Damnation! That fellow sees demons all over the place!

Blacksmith: That's because they are all over the place, Mr. Mayor, that's why. I'll be off now since you're busy . . .

Schmid: Just hold it a moment. You're a man who knows his way around and have your feet on the ground. I'm sure you understand that this whole situation is ridiculous. The idea of burning the one possibility we have of getting rid of all the rats! Of course there are witches, just as there are businessmen, blacksmiths, and farmers. They say witches are evil, but this one — assuming that he is one, now — wants to help us! Listen, let's suppose the Piper were to escape tonight . . .

Blacksmith: What are you hinting at?

Schmid: Anything could happen . . . If he is a witch, he wouldn't have any trouble escaping anyway.

Blacksmith: I'm having him watched every moment. And if what you're hinting at is that we make it easy for him to escape in exchange for a little flute concert in the streets of Pimburg, let me tell you that if I hear just one single note played, this sword will save the flames some work.

Schmid: Can't you see that your attitude is just helping the crooks who are speculating in the rat situation? Who knows if this isn't all a plot set up by Baun and Weis? And you're the one who's always complaining about speculators!

Blacksmith: Yeah, well, I like witches even less.

Lisbeth (*enters*): What's holding things up? Where's Walter?

Schmid: I'm afraid Walter isn't going to be able to play, daughter.

Lisbeth: Why not? The square is full of people waiting for him. Everyone's very happy about it!

Blacksmith: Look, Lisbeth, this piper is a very dangerous man — in fact, he's a witch. You know what a witch is, don't you?

Lisbeth: Yes.

Blacksmith: And you know that witches have to be burnt at the stake because they're in league with the Devil, don't you?

Lisbeth: But he wants to help us — he can't be a witch.

Schmid: If someone tells you he's a witch, he's a witch. Grown up people don't tell lies. And now get out of here. I've got things to talk over with the blacksmith.

Lisbeth: I don't want him to be burnt! Walter wants to get rid of the rats for us!

Schmid: Look, daughter, I've got a lot of work to do. Don't make things harder for me than they are already.

Lisbeth: I'm sorry, father. I'm going. But please don't let them burn him — all right?

215

Schmid: What do you care whether they burn him or not? (**Lisbeth** *runs out.*) And what am I supposed to tell them down there now, eh? How am I supposed to tell the people that we've got to burn the Piper and that they should get used to living with rats instead? They *do* have their feet on the ground, and they're not going to take this lying down, believe me!

Blacksmith: It's quite likely that there might be some trouble. I'll call the militia together.

Schmid: Right. Have them gather on the road behind the Town Hall. Come back here and tell me when everything is ready.

Blacksmith: Very good, Mr. Mayor. (*Exits.*)

The Mayor's Tango

Schmid (*sings*):

> When they picked me to be mayor
> I swore by the Holy Ghost,
> That I'd take care of the people,
> And be faithful to my post.
> But now if the Saints won't let me
> Use a witch to help the town,
> I wash my hands of the whole thing,
> And don't mind letting them down.

> Although it isn't too clear,
> I can do it this way without fear.

> If it's true that this damned Piper,
> While he's cleaning up the town,
> Puts our souls into perdition,
> Then let the rats run up and down.
> The Church knows what it's doing,
> In this I don't have a damn thing to say,
> If they want to burn him tomorrow,
> I'll wash my hands of it today.

> The whole thing's very confusing,
> And I don't want to end up losing.

> Before they'll die of hunger,
> The people of the town,
> Would rather risk damnation
> And call the Piper down.
> If someone, whoever he may be,

Comes and stirs up a fight in my lands,
Then come what may, it matters not,
I end up with dirty hands.

And thus and so and come what may,
I'll wash my hands and go away.   (*The lights go down.*)

Scene 8

Hans: Scene Eight, in which the Mayor is obliged to re-establish law and order in Pimburg, very much against his will.

The lights go up. Groups of people are gathered around the square.

Various Citizens: They say that when he was in Hamelin he had hardly played two notes before all the rats were following him . . . They say the streets looked like rivers . . . For once the Mayor's done what he's supposed to do . . . I was on the point of leaving town with my whole family . . . I've heard he wants ten thousand shillings . . . I don't care if he wants twenty thousand!

Shoemaker: As soon as they realized we were all united and meant business, they pulled themselves together and came up with a solution.

Various Citizens: He's right . . . Now we know how to make them pay attention to us . . . So what's holding them up right now? . . . Oh, they're probably still at dinner . . .

Soldier: Anyone seen Siegfried Zelten?

Various Citizens: No . . . I think I saw him at the other side of the square.

Soldier: Thanks.

Various Citizens: I heard from Grete — that's the mayor's serving girl — that they found a rat in their soup! . . . That must have been a pretty thick soup!

Soldier: Anyone seen Siegfried Zelten?

Zelten: Here I am.

Soldier: Let's go.

Zelten: Right now?

Soldier: Yeah.

Zelten: What's up?

Soldier: Search me. Come on. (*They go.*)

Various Citizens: Something must have happened: those two are both in the town militia . . . They've called everyone up.

Shoemaker: What's going on?

Various Citizens: They've called up the militia . . . What for? . . . They said they were going to start right away . . . And that was a good hour ago . . . This whole thing is beginning to look a bit queer, isn't it? . . . And now the militia? . . . Maybe the Piper needs some help.

Batts (*crossing the square*): If you please . . . with your permission . . .

Citizen: Alderman Batts!

Shoemaker: What's up, Alderman?

Batts: I don't know, I don't know a thing.

Various Citizens: Let's get a move on! . . . What are we waiting for? . . . You waiting for it to get dark?

Batts: Excuse me. (*He goes into the Town Hall.*)

Various Citizens: Let's go! . . . Come on! . . . Let's get started! . . . Hey, Mayor, you gonna get off your ass or not? . . . I'm gonna open a barrel of the good stuff to celebrate . . . We'll give you a hand . . . Okay, but bring a ham and a few sausages . . . Sure, if there's a ham left in Pimburg . . . Dammit, what are they doing up there? . . . Resignation and conformity, patience and humility — that's what we've got to have! . . . (*They laugh.*) Come on! . . . Let's go! . . . Get a move on!

Blacksmith (*enters*): At your orders, Mr. Mayor. The Militia is ready.

Schmid: About time, Blacksmith. If they wanted to come in here . . .

Blacksmith: Out of the question!

Schmid: I hope so. Let's go, Batts. (**Schmid** and **Batts** come out on to the balcony.)

Various Citizens: Finally! . . . About time! . . . Shhh! Shhh! (*They grow quiet.*)

Schmid: Fellow citizens, as I have already told you, the Town Council has contracted for the services of the famous Pied Piper of Hamelin. (*Cries of "Hooray!" and "Very good!"*) Our intention was to adopt a speedy, radical solution which would work once and for all and not cost us the earth. Unfortunately, we overlooked an extremely important detail in our eagerness to find our way out of our predicament. However, the opportune intervention of our beloved pastor, Reverend Grundig, has prevented us from falling into the clutches of evil forces to the great peril of our souls. Are there any of you, my fellow citizens, who would be willing to enter into relations with a person who has made a pact with the Devil by obscure and sinister means and has thereby obtained the secret of black magic and other devilish practices? (*Cries of horror from the crowd.*) Citizens of Pimburg, it is my unpleasant duty to dash your hopes and your illusions — the hopes and illusions that all of us up here have shared with you as well. I am sure you will understand with what deep pain and grief I do this.

Various Citizens: A witch? . . . He's a witch?

Schmid: Unhappily for the fortunes of the town, that is precisely what he is.

Various Citizens: Come off it, man! . . . Quit trying to put those old wives' tales over on us! . . . And what of it if he is? . . . If he can get rid of the rats, he's an angel from Heaven as far as I'm concerned!

Schmid: Reverend Grundig will be glad to confirm everything I've said.

A Citizen: We weren't born yesterday, Mr. Mayor!

Batts: In view of the fact that has just been communicated to you, the Council is obliged to go ahead with the plan it formulated previously in its special session. It has been decided to borrow ten thousand shillings in order to purchase enough rat-traps and poison to stop the advance of the rats. I would like you to know that the Council . . .

Various Citizens: Aaaaaah! . . . Now we get it! . . . The whole thing's a set-up for one of your business deals! . . . We want the Piper! . . . For us it'll come out cheaper!

Batts: You don't know what you're saying.

Various Citizens: We want the witch! . . . We want the Piper!

Shoemaker: We'd rather run the risk of getting together with the Devil on this.

Various Citizens: The main thing is he'll get the rats out of our houses . . . Who cares if he's Satan himself!

Schmid: Blasphemers!

Various Citizens: We'll take the responsibility, don't you worry! . . . Yeah, we'll risk it.

Batts: And what about your souls?

A Woman (*enters running*): Where's the fishmonger's wife? The rats have disfigured her children!

Fishmonger's Wife: Disfigured? (*Exits running.*)

Shoemaker: What about our children, Mr. Mayor?

Woman: The rats ate their ears and their noses and their fingers . . . (*Cries of horror from the crowd.*)

Shoemaker: We're all friends of that family, fellow citizens. They've got two children, Karl and Rosie — you've often seen them playing in the streets with your own children. Give us the Piper, Mr. Mayor! (*Shouts of approval.*)

Schmid: The Piper got rid of all the children in Hamelin as well — don't you remember that?

Various Citizens: Sure, and we know why he did it, too! . . . We want the Piper! . . . The Piper! . . . The Piper!

Shoemaker: If they won't let us have him, friends, we'll just have to get him ourselves!

Various Citizens: Damn right! . . . Let's go! . . . Everyone together now! (*The militia marches in and forms a line with levelled pikes.*) . . . The militia! . . . Treachery! . . . Tyranny! . . . They've got no right to do this!

Shoemaker: The militia's job is to defend the city, not to attack the citizens!

Schmid: As your elected official it's my duty to see to it that law and order are kept.

Shoemaker: Schmid, for the last time: give us the Piper!

Schmid: Fellow citizens, I order you with the full authority vested in me to clear the square.

One of the people tries to cross the barrier of pikes and is brutally shoved back; this is the signal for a general melee.

Shoemaker: Let's go, everyone!

Various Citizens: The Piper! . . . Think of the fishmonger's kids! . . . Our children are in danger! . . . Have you really thought about what you're doing, cousin?

First Soldier: I'm just obeying orders.

Citizen: Yeah, but have you thought about it? Would you really hit me with that pike?

First Soldier: If I'm ordered to, sure.

Second Soldier: Go on home, woman.

Citizen: You want the rats eating the noses off your kids? Come on over to our side!

Second Soldier: You go on home. My job is obeying orders. If you want to stay in one piece, you'd better do the same.

Citizen: Give me that pike. If this is all the militia's good for, you'd do better to quit.

Second Soldier: Get out of here!

Citizen: Give me the pike! (*They wrestle for it, and the woman is thrown to the ground.*)

Blacksmith: Load your muskets!

The soldiers obey, and the people flee in disorder.

Shoemaker: Follow me, friends!

Blacksmith: Arrest that man! (*The soldiers forcibly subdue the* **Shoemaker.**)

Blacksmith: You'll be spending the night in jail, Shoemaker.

Schmid: That won't be necessary — he's had enough with the beating he's taken. Come and see me tomorrow morning, Shoemaker.

Shoemaker: You want to see me, you know where I live.

Blacksmith: Why not let him cool off for a few days in jail?

Schmid: Let him go. (*The* **Shoemaker** *picks up his hat, spits, and leaves.*)

Blacksmith: Mr. Mayor, I have the honor to report that order has been re-established in Pimburg.

Schmid: Congratulate your men on my behalf and leave a few of them posted in front of the Town Hall just in case. (**Schmid** *and* **Batts** *exit.*)

Blacksmith: Thank you, Mr. Mayor! Atten–shun! Right — face! You've shown a high degree of preparedness and discipline, men. The enemy has fled with their tails between their legs. I'm proud of every one of you. (*One of the soldiers lets his pike fall.*) What's the matter with you? You asleep, or something?

Soldier: No, I'm fed up.

Blacksmith: What's that you say, you scoundrel?

Soldier: I think . . .

Blacksmith: You think, you think . . . If you're gonna start thinking I'll throw you right out of the militia! You and you stay on guard here. Everyone else, dismissed!

Everyone exits except the two indicated soldiers, who start singing.

The Song of the Fed Up Soldiers

First Soldier:

> I joined the army to roam,
> And to keep my city free;
> They sure put one over on me,
> 'Cause now I'm fighting my home.

Second Soldier:

> With my soldier's pay I bought a new suit,
> A hat and coat and a cloak, to boot.

221

First Soldier:

When the people charged against us just now,
They had good reason to do so;
The whole thing was a mistake somehow,
But nobody explained it to me, I vow.

Second Soldier:

I had the suit cut in the Dutch style,
And proudly walked around with a smile.

First Soldier:

I haven't fought with the enemy,
Instead, right in the middle of the fight,
I knocked down my old friend Henry,
Covered with blood he was quite a sight!

Second Soldier:

That suit didn't do me much good, I must say,
Two rats gnawed their way all through it one day.

First Soldier:

They told me I was big and strong,
Could make those pigs run home to bed;
I was dumb enough to believe that song,
Good thing that no one was left for dead.

Second Soldier:

They'll pay us a piece of gold for all that,
And the rats'll just frisk around and get fat.

First Soldier:

My friends will all cut me in the street,
They'll walk right past me and look at my feet;
Serve me right, too, no doubt about that:
If only I'd realize where I was at!

Second Soldier:

I've sold myself and so have you
For the pay they give us two by two! (*The lights go down.*)

Scene 9

Hans: Scene Nine. Nine already? In which is shown how the Piper escapes the snare set for him.

The lights go up. The prison. **Walter** *is in a cell. The* **Jailer** *is dozing. There is a knock at the door. The* **Jailer** *opens it to admit a colleague.*

First Jailer: You're late.
Second Jailer: My wife didn't have dinner ready in time.
First Jailer: Here're the keys. And watch him carefully — they say he's a witch.
Second Jailer: Bah, I don't believe in witches.
First Jailer: Well, there's one right there.
Second Jailer: Listen, if I saw all the rats following him I might believe it.
First Jailer: Don't you believe in the Devil?
Second Jailer: What d'you want me to say? All I know is I've got a house full of rats, and if this fellow can get rid of them for me, I'm not about to send him to the stake.
First Jailer: Well, I'll be off — I'm hungry as a horse. Good night. (*Exits.*)
Second Jailer: So long . . . (*The* **Jailer** *makes himself comfortable on a bench preparatory to taking a nap. There is a knock at the door.*) Who is it?
Lisbeth: I'm the Mayor's daughter.
Jailer: Yeah, I know.
Lisbeth: I want to speak with the Piper.
Jailer: Not allowed, sorry. Besides, it's dangerous.
Lisbeth: Isn't he behind bars? Well then, there's no danger.
Jailer: I've got very strict orders.
Lisbeth: Just for a moment. Look, I've brought a jar of wine for him, but . . .
Jailer: Just for a moment, then. (*Opens the door and lets her in. Then he sits down and starts drinking.*)
Lisbeth (*going up to the cell*): Hello, Walter.
Walter: Hello, Lisbeth.
Lisbeth (*in a low voice*): I've come to help you escape . . . (*She hands him a club which she has had hidden on her.*) Here, take this . . . (*Aloud.*) Is it true that you're a witch, Walter? Did you really make off with all the children in Hamelin?

223

Walter: No, I'm not a witch at all. Sometimes I find it's not a bad idea to let people think I am, but that's only to make them pay up.

Lisbeth: But now they want to burn you . . .

Walter: Yes.

Lisbeth: And what about your pipe?

Walter: I made it myself. When I tried it out all of a sudden toads and mice and all sorts of little animals started following me. I've never been able to make another one like it, though I've tried often enough. It must make some sort of special sound that attracts little animals.

Lisbeth: Oh, I see! . . . (*Low.*) Pretend that you're choking me, Walter, and when the jailer runs over, knock him out with that club.

Walter: This is dangerous for you, Lisbeth.

Lisbeth: Don't you worry about that . . . go on!

*There is a knock on the door. The **Jailer** gets up.*

Schmid: Open up, I'm the Mayor. (*The **Jailer** opens the door.*)

Lisbeth: My father!

Jailer: Good evening, Mr. Mayor.

Schmid: Lisbeth! What are you doing here? Why did you let her in?

Lisbeth: I made him do it, father. Just for a moment.

Schmid: Get out of here! And don't you ever dare to go out alone again!

Lisbeth: Yes, all right, father. Goodbye, Walter. (*Low.*) Hide the club . . . (*Exits.*)

Schmid: Nobody is to come in here — least of all my daughter.

Jailer: I'm sorry, Mr. Mayor.

Schmid: Open the cell door.

Jailer: Right away. (*Does so.*)

Schmid: Walter Romberg, you're free. The whole thing's been a misunderstanding. Please excuse the treatment you've received.

Walter: Thanks be to God.

Schmid (*giving him a purse*): There's a thousand shillings there. You can start work right away.

Walter: You're paying me in advance, Mr. Mayor?

Schmid: It's the least I can do. And please get started right now.

Walter, *seeing the door open, dashes over to it. When he gets there, he turns round and throws the purse at the Mayor.*

Walter: Here you are Mr. Mayor, buy yourself some rat-traps! (*Exits.*)

Schmid: Walter! Walter! I saved you from the stake! Why don't you get rid of the rats for me? There's a thousand good gold shillings there! (*To the* **Jailer.**) Blockhead! Why did you let him escape?

Jailer: Me? You yourself ordered me to . . .

Schmid: Go to hell! You have the nerve to accuse me? And don't stand there like an idiot, man! Run! Run! (*The lights go down.*)

Scene 10

Frida: Scene Ten, in which the Municipal Council plans the rat extermination campaign.

The lights go up. The Council chamber. Enter **Schmid** *and* **Webs.**

Schmid: Do you have the loan papers with you? I'll sign them right now.

Webs: Yes, Mr. Mayor. (*He puts the papers down and* **Schmid** *signs them. Enter the* **Bailiff.**)

Bailiff: The shoemaker refuses to come, Mr. Mayor.

Schmid: What do you mean, he refuses to come? Send two soldiers and have him brought here! (*The* **Bailiff** *exits.* **Schmid** *finishes signing.*)

Webs: I'll deliver them right now.

Schmid: See that you get back before the Council meeting. And ask the guild representatives to step inside, please.

Webs: So long, Mr. Mayor. (*He exits. Enter* **Weis** *and* **Baun.**)

Weis and **Baun** (*together*): Mr. Mayor . . .

Schmid: Good morning. And a very good one for you — it looks like you've won.

Weis: Naturally, Mr. Mayor. Nobody can compete with our organization.

Baun: And besides, what's the point of looking for solutions from outside if the best ones are right here at home — and such highly original ones at that?

Weis: The only thing I regret is the sad fate of that poor devil of a piper.

Schmid: He won't have to go to the stake after all. It seems he escaped last night.

Baun: What? How?

Weis: The way all witches escape, I imagine. There was a full moon last night.

Schmid: Precisely.

Baun: Live and learn, eh?

Schmid: Very well now, the Town Council has budgeted ten thousand shillings for the purchase of rat-traps and rat poison.

Weis: We shall supply them with the greatest of pleasure.

Schmid: How much are you going to sell us for that amount?

Weis: Let's say . . . twelve hundred ounces of poison at five shillings the ounce — that makes six thousand shillings, leaving four thousand for the purchase of the traps.

Baun: At twenty shillings each, that'll be two hundred traps.

Schmid: What happened to the discount?

Baun: We've made you a very special price, Mr. Mayor.

Schmid: I need a minimum of three hundred traps.

Weis: You'll find the poison a good deal more necessary, I assure you.

Baun: Mr. Weis!

Weis: Excuse me, Mr. Baun.

Schmid: How many rats do you figure all this will exterminate?

Weis: Approximately ten thousand.

Schmid: That doesn't even begin to be enough! I've got to have more traps and more poison! Much more!

Baun: We're perfectly willing to give up the contract if you have a better offer.

Weis: Though I would doubt that anyone could make you one.

Baun: All of the locksmiths are guild members.

Weis: And all of the apothecaries are guild members.

Schmid: The world doesn't end at Pimburg. I'll import exterminators from Gizburg.

Baun: Just as you please, Mr. Mayor.

Weis: Of course you'll have to pay the freight.

Baun: I assure you we can't do it for a penny less.

Weis: We're practically losing money as it is!

Schmid: Come off it, man!

Weis: My word on it . . . figuring in the commission we promised you . . .

Schmid: I'd rather you gave me more traps.

Baun: No, no, a contract is a contract. That's what we agreed on.

Weis: Business is business.

Schmid: All right. I want one third of the agreed on quantity delivered tomorrow morning.

Baun: You'll have it.

Schmid: Another third on Friday and the rest on Monday.

Weis: Perfectly all right with us.

Schmid: You'll be paid, as usual, at the end of the month. (*He gets up.*)

Baun: Delighted.

Weis: We're extremely obliged to you, Mr. Mayor. The Most Learned Guild of Apothecaries . . .

Baun: And the Most Ingenious Guild of Locksmiths . . .

Both: Are always at the service of the city!

Song of the Businessmen

Baun:

> Heart has nothing to do with business,
> Sentiment is out of place;
> Whoever has got all the money
> Is the fellow who holds the ace.

Weis:

> It isn't a question of luck,
> Or being born with a handsome face;
> You stretch out your hand and grab,
> Sentiment is out of place.

Baun:

> The laws are made by the rich,
> That makes good sense to me,
> Barons, and kings, and popes,
> Bow down to receive their fee.

Weis:

> Business is business, we know,
> That's true, come hell or high water;
> Business is business, we know,
> And God runs the world 'cause he bought her.

Both:

> Heart has nothing to do with business,
> Sentiment is out of place;
> Whoever has got all the money
> Is the fellow who holds the ace.

Baun *and* **Weis** *leave. The* **Bailiff** *pushes the* **Shoemaker** *in and leaves. The* **Shoemaker**'s *head is bandaged.*

Schmid: Good morning, my friend. Have a seat.

Shoemaker: No, thanks.

Schmid: Just as you like. The reason I've had you brought here is that after everything that has happened, one thing is clear: you'll be made an alderman at the next elections and perhaps even mayor. At this very moment the citizens have a good deal more confidence in you than in me.

Shoemaker: If that's all you've got to say to me . . . (*Starts to go.*)

Schmid: One moment. I saved you from being thrown in jail. In return, I'd appreciate your listening to what I have to say. The Council is about to convene in order to consider the rat extermination campaign. I'd like you to be here. I want you to convince yourself that everything is done in an open and aboveboard manner at our meetings.

Shoemaker: Oh, you mean now that you've rejected the sensible solution?

Schmid: You know just as well as I do that we couldn't have adopted that solution here in Pimburg without destroying certain values and principles that form the basis of our sense of community.

Shoemaker: Is it religious principles that you're talking about, Mr. Mayor? My own suspicion is that economic interests count for a bit more around here.

Schmid: I don't deny that economic principles exist too, but the one thing doesn't have anything to do with the other.

Shoemaker: Nonetheless, they got together to do away with a solution that looked like the best one going even if it hadn't turned out to be the definitive one.

Schmid: They got their fingers burnt with that solution in Hamelin.

Shoemaker: That was because they didn't fulfill the conditions of their contract.

Schmid: I personally discovered the Piper, Shoemaker. I tried to hire him to exterminate the rats, whatever it might have cost. I even did a few things I don't even want to mention to help him along. I assure you it just wasn't possible to do it that way.

Shoemaker: We were on the point of making it possible.

Schmid: Yes, but by using violence!

Shoemaker: It was the only way left to us.

Schmid: People got hurt, and you're responsible for that.

Shoemaker: Yes, you're right, I'm responsible for what happened. I lost my head. When I heard about the fishmonger's kĩds being disfigured by the rats, I just saw red. I thought we had the numbers to force things, but I was mistaken. There weren't enough of us, and I should have waited for a more opportune moment.

Schmid: Whatever happens, I can say I did my duty. I'd like you to understand that.

Shoemaker (*thinking it over*): Maybe. (*Enter the* **Bailiff.**)

Bailiff: The honorable aldermen of the city! (*Exits.*)

Schmid: Have them come in. Sit down here, Shoemaker.

Schmid *sits down in the chair at the head of the table; the* **Aldermen** *enter.*

Aldermen: Mr. Mayor . . .

Schmid: Good morning.

Batts: What happened to you, Shoemaker?

Webs: Oh, you've hurt yourself!

Kost: Somebody kick you in the head?

Shoemaker: That's right, and I bandaged it so no horns would sprout. (*The* **Aldermen** *laugh.*)

Rush: Well, at least you haven't lost your sense of humor.

Shoemaker: On the contrary, I happen to be in a particularly bad temper today.

Schmid: Sit down, everyone, please. (*They sit.*) I declare this meeting to be in session. I am pleased to be able to communicate to the Council that we have acquired twelve hundred ounces of poison and two hundred rat-traps for the rat extermination campaign.

Webs: Is that going to be enough?

Schmid: I don't think we'll be able to get rid of every single rat in town, but at least we'll be able to cut down on the worst damage that the plague has caused us.

Kost: What we have to do is decide on the distribution of the purchased materials in such a way as to bring about the maximum possible advantage to the town as a whole.

Schmid: Exactly what we're here for.

Rush: The most important thing is the protection of the food supplies.

Batts: Precisely — we've got to protect the essential goods.

Kost: And the inn! What about the inn? If we don't get out-of-towners in for the market of St. Rogatia, we're finished. Naturally the cloth warehouses have to be protected too.

229

Schmid: Right, I think we've hit on the two absolutely most important things: clothes and food.

Webs: We'll have to send some rat-traps to Reverend Grundig.

Schmid: Naturally. Webs, start taking this down. How many grain warehouses are there in Pimburg?

Rush: Four, but they're not all equally important.

Schmid: Very well, let's say twenty traps for the lot.

Rush: Twenty traps! I've got to have forty just for my own warehouse!

Schmid: We've got to make what we've got do for everyone, Rush.

Rush: The town can't survive without bread!

Webs: That's true. We've got to protect the flour.

Schmid: All right, thirty traps for you and ten for the other warehouses. Make a note, Webs.

Webs: Right.

Schmid: After bread, meat is next in importance. I suggest forty traps.

Webs: Butcher shops, forty traps.

Schmid: Fifteen for the cheese shops.

Batts: But Mr. Mayor, everyone knows that cheese is the rats' favorite food!

Schmid: All right, let's say twenty then. How much is that altogether?

Webs: A hundred. That still leaves the greengrocers . . .

Schmid: Yes, yes, let's give them another twenty, and ten more for the Town Hall, making thirty altogether.

Webs: And a total of one hundred and fifty.

Schmid: We've got to have at least thirty for the cloth warehouses since they're the town's principal economic resource.

Webs: Makes one hundred and eighty. Twenty left.

Schmid: The other twenty will be distributed throughout the town. Now let's move on to the poison.

The **Shoemaker** *gets up and walks toward the door.*

Schmid: Where are you off to, Shoemaker?

Shoemaker: If you've dragged me here so I can see how the aldermen share out the rat-traps that the citizens have paid for, I've had it! You make me sick!

Schmid: We've distributed the rat-traps strategically in order to save the town's essential goods. Would you have done it differently if you were mayor?

230

Shoemaker: No. It's just that by a curious coincidence all these essential goods happen to be in your warehouses.

Schmid: That's beside the point! What I asked you was whether you think the rat-traps have been sensibly distributed or not.

Shoemaker: Yes, but . . .

Schmid: But what?

Shoemaker: You own the essential goods. When the rats come, we have to pay for the traps which you then put up in your own shops . . .

Schmid: . . . for the purpose of protecting the town's essential goods.

Shoemaker: Yeah, but the essential goods belong to you and not to the people — and later you'll sell them to the people. There's something in all this I don't quite understand. No, there's something I don't quite understand . . . (*He leaves, still perplexed.*)

Webs: That shoemaker somehow gives me the impression of being none too bright.

Kost: You mean he's a bit cracked, don't you?

Batts: What is it he doesn't quite understand?

Rush: Search me. It's all plain as day to me.

Schmid: Gentlemen, while we're chattering away here, the rats are multiplying. Let's not waste any more time and get to work.　　(*The lights go down.*)

Hans: And so it came about that the rats multiplied, and multiplied, and multiplied, until finally the Pimburgers had to abandon their town. But the rats went with them, and plagues started in other towns; so that today there isn't a single town anywhere in the world that doesn't have to spend millions and millions of shillings in useless attempts to exterminate the rats.

The lights go up. The **Citizens** *sing.*

The Spirit of Public Calamities

> When a terrible calamity
> Falls upon our town,
> A few make a good thing of it,
> And the rest pay up and down.
> You and I, we ask ourselves
> What the solution is,
> But all they do is calculate
> The money in the biz.
> When rats come to a city,

Just as it happened here,
You can't sleep in your bed at home,
You stay awake for fear.
But a few in the town have the answer:
With money their ancestors gave them,
They cover their goods with poison
And surround them with traps to save them.
The plague decimates the city,
And causes many to die,
Without even packing their cases
They leave their houses and fly.
You and I and our families,
We get infected on sight,
So they sell us some blessed relic
Guaranteed to make it all right.
When hunger and famine threaten,
And your insides groan with pain,
There are some who are not so hungry,
You lose weight and they gain.
My legs get thinner and thinner,
And your teeth fall out two by two,
But the foodsellers' pockets get bigger
With the prices they charge me and you.
For the lads who shoulder the rifles,
War means they go to their death;
For the fellows who made the rifles,
For them war of life is the breath.
"The war's lasted long enough,"
You and I always say to each other;
But for those who make a profit on it,
It really isn't so much of a bother.

Frida: Fellow citizens, if we show them holes, they plug them up; if we demand cures, they give us tranquilizers. One way or another, we always get sat on. We've got to find more efficient solutions.

CURTAIN